W9-CIC-333

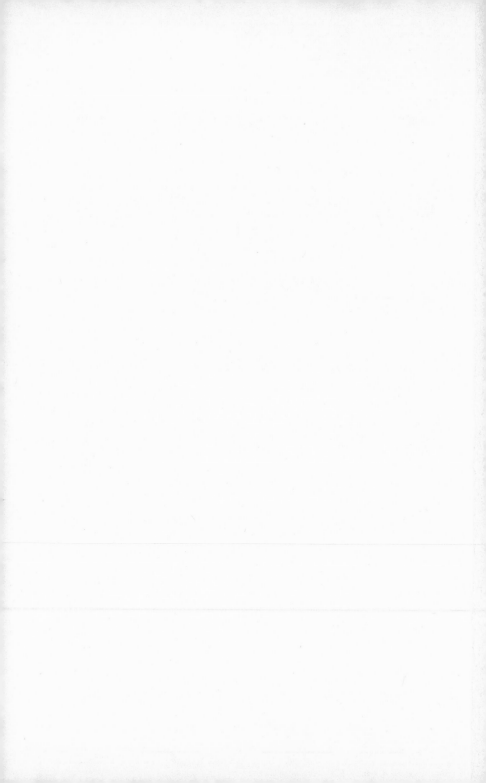

DO THE

KIND®

THING

DO THE

KIND® THING

THINK BOUNDLESSLY
WORK PURPOSEFULLY
LIVE PASSIONATELY

Daniel Lubetzky

BALLANTINE BOOKS

NEW YORK

2015 Target Special Edition

Copyright © 2015 by Daniel Lubetzky

All rights reserved.

Published in the United States by Ballantine Books, an imprint
of Random House, a division of Penguin Random House LLC, New York.

Simultaneously published in a trade edition in slightly different
form by Ballantine Books, an imprint of Random House,
a division of Penguin Random House LLC.

BALLANTINE and the HOUSE colophon are registered
trademarks of Penguin Random House LLC.

ISBN 978-1-101-88679-3
eBook ISBN 978-0-553-39325-5

Printed in the United States of America on acid-free paper

www.ballantinebooks.com

2 4 6 8 9 7 5 3 1

Book design by Christopher M. Zucker

To my children Romy, Jonah, Andy, and Natalie, and my wife, Michelle, who inspire me every day to become a better person

CONTENTS

DO THE
KIND®
THING

FOREWORD

Prior to picking up this book, had you heard KIND's motto—"Do the KIND Thing"—and wondered what it truly meant? At its core, it is about doing the kind thing for your body, your taste buds, and your world—by eating nutritionally rich foods without having to sacrifice taste, and by inspiring kindness to others. But for me, "Do the KIND Thing" is far more than that. It is about the way I think and do things, distilled into ten tenets that have helped KIND become a trusted and vibrant brand. It is a rallying cry to remind my team of the tools to build and cement our culture, and the values that we try to live by to make this world a little kinder. My hope is that, as you read this book, you will know what we mean when we say "Do the KIND Thing," and that it will help you think boundlessly, work purposefully, and live passionately.

CHAPTER 1

THINKING WITH AND

An Introduction to Avoiding False Compromises

It was May 1994. Mother's Day was a week away, and I sat anxiously by the phone. Across New York City, small ads in neighborhood newspapers proclaimed the launch of my new venture, through which Arabs and Israelis cooperated to make skincare products like Dead Sea bath salts, hand-treatment creams, and mud masks that I had assembled into gift baskets. These would make the perfect gift for moms, the ads explained, sending a thoughtful message of peace through business.

Cramped studio apartment/corporate headquarters; narrow black IKEA desk; second-hand chair: I had set up my "office" in anticipation of a flood of orders. My biggest worry was how to process and fulfill them all.

I had been starting businesses since elementary school, beginning with the magic shows I put on for neighborhood kids in my native Mexico City. But, at age twenty-five, I had just thrown away the promise of a Wall Street legal career to start my own company, based on a new concept I thought could change the world: economic cooperation between conflict-torn peoples as a way to help them get to know one another, create an incentive to build a shared future, and achieve peace. Building bridges between people was my passion, and I wanted to use commerce to help nudge neighbors closer together.

I was convinced that it was possible to build a company that was "not-*only*-for-profit"—one that sold great products *and* also did its small part toward making a better world. I believed I did not have to choose one or the other; our company could achieve both goals at the same time. First, though, I would have to get customers to buy the goods.

A week earlier, a delivery truck driver had rung up to apartment 8A, on the corner of Eighty-Fourth Street and Second Avenue, to announce the arrival of my Dead Sea cosmetics shipment.

"Come on up," I said over the building's intercom.

"You don't seem to understand," he replied tersely. "Please come down."

For my trial, I had asked my trading partners to produce a few hundred each of mineral-rich mud masks, hand-treatment creams with avocado oil, Dead Sea bath salts with various essential oils, and seven varieties of mud soaps. I had assumed it would all just fit in a corner of my tiny studio and would sell out quickly.

When I came down to the street, I saw that my order actually occupied an entire twenty-foot container truck. The driver and I hauled box after box up to a room already filled with samples of sundried tomato spreads made through cooperation among

Israeli, Egyptian, Turkish, and Palestinian trading partners, as well as packaging materials for the gift baskets. After stacking the boxes to the ceiling of my studio, I had to convince my landlord to rent me a windowless basement space next to the trash compactor to store the rest of the product. For the next two years, this crypt-like cubbyhole would become my new office.

The company had now officially taken over my life. When I lay on my futon bed, I stared up at a towering wall of boxes that threatened to fall on me any minute.

But it would all be worth it, I felt. The idea that Bedouins and Jews had partnered to make Dead Sea cosmetics would surely please any mom who cherished soft skin and peaceful cooperation. With such a fresh, novel concept, I thought, the challenge would be keeping up with all the incoming calls.

The week passed. Mother's Day came and went. Not one customer bought a single gift basket. Zero consumer inquiries. Zero sales. Most of my savings were locked up in inventory I could not move. And the smell of essential oils was suffocating.

I felt depressed. Terrified. In addition to sensing my dream slip away, I had no idea how I was going to pay my rent.

I worried about what my parents would think. They were already concerned that I was wasting my law degree. I was the first member of my extended family to get a graduate degree. As a Jew whose father had survived the Holocaust and a son whose parents had sacrificed so much to provide me with an education, I felt a keen sense of guilt and obligation.

And yet, this was my passion. This was my mission. I had to pursue it. I couldn't quit. I was going to make this work.

At the end of the week, I threw some product samples into

my battered fake-leather briefcase, closed the apartment door carefully so the boxes wouldn't crash down, and hit the pavement. I was going to sell my stock if I had to go door-to-door across the entire island of Manhattan and convince every buyer personally.

THE "AND" PHILOSOPHY—KIND'S FIRST TENET

This book is the story of what I discovered when I devoted my life to creating businesses that build bridges between people, from PeaceWorks' Dead Sea products to KIND, the snack foods company that evolved from those experiences. By 2014 KIND had sold over a billion KIND snack bars and KIND clusters in more than 100,000 stores. The KIND Movement, which advances our social mission by performing—and inspiring our community to perform—unexpected kind acts, has touched over a million people.

Like many start-up stories, mine has been rocky. The last two decades have been a series of ups and downs that alternately made me deliriously excited and desperately worried. Entrepreneurship isn't for the faint of heart, and it's impossible to tell how your story will turn out. All you have is your conviction, your ability to work hard, and your determination to never give up.

One thread that runs through this book is a revelation I uncovered along the journey—the power of thinking with AND. People often let circumstances force them into choosing between two seemingly incompatible options—like making a snack bar that either tastes good *or* is healthy for you. At KIND we pride ourselves on creating new paths and models that avoid that kind of false compromise. Instead of "Or," we say "AND."

The AND philosophy has become so central to our thinking at KIND that internally we call it the KIND BrAND Philosophy. At its core, it is about challenging assumptions and thinking creatively. It is about not settling for less, being willing to take greater risks and, often, it requires investing more up front. It is not just a way to think positively, or a feel-good attitude. It is about learning to think critically, frequently pursuing what in the short term may seem a tougher path: to be both healthy *and* tasty, convenient *and* wholesome, economically sustainable *and* socially impactful.

Some of the best ideas seem the most obvious in retrospect. The challenge is uncovering these opportunities when you have become accustomed to the way things are. In an effort to be efficient, your brain has a tendency to accept prevailing ideas or concepts that may no longer be correct (or may never have been). These shortcuts, called heuristics by psychologists, enable us to process information and reach conclusions swiftly. But they also bias us in favor of quick solutions that may not maximize our long-term potential. Thinking with AND means that we consciously try to break away from these mental shortcuts. At KIND we take it slow, relentlessly questioning our first principles and then using repeated rounds of brainstorming to find new solutions that don't rely on these assumptions.

This behavior lies at the very heart of our creative process. When designing products at KIND, we never allow cost considerations or other practical constraints like manufacturing efficiencies to be filters at the outset. Of course costs are critical; we prize resourcefulness and the ability to do much with little.

But that analysis has to come after the open brainstorming. Otherwise we would never have conceived KIND bars with whole nuts and fruits, as they are harder and more expensive to manufacture than bars made from emulsions or pastes. The AND process helped us realize that this extra investment would be worth it. Every one of our top ten competitors makes their best-selling bars from homogenous pastes. This is a logical path because slab bars (as they are called in the industry as a result of their manufacture from slabs of mashed-up, emulsified ingredients) run smoothly through the manufacturing line and cost less to make. But they leave many consumers dissatisfied, as they rob foods of their integrity and soul.

The AND philosophy has its costs. Because we use whole ingredients like nuts and seeds, which are not always of a totally uniform size, we often end up with bars that are slightly larger than advertised, but we can't charge more for the somewhat greater bulk. Sometimes whole ingredients yield bars that are *under* weight, and we have to give those bars away free, as samples. By contrast, the traditional way of emulsifying ingredients into pastes can yield bars of uniform weight. Our way is more expensive, but many consumers find the quality is superior to that of an emulsion bar. It's often harder to pursue the way of AND. But, as our market share growth demonstrates, if you have a commitment to excellence—a commitment to avoid false compromises—you will win in the long term.

Questioning assumptions also forces us to be nimble and staves off complacency. We've learned that just because everything is going well for the business, we can't assume that the trajectory will continue upward. We continuously think critically about our strategy: Where will our next competitive threat originate? How can we develop new products *and* protect our core lines?

The AND philosophy is a great tool for entrepreneurs, particularly for social entrepreneurs. A social entrepreneur is a person who tackles societal problems and seeks to effect social change through creative mechanisms. At its essence, the entrepreneurial mind spots opportunities to create value: Social entrepreneurs detect problems in society and try to find solutions to improve the world; business entrepreneurs discover gaps in the marketplace and try to fill them to achieve financial gain. A social entrepreneur with an appreciation for the power of market forces tries to advance both social and business objectives in unison. Thinking with AND can help you solve social problems *and* identify commercial gaps as it forces you to confront the underlying assumptions, and to uncover objectives that are in tension with one another. Once you have identified the conflicting objectives that you're trying to achieve and how they interact, you can start thinking about whether there are creative ways to accomplish both objectives at once.

ADDITIONAL KIND BUSINESS TENETS

There are, of course, other essential tenets that comprise my approach to life and business. The AND philosophy is the foundation for all we do at KIND. It is not just KIND's first and foremost tenet. It also undergirds nine other essential themes that run through what we do, and these themes correspond to the next nine chapters in this book:

2. Purpose

Purpose is why you get up in the morning, go to work, and give it your all. When your company has a real mission, it serves as a rallying point for your team members. They come to feel, as you do, that the efforts they put into advancing the shared enterprise serve a higher social goal. Chapter 2 explains KIND's integrated mission to advance our business while making the world a little kinder and how it informs everything we do and create, from our not-*only*-for-profit business model to our KIND Movement. Chapter 2 details the ancillary business benefits from having a purpose and the conditions necessary for those benefits to exist. Just as important, it dispels some myths about certain perceived advantages a business can gain from purpose and shares ways for companies and individuals to discover their purpose.

3. Grit

It's no secret that starting a new venture is hard work. The difference between those who keep going and those who give up is grit: the ability to persevere until the work is done. Grit can best be fueled by purpose: when you have a higher reason for doing what you do, it is harder for anything to stop you—but three additional anchors also underlie grit: conviction, self-evaluation, and sheer determination. Deep analysis and earnest introspection can forge a temper of tenacity. Grit, particularly when combined with the AND way of thinking, can move mountains. In Chapter 3, I share examples of creative perseverance that eventually paid off in a big way.

4. Truth and Discipline

Staying true to your brand is harder and more important than many realize. Every brand represents certain values and attributes. If you steer your brand in the wrong direction, or dilute its message, your customers may feel betrayed. The temptation to follow fads, try to please different constituencies or to expand too quickly without regard to your brand promise can kill your venture. But before you can uphold your brand promise, you need to truly understand what that promise is. What does your brand stand for? What is your unique value proposition? In Chapter 4, I contrast my early experience with Peace-Works—in which I was so excited about the concept and desperate for it to take off that I made crucial errors—with KIND's more focused and disciplined strategy, an approach that has allowed us to grow in a sustainable way without trying to be everything to everyone.

5. Keeping It Simple

In Chapter 5 I explore the too often underappreciated virtue of keeping things simple and staying grounded in business and in life. The tenet of simplicity imbues every aspect of the KIND brand, products, culture, and operations. Our straightforward brand name, descriptive product names, promise of foods that are as close to nature as possible, and forthright marketing style are also reactions against the spin we are exposed to in modern society. Our candid work environment and down-to-earth culture are important contributors to our success. Closely related to simplicity is humility. A strong leader avoids becoming overconfident to the point of impaired judgment. Skepticism or even paranoia about a company's market power and about one's own judgment is healthy.

6. Originality

We get our best ideas at KIND through brainstorming, using a rigorous process we've developed over many years. This approach to creativity initially welcomes the widest possible range of ideas, including wacky ones that seem impossible or implausible, and only later filters them down. The goal is to find fresh ideas that fit within the AND philosophy of achieving several objectives at once. But it doesn't apply only to new ventures; it is just as critical to reinventing and refreshing existing businesses. Critical thinking and analysis underpin our marketing campaigns, our sales strategies, and our new product development. While innovation is vital for an enterprise to thrive, you have to balance authentic innovation and authentic branding to ensure you do not confuse your fans or cause harm to your brand. In Chapter 6, I show what can happen when you don't get that balance right, along with illustrating how innovation at KIND helped cement what our brand stands for. I also describe techniques for thinking boundlessly that can serve our daily lives.

7. Transparency and Authenticity

Transparency and authenticity may be the values consumers most associate with KIND, largely because of the literal transparency of the clear wrappers we introduced into the nutrition and healthy snack bar category. But transparency is about a lot more. It relates to the authenticity that KIND conveys across every aspect of our operations. This is something people can sense. Transparency and authenticity also mean acknowledging mistakes when necessary, and not feeling you need to "spin" every issue to appear invincible. Whether dealing with suppliers or customers, transparency involves sharing information that transforms traditionally arm's-length relationships into a strategic trading partnership. When relating to our community and our consumers, transparency means being honest about our successes as well as our limitations. Internally, it means that we prize open and frank communication among our team members and share financial details of our business with them.

8. Empathy

Empathy—the ability to understand and share the feelings of another—is a vital if underrated leadership skill, as it helps build a loyal culture. One of the things that team members in any company are most concerned about is whether they sense that managers truly care about them and their professional growth. I may be particularly attuned to this because building bridges represents the common thread in everything I do, not because I am an altruistic soul but out of enlightened self-interest. As the son of a Holocaust survivor, I vowed to do what I can to prevent what happened to my dad from happening to others. In Chapter 8, I delve into my dad's story, and its impact on me. I detail the evolution of the KIND Movement, and share examples of some of the other work I have done to foster peace in the Middle East. I'm also forthright about the tensions between my philanthropic duties and my responsibility to my family, especially during some difficult times in my life.

9. Trust

Because I started KIND as a one-man operation, in the beginning, I had to do everything and I gained a general understanding of every facet of our operations. As KIND grew through its early stages, I relied on a core team of dedicated generalists to do several jobs at once. Once we became a larger organization, we needed specialists and my role shifted. I now provide a vision, and work to inspire and to coach the team. I need to nurture the culture at KIND, and part of that means knowing when to step back and let others lead. It's been crucial for me to trust and empower my team and to create space for them, but also to know when to intervene to preserve our brand and our values. In Chapter 9 I share the ways in which I have learned these hard lessons, as well as the advice I have received over the years from my advisory board.

10. Ownership

Ownership is, above all, an attitude. An ownership culture is entrepreneurial, resourceful, and resilient. It recognizes that we are part of something bigger than us—one big family—and have entered an implicit pact to be loyal to one another and think of our shared enterprise ahead of ourselves. As a first step, we align financial incentives: all of our full-time team members—from the president to the team members that clean the office—receive stock options entitling them to own a piece of KIND and have a direct economic stake in our business. But that is not enough. Ownership is about tapping the human spirit—about a sense of personal power and the responsibility that comes with it. That is why at KIND, and in this book, I avoid the word "employee" (which has acquired a connotation of subservience) to refer to my team members, who are empowered to become shareholders and think like co-owners.

★   ★   ★

As I discuss these nine other tenets throughout the book, I share examples of how the AND philosophy has helped KIND leverage the expected output from each of these tenets across all disciplines and departments, from new product development to marketing, from human resources to financial planning, from strategic planning to our social mission. Relatedly, my many failures taught me more about myself and business than my successes. Because I can directly attribute many of KIND's achievements to the lessons that I drew from my earlier mistakes, I share them quite prominently in these pages.

THE KIND WAY

For decades, people have accepted the dogma that you work hard for your money, and then find meaning or fulfillment outside your work, if ever. Increasingly, we are learning that you can find a way to achieve financial success *and* advance a social goal that you care about, that you can work for a company *and* contribute toward making this world a little better, that you can find remuneration *and* purpose in your work.

Thinking boundlessly often means challenging conventional wisdom in the corporate world. At KIND, AND is not just a top-level strategy. It's a guiding principle for every team member to use every day: What assumptions can I challenge? Which seemingly mutually exclusive options may actually be mutually achievable? Why can't we try to meet more than one goal with the same product or strategy? Are our assumptions and ways of doing things still valid? Do the supposed constraints still exist?

Thinking with AND transcends the workplace. You can

challenge the assumptions that threaten your personal fulfillment. You don't have to accept the way things are. All you need
to do is ask: Why does it have to be that way? When your de-
fault thinking is "AND" instead of "or," you start to break
down the roadblocks that prevent you from getting more out of
life.

Twenty years ago, as I sold my first products door-to-door, I
learned what it takes to see problems as opportunities and to
unleash the power of creative thinking, introspection, and self-
evaluation. I learned that dreaming can help you visualize and
forge a path to success, and that imagination has the power to
set you apart from your competitors, as long as you act on it.

Some people dub me an optimist, but I think that misses the
point. I consider myself an actionist: a person that does not accept things as they are and commits to change them (hopefully
for the better). Making a difference requires not just ideas, but
also the determination and mindset to execute them. For me,
this comes from my family history (a story of hope and perseverance against the odds), which burned inside of me and propelled me to do this with my life. I was raised to believe that we
have an obligation to be kind to one another as humans, and to
build bridges.

When trying to connect with others, I've found that there's
one unique advantage to being in the snack food business. When
I travel, whether for business or with my family, I always take
three cases of KIND bars with me to give away—particularly to
people whom I observe showing kindness toward others. Nine
out of ten people who eat a KIND bar end up as customers who
will repurchase and recommend it to others, so this isn't an en-
tirely selfless act, but there's an AND to it, too. My larger hope

is that they also become part of our Movement: that they not only buy our products and share them with their friends, but also join us in Doing the KIND Thing, even to strangers. So much has gone into each snack: vision, passion, purpose, logistics, the hard work of my team, and the ingredients themselves, which you can see yourself through the transparent wrapper. It's a lot to hold in your hand, and I love sharing it with you.

CHAPTER 2

PURPOSE

A Fuel for Your Passion

When you're training for a triathlon or a marathon, you run, bike, and swim wherever you happen to be. In the summer of 2002, I happened to be in Colombo, Sri Lanka, exploring a new business venture. I was training for the New York City Marathon, and I started my eighteen-mile run in the capital. By the time I completed the distance—gasping, sweating, endorphins pumping—I found myself on the remote outskirts of the city, along a quiet lake, surrounded by Sinhalese kids and friendly fishermen curious about my appearance. I was famished. I had a bit of money with me to get back to town. What I did not have were healthful portable snacks to refuel. It was a long trip back to the hotel.

The search for healthy snacks had formed the backdrop to my life since law school. I had started my first food company in 1994 after I sampled a delicious sundried tomato spread in

Israel. Given my passion for building bridges between people and cultures, I was focusing at that time on fostering Arab-Israeli relations. My company, PeaceWorks, brought together Israelis, Palestinians, Turks, and Egyptians to make delicious foods and encourage economic cooperation among neighbors striving to coexist. Then I started trying to set up similar ventures making specialty sauces and foods in other war-torn or conflict-ridden areas like Chiapas, in my native Mexico, in Sri Lanka, in South Africa, and in Indonesia. I traveled constantly. I was always on the run—more apt than calling myself a true "runner." I frequently found myself in places like Colombo, miles out of town, starving, and with nothing to eat.

Healthy snack options were just as scarce back at home. I was working sixteen-to twenty-hour days—as fledgling entrepreneurs are prone to—and I didn't have time to cook, even on the rare occasions when I was actually in my tiny apartment. But it did not matter where I was in the world; my choices for a snack to grab before embarking on an eight-hour bus ride through the Egyptian desert to visit a juice plant would be similar to the choices I had on the road in the American Midwest: over-processed, carb-heavy, sugar-laden foods. I could eat pastries, chips, or other salty snacks. But I was tired of the empty calories, and of feeling guilty. And I could not stomach traditional energy bars, which tasted to me like cardboard or astronaut food and were filled with added sugar and undecipherable ingredients. With some planning ahead, I could bring along fruit or raw nuts, which were better for my health. But the fruit was messy and spoiled easily. And it was too easy for me to eat the entire bag of nuts at one sitting.

What I was missing was a healthy snack option that could

travel well *and* fill me up. I didn't want to make the choice between healthy *and* tasty, convenient *and* wholesome, socially impactful *and* economically sustainable. There had to be a snack that achieved all of these goals.

There must be a way, I thought, for me to capitalize on the trend in society toward food that's convenient to eat on the go, combined with the increasing number of people who choose to eat real food. I knew that others also wanted to eat a snack that was nutritionally rich, and made with "ingredients you can see and pronounce." (This eventually became our registered trademark at KIND.)

Additionally, it was important to me to start a business that both made money *and* served a social goal. I didn't want the company to be a nonprofit; it had to generate earnings without taking outside charitable donations. A product, I believed, could serve two purposes at once. This stemmed from the AND philosophy that became such a crucial part of KIND's DNA.

At a trade show in the late nineties, I came across an almond-apricot-yogurt bar made in Australia that struck me as meeting a lot of the criteria I had been searching for. The owners pressed me to start importing the product. I resisted because all of my products had a PeaceWorks mission embedded in them (i.e., they involved cooperative efforts among neighbors in conflict regions), and I was barely keeping up with all the PeaceWorks ventures. But their product was tasty and healthy enough to persuade me to start a side business selling the bars into natural foods stores. Within a year, we were nearing a million dollars in sales. Soon thereafter, the small Australian manufacturer was acquired by a large conglomerate. The company proceeded to reduce costs and change the ingredients, adding sulfate preservatives and sorbitol, an artificial sweetener. As soon as we advised our customers of this change, they stopped carrying the product. We were devastated because our scarce profits from PeaceWorks had helped fund investment into this new space, and all of a sudden, from one day to the next, our entire investment was lost. We were on the verge of going out of business, and seven team members were relying on me for their salaries.

It was a frightening moment for me. I pleaded with the conglomerate to make a natural version of the product, but they declined. I lay awake at night thinking through all my options—none were readily apparent. I resolved to learn from the experience and to create a premium line of whole nut and fruit bars myself. This was the dawn of KIND Healthy Snacks. But the darkness before the dawn was indeed a dark time, as well as lonely and scary.

Yet, at the same time, it was energizing because it was so purposeful and liberating. We would never again be at the mercy of someone else's decision about what should go into our products. We would never again let anyone add artificial ingredients or make sugar or empty carbs a primary ingredient, or add fillers to lower costs while lowering the quality of our snacks. We would obsess about using nutritionally rich ingredients that can nourish your body and your soul. We would craft KIND Fruit & Nut bars to fulfill the goals I had set for myself: something healthful, delicious, *and* socially impactful, something easy to carry on the go that was at the same time wholesome and real.

We worked hard to define and refine the purpose of our product. First we established a commitment to fight the diabetes and obesity epidemic befalling society by introducing nutritionally rich products with a low glycemic index. A low glycemic index means that the product you eat, because it is nutritionally rich and dense, gets digested slowly. Its nutrients and energy, including its sugar, get absorbed gradually and gently into your body. In contrast, a product with a high glycemic index tends to be characterized by refined sugars and lack of nutrient-dense ingredients—the classic example is candy, but white bread and even fruit juices without the pulp and peel can also be high on the glycemic index. As soon as you eat these foods, the sugar levels in your blood immediately spike. Products with a high glycemic index not only give you sugar highs swiftly followed by tanking sugar levels that may make you tired or hungry again, they also mess up your body balance, because your pancreas must create insulin to try to offset these crazy spikes. This can eventually create insulin resistance, which leads to diabetes and can lead directly to fatty liver disease. Complications of diabetes can include kidney disease, heart disease, stroke, and dementia. The challenge to society is serious. Healthful eating of truly nutritious foods—no fads, and no empty calories—was established as a guiding principle for KIND. And, besides being healthful, the products had to be delicious.

But I didn't just want to make great food. Having learned from my PeaceWorks experience, I wanted to find a way to do some good in the area that most mattered to me: building bridges between people.

Initially, I thought about having the bars manufactured, as the other PeaceWorks foods were, by cooperative ventures in conflict-torn regions, but there was no obvious place where this could be accomplished. The production expertise was in Australia, a peaceful land whose only transcendental "conflict" was its painful treatment of Aboriginals by its Western settlers. (Well, a venture involving Aboriginals in the manufacturing actually crossed my mind! But it did not feel authentic. It felt forced and contrived, so I did not pursue that path.)

Initially we addressed this disconnect by donating 5 percent of profits from the KIND division to peace-related nonprofits. If we didn't turn a profit on a particular year, we would make a meaningful donation regardless, out of our gross revenues. This was a temporary fix, but it was important to us to integrate the *purpose* into the DNA of the company.

As we brainstormed about our brand name and mission, we rallied around a concept that could affirm our three anchors of health, taste, and social responsibility: being KIND to your body, KIND to your taste buds, and KIND to your world. Focusing on kindness stemmed from my belief, which I inherited from my parents, that kindness to others can build trust, and ultimately, bridges between people.

My father, who survived the Dachau concentration camp during the Holocaust, told me of a time when a Nazi guard took risks by throwing him a rotten potato that provided him the sustenance he needed to go on. Although that soldier could have gotten in trouble for helping a Jewish prisoner, he acted with compassion in the darkest of moments. My dad always credited the guard's action with helping him stay alive.

The question the brand asked was, In our modern society, where we have all these barriers between one another and are so desensitized to the suffering of others, could we find a way to build those human bonds between people and inspire them? Just as I tried to connect neighbors in conflict regions with PeaceWorks, could we use the power of kindness to get ordinary people to recognize their shared humanity and obligation toward one another? Could this be a step toward preventing what happened to my father from happening again to other human beings?

WHERE IT ALL BEGAN FOR KIND

I've been starting businesses since I was eight years old, but the first one I started with a social mission, and the first one in the healthy food arena—the precursor to KIND—launched in 1994. This was the first formal test, for me, of the idea that social objectives and profit-making could go hand in hand, a model I call not-*only*-for-profit.

When I finished law school in 1993, I went to New York to study for the bar. I spent that summer working at the law firm of Sullivan & Cromwell (S&C), which had offered me a job, while I prepared to take the exam. I then spent the fall at consulting firm, McKinsey & Company's Mexico City office, where I also had a job offer. With both firms' blessing and understanding, my plan was to try law and consulting and decide between those two career paths.

A big breakthrough in Middle East peacemaking occurred while I was in Mexico. On September 13, 1993, President Clinton hosted Yasser Arafat and Yitzhak Rabin in the White House Rose Garden to celebrate the Oslo agreement between Israelis and Palestinians. As I sat in Mexico City with some friends, watching this surreal ceremony, my career direction became quite clear. I had been writing about economic cooperation between Arabs and Israelis for years, when it seemed a distant proposition. I had dreamed about peace in the region since my childhood. I needed to support these nascent peace efforts.

I applied for a year-long scholarship to go to Israel and the Middle East—the Haas/Koshland Memorial Award—to turn a proposal about Arab-Israeli cooperation that I had written while in school into actual legislation, and to try building a consultancy business to foster joint ventures. As I was choosing between the legal and consultancy paths, I learned that I had received this fellowship, a $10,000 award to help support my year abroad. Financially speaking, the $10,000 itself was not remotely as attractive as the other two job offers. But the award, along with meaningful talks I had with my mentors, who encouraged me to follow my dreams, helped me to muster the courage to pursue my passion. All human beings at some point in their lives will encounter a juncture where they can either do what's more conventional, safe, and possibly even rewarding in the short term, or they can take a risk to do that which they truly believe in. The Haas/Koshland Memorial Award forever transformed the rest of my journey.

I declined the McKinsey offer. S&C encouraged me to take a leave of absence, instead of turning down their offer, in case I wanted to come back after completing my fellowship. The partners at S&C suspected that after I got the bug out of my system, I would return to the law firm. I (naïvely) thought I could set up the company and then come back to be a full-time lawyer on Wall Street and run the consulting company on the side. (Both of my mentors, S&C's Richard Urowsky and McKinsey's Jacques Antebi later joined the advisory board of my company. Later, Jacques would join KIND as our executive vice president for strategic and international development).

In mid-November, I rented a small studio apartment on HaKerem Street in Tel Aviv. I started delving into legislative research as well as setting up my new consulting firm. I began by looking into sectors where complementary comparative advantages and symmetrical respectful relations among equals could be fostered: agriculture and food processing, Dead Sea cosmetics, apparel and textiles.

I had so much conviction about my ideas that, through sheer determination, I was able to persuade people to open doors for me. Most, while skeptical about my prospects of success, were warm, encouraging, and supportive.

Despite this can-do attitude, I struck out with the consulting company idea. I quickly discovered that nobody in the Middle East felt they needed a consultant. "Why would we pay you?" they asked with typical Israeli frankness. "If we wanted to do this, we would just do it ourselves."

THE BUSINESS OF COOPERATION

One night, as I was doing research, I stopped at a small grocery store on Ben Yehuda Street. On one shelf, I noticed an obscure-looking jar of sundried tomato spread. Sundried tomatoes were not widely known among American consumers at the time, and I was curious. I bought the jar and a bag of pita bread. Later, sitting at my desk, I devoured the whole thing in one sitting. It was totally addictive.

The next morning, I went to the store to buy some more, but was told that they had run out of product. The company had gone bankrupt and was not making more. I had bought the last jar in stock.

After a few days of craving, it dawned on me that maybe this could be my vehicle for turning theory into practice. Instead of consulting others on how to launch businesses that fostered economic cooperation, I should create one myself.

I went back to the store, hounded the manager, and got the name of the distributor that supplied him the sundried tomato product. I called the distributor, and in my broken Hebrew, tried to explain that I was a crazy Mexican Jewish lawyer who wanted to use this sundried tomato spread to prove a joint-venture model for bringing peace to the Middle East. The distributor was perplexed, to say the least. But he agreed to give me the number of the manufacturer who had just gone bankrupt, Yoel Benesh.

When I called him, Benesh invited me to meet with him at his factory. It took me a few hours of long walks and bus rides from Tel Aviv to an industrial zone in Even Yehuda, near Netanya. I arrived at an empty building with virtually no equipment. Yoel's workers had been making everything by hand. They would manually mix the product in big kitchen vats, fill the jars, seal them, and immerse them in a gigantic pool of hot water to pasteurize them. They then would dry them and apply the labels one by one.

Yoel explained that he had been sourcing their glass jars from Portugal, their tomatoes from Italy, and other inputs from across the world. He had tried to penetrate the U.S. market, but it was too costly. He could not compete with Italian and Greek brands.

I'm sure Yoel wondered what a lawyer with no experience in the food business would be able to contribute, but he had nothing to lose. And when I told Yoel about my ideas, he sincerely and passionately connected with my philosophy. His father had

developed good relationships with some Palestinian olive grow-
ers. Yoel had several Arab Israeli friends, including his accoun-
tant Imad Salaimi, who'd go on to be part of this journey. The
idea spoke to Yoel on a deep level, probably as much as it spoke
to me—as a social mission more than as a business. Was it fate
that I met Yoel of all people?

I introduced Yoel to a glass jar manufacturer in Egypt, who
would charge a much lower price than his Portuguese supplier.
Together, we worked to identify a supplier of sundried tomatoes in Turkey that would be far more competitive than the
ones in Italy. And we sourced olives, olive oil, and basil from
Palestinian farmers in Ouja and other small villages across the
West Bank and from Palestinian citizens of Israel in the village
of Baka El Garbiyah, near Umm el Fahem, including Abdullah
Ganem, an eternally jovial grandfatherly figure. With geo-
graphically closer and more competitively priced ingredients
and jars sorted out, we decided to give this business a shot.

In parallel, I had been researching skincare products made
with Dead Sea minerals. I had met a group of French and Israeli
entrepreneurs who purchased mud soaps from a Bedouin family
and Dead Sea minerals from Jordanians. I agreed to do a pilot
with them to see if we could market the products in the United
States. I ordered five hundred samples of each of their products,
including seven varieties of mud soaps, hand cream with vitamin E and avocado oil, mud masks, and big tubs of Dead Sea
bath salts with aromatherapy essential oils. (If you read Chapter
1, you know where those will end!)

The business idea behind Yoel and my sundried tomato effort
came directly from my college thesis and the legislative proposal I wrote thereafter. Both built on the existing theory of
economic cooperation, which holds that warring populations

will be more inclined to a lasting peace when economic links exist between them. Setting up ventures owned and staffed by people from groups in conflict gives them a reason not to fight, and, eventually, a reason not to hate one another. When people work together or trade with one another, three distinct benefits emerge. At a personal level they discover their shared humanity and shatter cultural stereotypes. At a business level, they gain a vested interest in preserving and cementing their relationship because they are benefiting one another economically. And at a regional level, success gives people a stake in the system.

I get a lot of questions, then as well as now, about this business model. Usually people are polite, but the gist of their questions is this: How can you be so naïve as to think peace in the Middle East will come as a result of selling little jars of sundried tomato spread? My answer: It won't, but it will be a start. None of this was ever intended to be a substitute for the necessary geopolitical solution: ending the occupation and achieving a Palestinian state that recognizes the right of Israelis to have a Jewish and democratic state at peace with it. My little effort was always meant to build cooperation and collaboration, to give long-warring cultures peaceful and fruitful experiences with one another. I simply wanted to build small bridges that could perhaps serve as foundations for larger ones in the future.

What became my core passion and expertise was the idea of business with a social bottom line along with the business bottom line—built right into the DNA of the company. What excited me most about this model was and is that the social and business missions are not only in harmony, but also reinforce and advance one another.

The more sundried tomato spread I sold, the more Yoel could scale up his venture and increase the impact of the cooperative footprint. He would find more Palestinian farmers from whom to buy olive oil. He would have more Turkish, Egyptian, and Arab Israeli trading partners. And each of them would have more staff impacted by this cooperative venture and exposed to working with the other side.

Market forces are among the most powerful drivers in our society. If you're able to structure your ventures or give validity to your dreams through a business model that is in true harmony with the social objectives it sets out to address, you can scale faster, you can do so in a self-sustainable fashion, and the impact can be measured. This is a perfect application of the AND philosophy. Social enterprises challenge assumptions and refuse to compromise between social and financial impact.

PURPOSE GIVES YOU STAYING POWER

After a couple of months of working with Yoel, I wrote to the Haas Koshland family to update them on my research. I explained that the consulting idea had gone nowhere, and shared my plan to start a company that would try to foster those joint ventures itself. I requested their permission to return to the United States earlier than planned so I could start setting up the venture. They were very supportive. By the spring of 1994, I had rented my tiny studio apartment in Manhattan and was by then deep into my Dead Sea soap idea as well. I was getting ready to start making the biggest business mistakes of my career, as well as to set the foundation for what would become my successes.

To say PeaceWorks had modest operations at first is to overstate its size. When product shipments arrived, I brought them down to the "warehouse"—the basement storeroom of my apartment building—by sliding the boxes down the stairs on recycled planks of wood. I equipped my basement cubbyhole with used furniture that I scavenged from curbside garbage piles. The same windowless storeroom also served as my office. My friend Andy Komaroff came to visit and humorously gave me a "tour" of my own facilities. "Welcome to the worldwide headquarters of PeaceWorks Inc.," he said proudly as we walked down the building's back service stairs into the dark basement. "Here we have the finance department," he said as he pointed past the laundry machines in the basement. "And here we have operations and logistics," he indicated as we walked through the room housing the garbage compactor, ignoring the stench.

What kept me going was my sense of mission: I was in this to help build a footing for peace. Although PeaceWorks floundered as I paid for my failures and lessons in inventory control, marketing, new product development, and strategy, what never wavered was the company's purpose. That was essential because it enabled me to persevere and to view every setback as an opportunity to learn and improve. After all, I had to make a difference. I had to help my Israeli, Arab, and Turkish partners. Failure was not an option.

Every time I had to struggle out onto the street at dawn with my heavy bag of samples, ready for another twelve hours of cheerful door-to-door selling, I remembered the scenes I had observed in Israel and Palestine. The people there deserved to live in peace. I also thought about my father, and what he went through as a child during the Second World War and as a kid in a concentration camp. That put my problems in perspective—and reminded me of my mission.

If you can find a purpose that defines you and imbues you

with meaning, then channeling that passion and energy toward your business or vocation can be a source of near invincibility. Pursuing what you believe in already constitutes success regardless of the outcome.

Incorporating both a social and a business mission into a venture's DNA does not happen overnight. It can take days, weeks, months, or years to decode how to let those objectives reinforce one another harmoniously and authentically. It requires out-of-the-box thinking and disciplined questioning of assumptions. It would be disingenuous to guarantee that, by reading about my experiences, every reader filled with purpose will come up with a magic formula for making money while solving society's ills. It took me many years to figure it out and it involved making big mistakes and being willing to learn from them. But what got me there was sincerity of purpose, and the steadfastness that comes with it.

It was purpose that helped me overcome the gravest doubts and the biggest challenges. In the mid-nineties, a spate of terrorist bombings that targeted the Tel Aviv bus routes made me question the feasibility of my work to advance peace in the Middle East. I was trying to bring together two populations through the slow build of a linked prosperity, while an act of violence from one individual could cause such carnage and change the mood of the region overnight. Images of devastation from a terrorist bomb in Dizengoff shopping center shook my commitment and made me question whether our work was a mirage or even a lie. I called Yoel, Abdullah, and other trading partners, and asked them if they, too, felt that perhaps we were making a mistake, and we should suspend our efforts, at least temporarily. "Daniel," Yoel instantly retorted, "these are our lives we are talking about. This is not a game or a school project. Now more than ever we need to continue our work and deny terrorists a victory." I never questioned the value of our mission again.

In those early days, I spent long hours on the road pitching my wares to stores. Sometimes my gas and travel expenses outstripped what I had sold for the day. Life as a traveling salesman is not easy; it undermined my motivation at some points. I once found myself sitting on a vinyl chair in a dingy Waldbaum's purchasing office on Long Island, waiting my turn to see the grocery chain's buyer. At my feet was the dilapidated fake-leather briefcase left over from my days as a law-firm intern, now stuffed with jars of sundried tomato spreads. I looked around. Elderly salesmen sat with kind but tired faces as they waited for a chance to be seen. I sensed they had been following this routine for several decades. Was this *Death of a Salesman* tableau my future? Could I turn the company around, both in profitability and in its social mission, or was it doomed to mediocrity? During the worst periods, when I had trouble meeting payroll and could barely afford to pay myself my $24,000 salary, I thought seriously about taking a job as an attorney. Overarching purpose gave me determination not to give up.

PURPOSE IS *NOT* A CRUTCH

While a social mission can fill you and your team with purpose, and can generate loyalty and support from consumers and customers, it is no replacement for ensuring that your product or service wins on its core features. A social mission should never serve as a crutch to bypass quality, nor serve as the basis on which to try to attract consumers. Studies that indicate consumers buy products because of their social mission, in my experience, are wrong. Consumers may want to think they do—and indeed, a company's social mission may be a reason to buy once—but, in practice, they repeatedly buy what they truly need and feel fits their lifestyle best.

The mission does not sell the product; the product sells the product.

Yes, increasingly consumers are focused on ensuring that the companies they buy products or services from are genuine members of their communities, doing their part to make this a better world. But that is not a substitute for delivering on the functional merits. First and foremost, the product must stand on its own. And if your social mission gets too far ahead of itself on the marketing front, consumers may feel it is masking inadequacies in the product.

I was so passionate about the PeaceWorks mission, that initially I put it front and center on our products. We branded that first sundried tomato spread "Moshe & Ali's." The marketing story featured Moshe Pupik, a fictional Jewish chef, and Ali Mishmunken, an Arab magician, who concocted a Mediterranean spread so delicious that it hypnotized rival armies and put them in a friendly trance. Instead of fighting, the warring armies would then drop their weapons, melt them into spoons, and use the spoons to partake of the entrancing spreads. I crafted a video and booklets telling this story in my attempt to explain, in a disarming way, how the PeaceWorks model functioned and how we were using food as a common bond to help people work together. "Cooperation never tasted so good" was the motto. People appreciated the story, but the tongue-in-cheek marketing and social emphasis didn't properly celebrate the high-end specialty spreads and their premium ingredients.

Fortunately by the time I launched KIND, I had incorporated this lesson from my experience with PeaceWorks. While KIND's mission of inspiring kindness means a lot to our team, from the beginning we decided it would not be a basis for how we position or sell the product. At least prior to the publication of this book and the concomitant decision to begin sharing the full story behind KIND, probably less than one percent of our consumers had ever heard of that part of our social mission; to sell more, we emphasize our products' healthful premium ingredients and delicious taste. We do want our community to learn more about our efforts to make this a kinder world, because we want them to join us in its pursuit, and because we believe this will engender loyalty and passion toward KIND and its products. But we drive our sales by focusing on being number one in how we solve the needs our consumers have.

Our company motto, "Do the KIND Thing for your body, your taste buds & your world," highlights our business and social priorities. Healthful products—and the implicit social purpose of fighting diabetes and obesity—are a prerequisite to anything we make: Be KIND to your body. Taste is the corollary prerequisite: Be KIND to your taste buds. Only after those two product features do we have the luxury to commit to be KIND to our world through the work we do to inspire and celebrate kindness.

Balancing how we speak about and structure our social work requires tact, thoughtfulness, and humility. If you get it wrong, you lose legitimacy. Third-party studies have highlighted that

KIND commands the highest level of trust and belief in its integrity, transparency, and authenticity among brands in the nutrition, cereal, and granola bar categories. This is of foremost importance. We constantly remind ourselves that, after all, we are a business—not-*only*-for-profit, of course—proud to be competing in the marketplace on our own merits and winning on commercial and financial terms. We have to be up front about this, and never try to leverage our social mission in a way that seems inauthentic or manipulative. We never do good to improve our sales; we do good to do good. If we follow this formula, we believe, KIND karma takes care of the rest.

AUTHENTIC PURPOSE
VS. SHALLOW "CAUSE MARKETING"

"Cause marketing," in contrast, is something I am quite wary of, both as a consumer and as a social entrepreneur. Over the last couple decades, it has become trendy to append social causes to a product's marketing campaign to get more people to buy the product. Rather than trying to tackle a social ill through a sustainable business model, some "cause marketers" attach some shallow bells and whistles to make brands or products seem socially conscious. My sense is that consumers are extraordinarily savvy and can detect and ultimately dismiss these marketing gimmicks. Perhaps in the short term a shallow campaign may achieve tactical objectives; but in the longer term consumers catch up. To build enduring brand value, the social effort needs to be authentic and permanent.

Corporate social responsibility comes in two flavors. Some

large corporations genuinely see the imperative to act responsibly in society and take steps to do good. A lot of good deeds come from some of the largest corporations, and frankly they often don't get credit because consumers question their motives, even when they are sincere and sustained. Then there are artificial and shallow initiatives that are clearly designed to create a semblance of goodness. These often feel forced, particularly when the underlying business is at tension with the social mission to which it claims to attach itself. If you are making unhealthful products (say candy or sugary beverages), trumpeting a donation to a charity that fights childhood obesity, for example, may actually hurt the brand because it will seem hypocritical and may actually highlight the brand's detrimental impact on society. (There are also business leaders like Warren Buffett who feel it is not for the corporations to decide how to do philanthropy, and they should disburse dividends and let their shareholders determine how to allocate their resources; I respect the viewpoint intellectually, even if I feel that in this day and age, where market forces and the private sector dominate our lives, corporations themselves have the power and responsibility to be positive actors in society.)

Here is how I see it: If your product's features fall short of those of your competitors, consumers will reject it even if it had been made by Mother Teresa and aimed to do a ton of good. If consumers are choosing between two products of equal quality and features, one of which has a sincere social purpose, the majority will opt for that brand. But if the product feels inauthentic, that will backfire and turn consumers off and prompt them to reject such brand. Consumers will choose a "fun" brand (say Doritos) that is authentic in just being indulgent before they choose a "fun" brand that pretends to be something it isn't. At the end of the day, if your goal is to sell products, focus first and foremost on winning on the product's merits. Then ensure that any stated social mission is genuine.

Take Maiyet, a luxury apparel brand I cofounded with Kristy Caylor and Paul van Zyl, initially borrowing on the Peace-Works concept I had pioneered in the food arena. Maiyet elevates the crafts of artisans in conflict regions, involving Christian and Muslim women in Liberia, Hindu and Muslim weavers in India, and jewelers with complementary techniques from the Hutu, Kikuyu, and Luo tribes in Kenya. Kristy and Paul have received wide praise for their aesthetic excellence. Maiyet products sell at Barneys and high-end boutique chains. It has been praised as the first upscale apparel brand to have truly melded a deep social mission with uncompromising craftsmanship.

Shoppers may appreciate that Maiyet strives to alleviate tensions between Indian Hindus and Muslims, but they buy the clothes because they are beautiful and well made. Customers do, however, understand the brand and what it stands for, and that makes them more loyal and more likely to look for Maiyet in stores.

MONEY IS NOT A PURPOSE

Here's where some people will say: "But my business doesn't have a purpose. Its goal is to make money." It's true that not every company is set up as a social enterprise. And it is true that financial health is vital for any business. But every successful company has a purpose and a value to give to society, beyond making money, or else its products or services would not be attractive. Beyond generating jobs and incomes for employees, successful businesses solve needs in the marketplace. People pay them money precisely because they are addressing a need they have. Social businesses identify opportunities that also address societal problems. But every business, if sustainable, addresses existing needs.

Whether you are thinking about your business or about yourself, striving just for money will limit your potential and never fulfill you because money is just a means to track and trade value.

To keep myself grounded, I constantly think about the parable of the forty-nine coins:

> In a faraway kingdom, there was a humble man who cleaned the floors of the king and was always smiling and happy. The king approached his senior counselor and complained, "How come I am the richest and most powerful man in the kingdom, and I am always worried and down, yet this pauper is always beaming with happiness?"
>
> "Don't worry, Your Majesty," said the adviser. "I will take care of this."
>
> That night, the adviser traveled far into the poorest reaches of the Kingdom, where the happy man lived in a little hut. He peeked through the window and saw him playing with his children on the floor as his wife cooked dinner.
>
> The adviser took a pouch with fifty gold coins, and placed it on the floor in front of the poor man's

house. But just before doing so, he removed one of the gold coins and put it in his pocket. Then he knocked on the door and hid.

The man came out, saw no one, but noticed the little pouch, and opened it. He was in shock. Gold coins. Just one of these gold coins was more than he could have ever hoped to see in his life. And yet it wasn't just one. It was two, and three, and four, and he counted them, forty-eight, forty-nine. FORTY-NINE GOLD COINS!!! "Wait a second," he thought to himself. "Forty-nine? That is an odd number. I must have miscounted." So he counted again and found, again, only forty-nine coins. How could this be? He was missing one. Where was it? He opened the door and looked in the porch. He ran back in and asked the children if they had taken one of the coins. He shook his son and pressed him, "Are you sure you didn't take a coin?" He didn't understand where the fiftieth coin had gone. He had forty-nine. That was incredible. But if he just could get to fifty! That should be the goal. If he could round out to fifty gold coins, he'd be immensely rich. He hid the coins under the earth and went to work the following day.

Throughout the day he was preoccupied with how he was going to save enough money to get to the fiftieth coin. He should take a second shift. His wife could take another job. And maybe his kids could stop going to school and help out. The king passed by and said hello to the janitor. But he was too preoccupied and irascible to be warm. When he got home, he was anxious and nervous—what if someone had stolen the coins? He ran and checked: Okay, they were safe. Then he proceeded to instruct his wife and children on the new jobs they would be assigned.

He took on two, and then three, shifts at work. His exhaustion and paranoia made him so irritable and unpleasant, that at some point the king just had him fired. He was so obsessive and demanding that his wife and children left him. The pressure made him lose his mind. He ended up all alone, searching for his fiftieth coin.

I was brought up not to care about money as a scorecard. But it gets harder for me not to keep count, because the more successful KIND has become and the more that money has become available, the more it becomes a dangerous poison that can seduce me into defining myself and my success by the amount of money I make.

As a kid, I had no financial needs. I was lucky that my parents were able to provide for me and my siblings, especially after they had struggled greatly. I always had a job or a small business that I was running, but I did it because I enjoyed the entrepreneurial pursuit. Making money was a source of pride, but it was never the money itself that gave me meaning or pleasure—it was the sense of accomplishment. I did track my earnings, because my dad taught me that as a businessman you have to keep records. And I was tenacious and focused on both the top line and the bottom line. But the money itself was just a means to measure my effectiveness.

Now that KIND has become a significant business, I never

lose sight of the importance of financial performance, but I strive never to concern myself with my personal net worth. And I do my best not to let financial success change my lifestyle. Particularly now that I have kids, I constantly remind myself to set a proper example for my children and not create a culture of abundance, but one of self-imposed limits. I try to stay focused on what matters, and not to glorify wealth for its own sake.

I also have to be careful not to forget my personal commitment to build bridges and press for Arab-Israeli reconciliation. As my business grows, it places more demands on my time. I try not to let KIND, even with its important social purpose, become an excuse for me not to pursue the harder challenges. I have to remind myself that I can't retreat from those responsibilities.

Does having a sense of purpose mean that you are deluded into thinking you are so special that you will necessarily achieve what nobody else has? I often get asked, "Why do you think you can help bring peace to the Middle East when so many have tried and failed to do so over half a century?" Well, I actually do think every one of us is special in his or her own way and can bring some specific strengths to the table. I bring tenacity, creativity, and sincerity of purpose. But I certainly do not believe I can do what others can't. I just believe I can be one of the many who need to join forces to seize back the agenda for conflict resolution; at best I can be one of the catalysts to get others to join in. And I know that it won't get done if we moderates keep making excuses about why we don't need to play a role to stand against violent extremism. I have a responsibility to do my part.

More important, the question misses the point about purpose. Once you've found your purpose, it doesn't matter if you are certain of whether you are going to solve the problem. If that is truly the mission that gives you meaning, how can you not pursue it? Meaning and fulfillment come from doing what you know you need to do—you can be at peace when you know you are giving it your best. You certainly can't wait for others to do it for you. As the celebrated Rabbi Hillel said, "If I am not for myself, then who will be for me? And if I am only for myself, then what am I? And if not now, when?"

TALKING WITH YOURSELF TO FIND YOUR PURPOSE

Many people who care deeply about a cause choose to donate some of their income. They are advancing causes they believe in in a sequential fashion: work hard, make money, then do some good with it. That's certainly commendable. But given the amount of time you spend at work, it's ideal if you can enjoy what you do. A lot of people now are quitting those safe jobs to find meaning. Under the right circumstances, your work can be something you enjoy and are proud to do.

I realize that it's a privilege to be able to select a career based on how it helps you fulfill your purpose; sometimes you just don't have those options. But even if your financial situation doesn't allow you to launch a whole business, you are more likely to make those ends meet and to grow professionally if you dedicate yourself to a company or organization that energizes you. And if you have the time to figure a better way by following the AND philosophy—an integrative instead of a sequential approach—then you may be able to find meaning and purpose while advancing business objectives.

Finding purpose in what you do is not an exhortation to sacrifice yourself for the greater good. There is nothing selfless or self-important about what I am advocating. When I dedicate myself to build bridges, it is not an act of sacrifice for humanity. It feels like an act of self-preservation. I derive enjoyment from it.

Indeed, if you do uncover a way to find purpose through your work, then you also need to be careful to not allow your career to consume you and your family and personal life. Satisfying work can be so immersive and engaging—can give you so much joy—that you can end up sacrificing other aspects of your life that are also important. Prior to getting married and having kids, I didn't realize how unbalanced my life was; and I could possibly have missed out on the blessing of raising kids and the meaning that comes with it (including raising them to become good human beings) because of my obsession with Middle Eastern peace and social business enterprises.

If you're at a crossroads or starting a new business or simply want to evaluate whether you can better incorporate purpose into an existing venture, you will need to truly understand yourself. You need to know what gives you purpose before you can translate it into business practice.

It could be to make others happy. To be a good parent. To take care of others. To invent a cure for a disease. To keep this planet clean. It could be a big global problem, or one that affects your community. Or something important to your family. Or something just for you. Purpose and passion are not just about your business or your job, and they will be different for each individual.

You may not have identified what force within drives you.

This is where introspection is key. Thinking hard about your life, and questioning your assumptions, will help you to be honest with yourself about what you believe and how you want to live as a person. A sense of purpose makes you happier and more effective in your job and in the rest of your life.

Talking with yourself often and deeply is not always an easy task but there are no shortcuts to understanding what makes you tick. You must take the time to ask yourself questions. Your answer most likely will not come overnight. And it may evolve as you gain other experiences. But that is why it is so important that you consciously invest the time to listen to your inner self along the way.

Knowing what makes you happy is presumably the first step to actually *being* happy. So why is it that so many people go their entire lives without considering it? It is tough work, actually, not just because our modern culture of tweets, blogs, emails, and Facebook posts extinguishes our time for deep reflection, but because these are tough questions that are not easy to answer. If you never ask them, though, you will never even start the journey to find the answers. And the journey itself may be the answer.

If you can find what you love, and do it, your success is guaranteed—because every day pursuing what you care about will fulfill you. But if you let societal pressure fool you into thinking that your "goals" are financial success, or power, or fame, or other empty concepts on which you benchmark yourself against others, you'll be like a hamster running on a wheel, never quite reaching the goal.

Even though this advice may seem obvious, in a culture that celebrates materialism and consumerism, at many points we are tempted to measure our success against that of others. It happens to me and I have to remind myself of my priorities. Many talented and smart people get lost chasing the wrong goal.

To find our true north, we need to talk to our innermost selves. We need to dream—to consciously daydream. To let our thoughts and our consciousness take us wherever they may. Daydreaming helps us to visualize the heights we can reach, to imagine new worlds, to imagine ourselves in new places, to never believe someone who says "it can't be done." Every major accomplishment starts with some people thinking it is impossible to achieve it and naïve to try.

Our fates are interlinked nowadays now more than ever. The challenges that new generations are inheriting are daunting. From resource scarcity to global warming, tackling these challenges will require that we recognize our shared humanity and work together. We cannot look around for someone else to solve these problems. We are the ones with the power and responsibility to lead the way.

Talk to yourself because along the road, as you commit to excellence and aim high, there will be times when you fall. And the higher you climb, the bigger the fall. Sometimes that fall will hurt. A lot. And at those times, when you talk with yourself, it is most important that you love yourself and cut yourself some slack. Be comfortable making mistakes. As long as you learn from them. But don't be afraid to keep climbing, and falling. For failures, and the lessons we draw from them, most often precede our greatest successes.

I cannot think of any venture I have initiated where an earlier failure wasn't an important precursor to an eventual success. Failure holds the seeds for greatness. So long as you water those seeds with introspection, they can be the root of your success.

Whatever you set as your mountaintop, all that matters is that you be true to yourself in figuring out what that is, and that you give it the best you've got. So that when you look back, as you continue that conversation with yourself, you will know you've lived life fully, with integrity, passion, and purpose.

CHAPTER 3

GRIT

Steadfastly Advancing Your Vision

One of the toughest challenges when starting a company is when your "brilliant" idea, the one you just know the world will love, involves altering consumer behavior or introducing something that didn't exist before. With KIND, we were creating a whole new category of products. We had to convince food-store buyers that our products not only were great sellers, but also filled a need consumers didn't even know they had.

The first question was what to call our new category. We spent years mulling over a name. Initially, to capitalize on the energy-bar rage, we called KIND a fruit and nut energy bar. Then we realized that the term "energy bar" bore the negative connotation of not being made from real food and not tasting good. We switched to calling our products fruit and nut bars. Then we began referring to the broader segment in which we competed as the "healthy snack bar" market—in line with other emerging competitors in this space. To distinguish KIND from bars made with fruit and nut pastes that were being introduced around the same time, we refined the name of our products as "whole nut and fruit bars" to highlight that our products were made from whole ingredients without emulsifying them.

These distinctions seem so trivial or obvious looking back, but they matter a ton, and figuring out the taxonomy took us hundreds of hours. When you're creating something new, everything has to be done for the first time.

Making a KIND bar brought its own challenges. We had to develop a recipe to bind the nuts and fruit with natural ingredients. One of these was honey, which also helped protect the nuts from oxidizing. We initially made small batches by hand and laid out the finished product in large baking trays to dry. Then we'd cut every bar individually. It was a labor of love, and very expensive and inefficient. We had to devise a process to automate the formation and packaging of the bars, which was extraordinarily trying because delicate whole nuts were moving through the line. We tinkered with every aspect of operations until each step worked, sweating long hours to figure out new ways to do things, and hiring experts when they were available and we could afford it. Our arduous manufacturing process is the result of thousands of brainstorming and trial-and-error hours.

I am aware that an often-accepted maxim of business strategy is to pursue the path of least resistance. It makes sense to avoid unnecessary headaches. And it's true that entrepreneurs do often have a penchant for embracing challenges, which can make us miss more efficient ways to get somewhere. But the easiest path is not necessarily the right path when pursuing a new venture, particularly one anchored around the AND philosophy. When it comes to defining your unique value proposition, you have to be wary of shortcuts. If in finance "cash is king," in consumer goods, product is king. So when crafting our products, we could accept no compromises. Yes, it was much harder to make a whole nut and fruit bar than a slab bar. But we could not cut corners on the essence of our concept. It took a lot of determination to stay the course.

Once we had a product to sell, we went door-to-door around the country to present our new bars. We had been selling healthy foods to specialty and natural stores for the past ten years, so we had relationships with stores that got us meetings about KIND.

One of these early meetings took place at a natural foods store in Colorado. I sat down at a table in the store's cafeteria with a nice buyer who looked me in the eye and said, "I don't know where to put your products." He explained that KIND bars did not look like they fit in the nutritional bar section of the store. And clearly they were not candy bars or cereal bars. He didn't think they would work in the checkout aisle.

"I don't know where to merchandise you," he said. "This is not what a nutritional bar looks like."

I took a deep breath. What was so obvious to me was apparently not getting through to him.

"The whole point is, it's not made as an emulsion because we're using ingredients you can see and pronounce," I said, reciting KIND's tagline.

He smiled politely. His concern, he said, was that consumers had become accustomed to eating pastes with a homogenous puréed texture.

"People are used to a smooth texture in their bars," he said.

After highlighting that our products were minimally processed and closest to nature, I convinced him, as a personal favor, to allow KIND in on a test basis, with a small rack over by the nutritional bars (but not on the same shelf).

In many natural foods chains, because buyers said KIND did not fit into the traditional nutritional bar selection, it was the grocery-section buyers who gave us a chance. At Whole Foods Market, for instance, most nutritional bars can be found in the natural Whole Body section. Because the original buyers didn't think we belonged there, KIND initially launched in the candy bar aisle, at the bottom of the shelves. Customers had to bend all the way down to pick up our bars. That was tough, because traffic was slower on that aisle, and people looking in it were looking for chocolate or candy. At the time, consumers who were looking for a "performance" bar tended to head for the nutritional bar aisle instead. And, as there was no "healthy snack bar" segment, or familiar products in that space, consumers didn't even know to look for anything like that anywhere. They had to discover us.

Despite the difficulties, KIND attracted consumers' attention with our transparent packaging. Eventually our products performed so well that they were moved from the candy section to the granola and cereal bar aisle. Now another roadblock emerged: Cereal bars are drastically less expensive than KIND bars, because they contain grains rather than pricier nuts and fruits.

We had to rely on the KIND bars themselves at this point. Luckily, once consumers tried them, they overwhelmingly bought our products again. Eventually we helped pioneer a whole "healthy snack bar" section within the grocery area. After some time, the healthy snack bar section became so popular that other nutritional bar companies started asking to move from their dedicated aisle to the section where KIND was located.

SOLDIERING THROUGH THE LEAN YEARS

Grit is about perseverance, the ability to keep going at all costs. At a small, struggling company, where every sale can spell the difference between the ability to pay your bills or not, grit means getting up every morning and selling as hard as you can.

As KIND was born in the aftermath of our losing everything PeaceWorks had invested to import the Australian brand of bars, we were in danger of going out of business. I had no idea how I would make payroll. Frequently I deferred paying myself part of my annual salary of $24,000. On top of all this, there was the pressure to deliver for PeaceWorks' investors.

I had taken on a $100,000 investment several years earlier, in 1998: $50,000 and $25,000 respectively from my childhood friends Jaime and Gregorio, and $25,000 from a friend Gregorio had brought in.

A couple of years before the launch of KIND, Gregorio's friend came to me and said she wanted me to buy back her stake. I wasn't legally bound to do so, and I could have just told her we did not have the money, but I felt morally obligated and I did not want an unhappy investor on my hands. So I bought out her shares. That took most of the cash PeaceWorks had, and it was money that was no longer available to put into the business when our situation worsened later.

I did have a safety cushion that others starting businesses do not. I knew that my parents would have bailed me out if I had been in danger of starvation. In the mid-nineties, my dad lent me $100,000 for the company, and I was enormously proud when I was able to pay it back a few years later. If things had gotten worse in PeaceWorks' early days, my family could have thrown me a lifeline. I didn't want to rely on them, and I wanted to make it on my own. But knowing they were there in case of an emergency gave me the fortitude to keep going.

For several years after I repaid my dad, PeaceWorks was going sideways. The most painful times were immediately before we launched KIND bars, when I had a half-dozen team members and we suffered a drop in sales. When that happened, our cash flow issues got worse, because our accounts receivable—the money stores owed us—were not being paid on time. A small company without an essential product is always the last in line to get paid by retailers, because they don't require more shipments from you. You have to beg and cajole and just stay on top of the people working in accounts payable at the stores. In addition, because we were a food company, our inventory had an expiration date, after which we had to throw it out or sell it to a liquidator at a steep loss.

The situation took a toll on me. I was too busy to be depressed, but I was terrified and felt isolated. To handle the financial constraints, I turned to time-tested methods familiar to anyone who's ever been broke in a big city. I spread my limited budget as thinly as I could. I searched out all-you-can-eat brunch restaurants and filled up—one satiating seating to last me an entire day. Or I bought a falafel or shawarma, loaded—and reloaded—on the vegetable toppings, and considered that my one meal for the day.

I consider myself a guy with a lot of vision, but at the time I was just trying to survive. When you are desperate, your ability to strategize and visualize is far more limited. PeaceWorks was nearly fatally wounded, on the cusp of going out of business. Luckily, after we developed KIND, the business took off, and all our hard work paid dividends. But it took a good decade.

If you can believe it, the minefield environment around the years immediately preceding KIND's launch (2001–2004) was nothing compared to PeaceWorks' first years (1994–2000), when I was young, naïve, and inexperienced. The mistakes I made during the decade before KIND could fill a business-school course primer on how not to run your start-up. And fortunately for me, KIND was able to benefit from ten years of lessons from my earlier efforts.

It's still not hard to remember—viscerally—lying on my futon in my old studio: I literally faced a towering column of boxes of mud soaps threatening to fall on me any minute. As I sought a ray of sunshine during the day, rows of cartons of sun-dried tomato spreads blocked the light from the windows. Going to get a bowl of cereal or to take a shower required advance planning because I had to trace around a maze of cases and assorted supplies that doubled as an obstacle course within my tiny studio apartment. Neighbors in my building swore that I was running a spa because the pungent smells of aromatherapy permeated the entire eighth floor. The Mother's Day gift baskets had not worked out. I had tied up all my savings in inventory. I needed to sell that inventory swiftly to generate a little income and to enable me to buy a second generation of product, which would hopefully benefit from the lessons of what I had done wrong in the first round.

SELLING: HOW I GOT IT WRONG

I thought I knew how to sell products. I was convinced that my experiences with booths, fairs, and kiosks back when I was selling watches as a teenager, my first start-up, would be translatable into my new lines at PeaceWorks. All the grit in the world couldn't make up for my lack of knowledge, unfortunately.

In 1994, I rented a kiosk at the Port Authority Bus Terminal and one at the World Trade Center, and offered both the skincare products and the Mediterranean spreads. I also took booths at trade shows and at Manhattan's ubiquitous street fairs. The booths at the trade fairs were barely breaking even; sales from the kiosks were not enough to cover the rental fees, let alone other overheads. This clearly wasn't the way to scale the business.

I quickly learned that kiosks did not elicit sufficient trust to sell food. I also picked the wrong locations. Harried commuters rushing in and out of the train tunnels at both the World Trade Center and Port Authority were not looking for groceries and did not want to buy and travel with jars of spreads; they just wanted to rush home. It was an uphill battle trying to cover the costs of the booth rentals every day.

I gradually realized that we needed the validation of an established food store, especially one that specialized in gourmet foods. There, the customers were looking for specialty food and were willing to pay for it. The imprimatur of a top retailer would carry considerable weight with consumers. If I could get my products into a specialty store, I would generate far smaller margins because the retail prices would need to incorporate a margin for the retailer and even for a distributor, but I would make up in volume what I lost in margin.

A new problem arose: My presentations to specialty retailers were not yielding any approvals. My products had many deficiencies—from the price structure to the nutritional information on the label, to the look and feel of the brand—but I didn't know what the problems were, let alone how to fix them. I started going into retail shops and refusing to leave until the buyer or store manager either ordered my products or taught me what I needed to do right. The managers appreciated (and were entertained by) the sincerity and incongruity of my efforts: Here was a crazy Mexican Jew who had abandoned a law-firm career to carry around bottles of sundried tomato spreads in a gigantic brown vinyl briefcase, all for the sake of advancing economic cooperation in the Middle East. They liked my story and my willingness to learn and do anything to make things work. So they were a bit more patient. It helped that the product was really tasty. Some gave me a shot; some gave me advice.

I remember walking into the famous Upper West Side grocery store Zabar's, the pantheon of specialty foods. I loved the energy and all the characters there—Neil Simon and Woody Allen characters alike, and all together in one store. I approached a clerk and asked to meet with the general manager or the owner. I waited perhaps an hour to talk with someone. Eventually, Saul Zabar himself and Scott Goldshine, his loyal manager, came over. I didn't get the chance to go present the product inside an office or even at a buyer's desk. "You have one minute," Saul said to me as he tapped the far end of the last register, where people were bagging their groceries.

Right on that metal table, I positioned the jars and explained the concept. Saul and Scott proceeded to insult me in a friendly way: "You have no idea what you are doing. Your labels are too busy," said Saul. "Your pricing structure is all off," said Scott. "The product is too salty," exclaimed Saul. "And too oily," added Scott. "This is all wrong," they both concluded. In between insults and curse words for how completely inept I was, they gave me exceptional advice. I listened intently and promised to work on it all. The whole ordeal may have lasted ten or fifteen minutes in the end, but it felt like I had been in a boxing match with two heavyweights for an hour. Zabar and Goldshine agreed that if I made the changes they suggested, I would get a chance. I am sure they doubted I would come through, but a few months later I did, and they placed what at the time was a huge opening order (ten cases). We ended up building a twenty-year relationship; we're still friends, and our products are still sold at Zabar's.

At the beginning, PeaceWorks' Mediterranean spreads had even more problems. The jars were leaking oil because they had not been vacuum-sealed correctly. The labels were misaligned because they were placed by hand. Our pricing was a mess because we had not created the appropriate margin structure to allow retailers and distributors the profits they needed. I had to go back to the drawing board again and again.

That was how I educated myself about the food industry. In retrospect, it was one of the greatest learning opportunities I was given, because these were the people who were in the trenches. I brought in my jars of samples; they told me what I was doing wrong; I fixed it; I closed sales, and I ordered more products from my trading partners.

While I was trying to get into the specialty stores, I was also casting as wide a net as I possibly could. I had no distributor and had to make every sale myself. My system was not exactly time- or cost-effective: I walked the streets of New York City selling to any store that would carry my products.

I was a newcomer to Manhattan so I didn't really know the city well. In the early days, after a night out with my friends, once the streets were quiet, at around 2 a.m., I would drive my old Cougar down every avenue and street, doing reconnaissance. I would stop every few blocks after observing any food stores to indicate their presence in my notes. It took several nights of driving, but eventually I had a hand-drawn map showing the location of every grocery store, convenience store, bodega, department store, and any other shop I thought sold food on the island of Manhattan.

Then it was time to hit the pavement. I started off on foot at 7 A.M. at 122nd Street and Broadway, up near Columbia University. Walking down the west side of Broadway, I headed downtown, stopping at every store that I thought might carry my products. I carried my fake-leather briefcase filled with thirty pounds of Moshe & Ali's spread samples in glass jars and a loaf of bread for taste-testing purposes. I would not leave unless the store owner gave me a chance. If the person in charge of the store didn't have the authority to place orders, I asked for the phone number of the person who did. Later, I would call the buyer at headquarters.

Sometimes it would take a full day for me to walk the length of an avenue all the way to the tip of Manhattan, just doing one side of the street. Then the following day, I would do the other side of the street, store by store. On other avenues like Madison or First, with fewer food stores, it was more efficient for me to crisscross the street as I walked. I covered every avenue in Manhattan in this manner. Most of the opportunities lay on Broadway and on Second and Third avenues, with some exceptions on the Lower East Side and in SoHo.

When I received my boxes of goods from the Middle East, I packed up my battered Cougar and delivered the orders myself. Since the trunk's lid was broken, I used duct tape to keep it shut.

After I had some small success selling the products into retail stores, I was permitted to set up demonstration tables so customers could sample my goods. Doing demos at Zabar's was the highlight of selling for me. I spent about $50 buying delicious crusty baguettes from their famed bakery counter, and saved money by conducting the demo myself. Over the course of several hours standing in their store and telling customers about PeaceWorks' products, I would go through two to three cases of spreads in samples alone, and would sell thirty cases, or about $1,000 worth of spreads in one day. The store was the epicenter of gourmet food in New York City, and I loved to make customers laugh as I told them why I was so passionate about my products. I had similar experiences at Fairway Market, West Side Market, and other independent retailers across Manhattan.

Once I had about two hundred stores in New York City buying products, I engaged small distributors to service them. I would open the account and make the first sale, and my distributor would maintain the business, delivering the reorders. I still had to do all the selling but I no longer had to make deliveries, which freed up some of my time for more sales.

My next target was Philadelphia. I was twenty-five at the time, and dating a senior at the University of Pennsylvania. I followed the same procedure I used in Manhattan, driving the streets around the university and drawing out a map of all the food stores I could see from the car. I looked through the Yellow Pages and made a list of everything listed under specialty stores, natural stores, health food stores, kosher stores, or grocery stores. Then I tried to call each store to make an appointment with a buyer.

This was a completely inefficient way to sell, but I didn't realize how wasteful I was being with my time. I often drove for an hour to an appointment in the Philadelphia suburbs, only to discover the store specialized in Hungarian meats or Hispanic food or was a tiny convenience store with little chance of attracting consumers who would shop for specialty Mediterranean spreads. Or I arrived at 5 A.M. at the Germantown farmers' market to meet a buyer at his stall, only to learn he had taken the day off.

One account that I was able to sell to was Ashbourne Market in Elkins Park. This customer represented a typical sale: a two-hour round-trip drive, for an order of less than $40, with a potential for a second order later in the year. I realized how scant the progress was at the time. A logical human being would have given up, but I was determined and naïve. And the naïve aspect was part of what kept me going because I was somewhat unaware of the huge obstacles I was going to have to overcome.

One of my first big scores was a big distributor on my way to Philadelphia, Haddon House. They were a serious national distributor, and getting them on board was an energizing win for me. Once they were stocking my products, I made a point of getting to know the sales representatives who serviced my customers. I would take groups of them to lunch at a nearby Applebee's, a huge expense for me, but worth it because it bought me time to explain my products as we ate. My hope was that they would open accounts for me, and sometimes they did. I also went on ride-alongs with them when they visited customers. They would introduce me, and I would pitch directly to the buyer at the store. Moshe & Ali's spreads barely registered on Haddon House's radar; in contrast, KIND is now one of Haddon House's most important lines.

TWO PHASES OF ENTREPRENEURSHIP:
FORGING GRIT THROUGH CERTITUDE

Grit is about attitude and temperament, about staying power forged from character. But where does that determination emanate from? Besides sheer character, can the process through which you reach a decision to pursue a venture influence your level of steadfastness? I believe so. Furthermore, a two-stage process can save an entrepreneur from himself before the venture starts. An entrepreneur has to have conviction to get to the finish line no matter the obstacles. But what if one is pursuing the wrong idea? You could end up mired in the mud your entire life. That is why it is essential to separate the research and development phase from the execution phase.

Once you get an idea, it is vital to first test it. Had I delved into a big marketing campaign before testing the Dead Sea minerals as I did through the newspaper ads and the street fairs, I could have wasted millions instead of thousands learning from my mistakes. During this initial phase, one must question every aspect of the idea. Does the idea make sense? Is someone already pursuing it?

If you do your research and find that you don't have any competitors, you clearly have not done enough research. Every idea under the sun has some competition. For instance, even though I had never tried sundried tomatoes, I quickly learned that an entire cottage industry in Italy and California existed around them. This is a time for healthy skepticism. Is there truly a problem that needs to be addressed? Does the idea address it in a credible and satisfactory way? Is it efficient and effective? Is your process for getting there sound and realistic? Do you have what it takes? Invest the time during this phase to ask all the tough questions, even about yourself and your temperament and financial situation. The research phase has to incorporate true introspection as well as empirical research. It is prudent during this period for you to ask those you trust for their earnest assessment.

Only once you question yourself and your concept thoroughly and deeply—only once you've walked through the fire of doubt—should you feel comfortable moving forward with your idea. If after a serious period of research and introspection you are still convinced that your venture is sound, you then flip a switch within your heart and your brain—and move from skeptic to evangelist.

The evangelist phase begins with the first moment of execution. From that point forward, you can never look back or give up. You are invincible and cannot be stopped. You draw strength from knowing you tested and retested, and that you can get there. Nobody's doubts can discourage you. You can have moments of failure and weakness. But inside you carry that fire that tells you, "I must stay the course, and I will achieve my goals—failure is not an option." Of course it is normal and necessary for you to constantly ask yourself questions about how to adjust strategy, about how to incorporate feedback and new information, and about how you can improve your product or delivery system. You have to be a critical thinker at all times. But, during the evangelist phase, you cannot doubt the essence of your pursuit. You have to put all such doubts aside. Nobody and nothing must stop you or discourage you, only strengthen you and your conviction. You become an actionist, a person who gets things done in a single-minded fashion.

The process of moving from skeptic to evangelist is vital. If you confuse or mix up these separate phases, you can cause yourself and your dream a lot of harm. If you have false assurances about the certainty of your idea because you didn't test it thoroughly, you can end up in the wilderness for decades and waste your energy and your life—is that motivation enough to take the research phase seriously? On the other hand, once you flip that switch, it is vital that you not let setbacks stop you. Anchoring around the conviction you draw from the righteousness of your purpose *and* from the certainty of your path, backed by the thorough research and thinking you did during the skeptic phase, should give you the sheer determination to stand up when you fall.

Not everyone is cut out for a life of entrepreneurship. It is like parenting—enormously rewarding *and* enormously challenging. There's a great satisfaction in doing something that you love. But you need to understand you will experience both higher highs and lower lows than in a traditional office job.

Unanticipated things will go wrong—sometimes horribly wrong. It's okay to feel scared and isolated; you can accept those emotions and get back to work. You may have some of the most difficult moments in your life. At the end, though, if this is truly your baby and your mission, you will end up loving the journey because it is the journey you are meant to walk. Even with those setbacks and horrible failures, you will draw meaning from your efforts.

I wish I could say it never crossed my mind to give up, but in the years before we launched our first KIND products, I did consider quitting and going back to a safe career in law. Sometimes I thought longingly about what it would mean to draw a steady salary and not bear the responsibility for other families' sustenance. I worried that my company might never be successful and that I would not achieve my mission.

What kept me going were the underlying anchors of grit, purpose, and conviction. I just couldn't let go of my dream, and I couldn't let my team down.

CAN YOU TEACH GRIT?

As a kid, my favorite story was "The Three Little Pigs." The lesson about investing time in quality work stuck with me, and in everything I do I always try to build a solid structure. Now my wife and I read this folktale to our children. We also read them the story about "The Little Engine That Could" ("I think I can, I think I can, I think I can").

Can you teach resilience? How do you forge a young (or less than young) personality to know to get up and not stay down? How do you inculcate the sense in your kids that they should not take no for an answer when they truly believe in something? As parents, we sometimes face the perverse incentive for our kids not to question us and to accept whatever we tell them. But teaching your kids that it is okay to question authority, that it is okay to press you, is sometimes useful. You don't want to raise someone who can't get along with his peers because he is too pushy or stubborn. But you also don't want a pushover who accepts whatever life throws at him or her and will blindly obey when someone imposes an arbitrary rule or condition.

The lesson has to be taught and then restated for them: If something goes wrong, don't be afraid to try again. What matters is effort. What matters is that you don't give up. *Don't be afraid to fail. Be afraid to not try.* Children (young and old) want to avoid disappointing their parents. It is important for us to learn to compete with *ourselves* and be proud of our effort and not to try to succeed to impress others. A great book that shares insights on this front is *NurtureShock,* by Po Bronson and Ashley Merryman.

Much of our success—or lack thereof—in life stems from luck. But much of that luck is also related to our persistence in the game. If you don't play the game, after all, you can't score. Life will certainly throw many curveballs, so teaching ourselves and our loved ones to have a resilient mindset can help us deal with that uncertainty and persevere. It is critical that we build—in ourselves and in our offspring—the self-confidence necessary to keep playing the game, even if we don't think we are that good at it. The more we play it, the better we get at it.

From an early age, I saw my father working hard on his business selling timepieces. Often people would come to ask for his advice. I loved to sit next to him as he worked in his study, doing my homework and listening to the conversations he had with his colleagues. Watching my father's work and life ethic had a lot to do with my drive to become an entrepreneur and to try to improve our world.

I started earning money from an early age. Although my family was well-off by Mexico City standards, we were taught the value of being as financially independent as possible. Even when I was too young to truly understand what that meant, I put money away in a piggy bank.

When I was six or seven years old, I started my first business, organizing carnival games for my three siblings and my cousins. I would charge each kid a couple pesos to play a ringtoss game, with a spicy Mexican candy called chamoy or a stick of gum as a prize. My sisters Tammy and Ileana, my brother Sioma, and my cousins Sandy and Eddy played all the time.

When I was eight, I did my first professional magic show. Eventually, my magic business grew and I needed to acquire a stage name. Taking inspiration from Houdini, my "uncle" Jordan suggested The Great HouDani. When I partnered with my friend Jaime Jaet, he insisted on becoming HouJaime (which doesn't sound like Houdini at all). Another friend, Gregorio Schneider, joined me and Jaime as the fantastic clown Huevolete (which would roughly translate as "Eggoletto"). Together we did shows at kids' birthday parties, bar mitzvahs, retirement homes, schools, children's hospitals, and at a center for kids with severe developmental delays.

Our best gig was at a department store that Jaime's parents partially owned. On Children's Day, the Mexican holiday of Dia de los Niños, we would do eight back-to-back shows for two hundred kids at a time. We would make about 500 pesos (roughly $80 today after adjusting for inflation), which was a lot of money for us.

My partnership with Jaime and Gregorio continues. As I shared, they were the first investors in PeaceWorks, and they still hold stakes in KIND.

Around the age of twelve, I wanted to learn more about business, and I wanted the experience of doing things on my own. I asked my parents if I could get a real job for the summer. They were hesitant to let me go off by myself, but they spoke to my godfather, and he arranged a job for me, helping in a textile wholesaler in downtown Mexico City.

I would ride the bus to the subway and then take the subway all the way downtown and walk a few blocks in the heat of the Mexican summer. The city was even less safe then than it is now, and children from well-off families—and certainly Jewish children—never left their homes unattended. Playtime occurred behind the high concrete walls of each family's home. So it was unusual for a kid my age and in my situation, from a private school, with plenty of opportunities, to go downtown on the subway every day.

"I think it wasn't very easy to discourage you from anything," my mom told me when I asked her recently how I managed to convince them to let me take the subway downtown alone. "When you set your mind to something, you did it."

My job was to carry big rolls of cloth on delivery runs to different locations several blocks away. I also would measure and cut cloth for customers, and work the cash register. In the middle of the eight-hour workday, at 1 P.M., I would get a soda break and could buy myself a cold orange Crush. That was my favorite part of the day.

When my family immigrated to San Antonio, Texas, when I was in high school, I lost the customer base for my magic-show business. I still wanted to work but only my dad had a work permit. I had a new friend who had immigrated to San Antonio from Russia, Max Reshetnikov. He convinced me to take a job getting leads for an aluminum siding salesman.

That was perhaps the weirdest job I've ever held, and the most unpleasant. Just like the movie *Tin Men,* with Richard Dreyfuss and Danny DeVito, aluminum siding salesmen often come up with unscrupulous, laughable, or dishonest techniques to entice poor families to install siding over their wooden homes, ostensibly to protect the house.

Max and I earned less than minimum wage on an hourly basis, plus $50 if any of our leads turned into an actual sale. The salesman we were helping, who I'll call Bill, would pick us up in our neighborhood in a big old seventies Cadillac with burgundy velvet seats. He would drive us for a half-hour into the gang-infested south side of San Antonio. Dropping us off on a corner at eight in the morning, Bill asked us to walk the streets for the next four hours under the scorching Texas sun, knocking on every door.

If somebody answered, we would tell them about the benefits of aluminum siding. Here's the sleazy part of the job, which I to this day regret: Bill had told us what to say to get people excited. We would tell them that the head of our company was coming to town, so we were running a promotion. Or we would say that *National Geographic* magazine would be visiting to take pictures of the most-improved homes. Using these tactics made me feel uneasy.

The downsides of the job were significant. I was propositioned. I was bitten by a dog (which required rabies shots). And I never earned one of those $50 payments, because I did not get even one appointment for Bill. Max got two or three, which made me wonder what I was doing wrong.

Once I realized that selling aluminum siding was not my calling, I switched to more entrepreneurial activities. I created a lawn-mowing business with another kid named Danny, which we aptly named DND Mowing Services. We offered to mow lawns in my neighborhood, Hunters Creek, and elsewhere. The business floundered, however, because we had neither a car nor a client list—nor, in fact, a lawn mower; if a homeowner wanted to hire us, we asked to use theirs!

Eventually, I started selling watches. My dad did me a big favor by introducing me to one of his suppliers from his duty-free business, a friend of his, who handled the MICHELE brand of watches. He agreed to sell to me initially just as a favor, at wholesale prices. Eventually I sold a significant volume, and I was proud that they wanted me to sell because I was good at it, not because they were doing my father a favor. My dad also hooked me up with a few low-end Chinese-made novelty watch brands. Once my watch-selling business got off the ground, I also got Citizen to sell me some watches and some of their clocks. I would eventually buy full lots of clocks that Citizen needed to liquidate, five hundred to a thousand clocks at a time.

I started selling at the Eisenhauer Road flea market in a bad part of town, the year I was sixteen. I would drive there at 7 a.m. on a Saturday, often bringing my younger brother Sioma, who was twelve, along as my assistant. I priced my watches between $20 and $60.

The flea market had dirt floors and a labyrinth of small booths with people hawking everything from counterfeit Chinese merchandise to novelty goods. There was a pawnshop, and stores selling the kind of trinkets you find in an Oriental Trading Company catalog. Bizarre characters walked the aisles. Our favorite thing, once we had sold one watch and had some income, was to buy one of those huge smoked turkey legs and share it. (I don't think I could eat one of those monstrosities today.)

My time at the flea market helped me hone my business skills: negotiating, bargaining, pricing, keeping books, factoring in all costs including shipping and overhead. In essence, I learned about retail merchandising.

When I started college, I upgraded my watch business by renting little kiosks in shopping malls, most frequently at North Star Mall—San Antonio's fanciest—and at Ingram Park Mall. I called some of the kiosks Da'Leky Times (which sounded better than Daniel Lubetzky's Times); others were dubbed Watch-U-Want. I started developing a network of students who would help me man those booths. Staffing the booths was tricky because our leases required us to be open whenever the mall was open. On a couple occasions I had to skip classes.

The most dreadful moment was when there were no interested shoppers and no foot traffic in the malls—while I had to listen, over and over again, to a track of "oldies but goodies" songs wafting from the shop next to my kiosk. But it was a lot of fun when customers stopped by. I could sell more than $1,000 in a weekend, and I managed to turn a profit almost every week. My favorite customers were the tourists. I enjoyed negotiating with them. Many were Mexican, like me, and were used to haggling, which is a time-honored way to buy things in Mexico. I would sometimes sell five to ten watches to one family at once, as gifts for their relatives back home. Because I didn't have much overhead, my prices were very competitive.

My biggest challenge was dealing with shoplifters. When customers swarmed the booth, it was difficult to keep an eye on all my watches. I came up with a system of tying my watches in groups of five or seven with a ribbon, and memorizing the precise order of those clusters. Some of those watches cost me more than $100 each, in particular some cool Citizen scuba diving models I carried, and I didn't want to lose them.

There was one strategic spot where I could stand and see all my merchandise at the same time. If I was trying to close a deal with a customer and didn't happen to be standing in that spot, I would have to keep apologizing and leaving his side to circle the kiosk, just to check on the other side's displays. Having two team members was too expensive for my business model.

Once, when the booth was busy, there were a bunch of people on one side of the kiosk and one young woman, alone, on the other side, unattended. Within seconds of seeing her there, I checked the displays and a whole swath of watches, about a dozen, was missing. The young woman was the only person who had been near them.

As she walked away, I asked her to stop, but she ignored me and kept walking. So I quickly asked a salesman in the next booth to watch my kiosk and I ran after her, shouting, "Call the police! Shoplifter!" The kiosk workers around me, who shared my fury against thieves, tried to help by flagging down mall security guards as I ran after the woman. She was walking quickly, and I couldn't tackle her lest I be the one accused of assault.

Finally, she reached the doors leading to the parking lot. I was sweating, knowing that if she got through I would lose my merchandise (which would put a big dent in my college savings). So I held the doors closed until the police came. She kept trying to push me but I would not touch her; I just kept holding the doors.

Finally a police officer came up and asked what had happened. I explained what I had seen.

"Did you see her take those watches?"

"No, I did not," I answered.

"Then how can you be so sure that she stole them?"

"Because she was the only person on that side of the booth, and I check my watches periodically," I said.

The lady was carrying a purse and a white bag with a teddy bear on top. I asked the guard to get her to open her purse. He hesitated but I finally persuaded him to tell her to open her purse, over her objections.

The purse was absolutely empty. I gasped.

The security guard gave me a stern look. "Let go of those doors and let her through."

I started looking down at the floor in defeat. Then, as a final try, I said, "Ask her to show you what's in the white bag, under the teddy bear."

He hesitated; then he finally told her to lift the teddy bear. She started crying. Under the bear were not only my dozen watches along with their display packaging, but also a host of other items that she had clearly been shoplifting all day. Even the empty purse, it turned out, had been stolen.

Da'Leky Times went on hiatus while I went abroad to spend my junior year studying in France and Israel. For the first semester, I studied at the Institute of European Studies in Paris and took some courses at the Sorbonne.

I hadn't brought my magic trunk with me, but I became enthralled by the street performers I saw. I observed how they approached total strangers. It seemed daunting and intriguing. I decided to try it, so I compiled tools for a routine: a deck of cards, some rope, some coins, a ring. I practiced and practiced. Then I went back to the tourist area of Les Halles.

After a bit of hesitation, I meekly approached a table and asked in a low voice and broken French if the guests wanted to see some magic. They flatly said, "No" and waved me away as if swatting a fly. I went to another table and timidly asked again, *"Voudriez-vous voir un peu de magie?"* "Would you like to watch a little magic?" They, too, looked at me as if I were an insolent kid interrupting them and went back to their conversation.

I was frustrated and upset at myself. I walked back to my host's apartment in shame. I remember sitting on a bench, staring at the wall of the Métro, and feeling an enormous hole of anger in my stomach. Why was I so nervous? I was clearly emitting that insecurity to the prospective audience. Why would they want to waste their time believing I may have something worth showing them if I didn't believe in myself? Why was I even asking, rather than showing them something up front? I went home. That night, while lying on the bed unable to fall asleep, I came up with a different strategy.

The next evening, I showed up at the same spot wearing a sports jacket and self-imposed confidence. I approached a table and, rather than ask anyone's permission, just smiled at them, tossed a coin into the air, and made it disappear before their eyes. They all were surprised and exclaimed in unison, "How did you do that?" I smiled again, approached the woman seating closest to where I was standing, and "discovered" the coin from behind her ear. My small audience was having fun. I was enjoying it—so I kept going. Fifteen minutes later, I thanked them, and everyone at the table gave me a few coins. The table next door had seen some of the commotion and laughter and immediately called to me. That night I made $300 in tips, a very hearty sum for a college student having fun at work. But of course the greatest reward was that I had conquered my fears and insecurities and figured out how to become a street performer.

The next step was doing large shows. This was an even harder challenge. At a plaza outside the Centre Georges Pompidou, a series of street performers competed for tourists' attention at the same time. You could watch the sword-eater, or the breakdancer, or the mime. A performer needed to keep the audience's attention, or else they'd just keep walking or go see someone else. I invited three friends to come watch me, and I started inviting people to gather around as I launched into my stage-magic routine. About thirty people surrounded me at one point, but they soon moved on to watch other shows. I got nervous and started stammering and losing my voice. All I could muster were small grunts. People thought I was affected and stayed away. I was left with three people watching—my three friends.

Again, I was embarrassed and disappointed with myself. But I reflected on what I was doing wrong and determined to fix things. I realized that good street performers marked their stage and took time to prepare people for the performance. They wouldn't start the show right away. Instead, they carefully created an imaginary perimeter: People in the front row held the "best seats in the house," so they'd have an incentive to stay and see the show. I also convinced my friends Fiona and Hendrik to play the violin and the drums. I'd start the show by asking someone in the audience to "volunteer" and would pick my friend Wendy. I would slide a gigantic needle through her tummy, and would leave her in hypnotic suspension throughout the performance. I would only remove the needle after passing on the hat for contributions from the audience. The money was not nearly as good—we'd collect about $60 for a performance, which we'd need to split among the four of us, and then we'd have to wait our turn in the self-organized queue of performers to get another shot at the stage. But the intensity of having four hundred people on the streets watching your performance when you know you have nothing holding them—other than a needle through Wendy's body!—was electrifying. The experience of engineering the stage so that people stayed to watch taught me a lot about organization and behavior. Eventually I took my show on the road and traveled across Europe, paying for my travels with money from my magic shows.

Although I saw myself as a businessman, my experience in Israel sparked a new nerdiness in me. During my senior year, back in San Antonio, I got prescription glasses for the first time, after spending countless hours in the library researching my thesis on the Israeli-Arab conflict. In place of my social life, I now stayed in, working, at nights and on weekends, because I was so passionate about the subject. The thesis in the end was 268 pages long. (I still keep a copy in my office, and lend it to friends who are suffering from insomnia and need something to fall asleep.)

I applied to several law schools and was fortunate to get into Stanford Law, which was my first choice. With my acceptance in hand, I had to choose whether to continue with my watch business or head off to Stanford. It was a hard decision. My dad, who had never had anything more than a third-grade education, cherished the thought of his son going on to be a nice Jewish lawyer. He also wanted me to pave my own path and not go into the watch industry. He himself had dreamed of becoming a doctor, but his education had come to an end when the Germans invaded Lithuania. He had started selling watches because he had no other options, whereas I, through his sacrifices, did have choices. I had several long conversations with my dad where I tried to encourage him to let me come work for him at his duty-free company. It was clear that, in his heart, he would have enjoyed it if we worked together. But it was a testament to his selflessness that he wanted me to aim higher.

The two abiding interests in my life—commerce and peacemaking—were pulling me in opposite directions. It's possible to do magic shows on the side while in university, but eventually one has to choose a career path. I was conflicted about how best to achieve my goals. Eventually, I was lucky enough to figure out a way, using the AND philosophy, to do both. The way I avoided having to compromise on either of these dreams was to start my own business with a social mission. As an entrepreneur, I could set the terms.

WHEN OTHERS DON'T SHARE YOUR COMMITMENT

One of the most painful experiences of KIND's early years was the rash of defections that the company suffered as key team members jumped ship. I couldn't blame them. After ten years of trying to get PeaceWorks to take off, a significant minority of my team thought we were going nowhere with our new KIND Fruit &

Nut bars. I had private meetings with some team members whom I really liked, serious hardworking salespeople who were good at their jobs. They all told me they didn't see a future in the company and its new line. These departures wounded me personally, because, while I could see why they were making these moves, I believed fervently that KIND held opportunities for us all.

I had one team member who was a truly gifted saleswoman. I had invested in her, training her to make her even stronger. When she came to me to tell me she was leaving, I pushed her to explain why. She said I wasn't launching enough new products and expanding in enough directions.

"We just launched KIND," I said. "We need to let it take off first." But she would not be persuaded. I received the same feedback from several sales brokers who worked with us. They were happy to sell KIND bars, but they were eager—desperate, even—for new products. All these questions made me wonder if I wasn't moving quickly enough to innovate.

Despite this clamoring for more KIND items, I was terrified of overextending the brand into irrelevance, a mistake I had made before, which almost tanked PeaceWorks. How could I know if it was time to be disciplined and stay focused on KIND's core items or if the time for expansion had arrived?

CHAPTER 4

TRUTH AND DISCIPLINE

Staying True to the Brand and to Yourself

At KIND, we are laser-focused on maintaining our brand promise. I learned to obsess about the quality of our products and the consistency of our brand the hard way, through an earlier failure. Lack of brand discipline almost killed the Moshe & Ali's food line PeaceWorks first launched. The source of my failure was one of the most common and destructive mistakes fledgling entrepreneurs make: expansion at all costs and with no clear strategy.

In addition to the Moshe & Ali's sundried tomato spread, I also created and sold basil pesto and green olive spreads that were produced through cooperation among neighbors striving to coexist in the Middle East. The quality of our products was very high: *The New York Times* wrote they were "delicious . . . and lack the saltiness of other spreads." The products earned a devoted following among retailers who sold our goods and consumers who enjoyed eating them.

Based on our initial (if modest) success, we quickly expanded into seven flavors, including black olive, cilantro pesto, and garlic dill. All were based on Mediterranean flavors and maintained high quality, ensuring brand consistency, and performed reasonably well also.

"This is so easy," I thought. "Let's keep going." Food-industry experts had told me I should try to grab as much shelf space as possible. The simplistic mantra was "more products get you more shelf space; more shelf space gets you more attention; more attention gets you more sales." That is all basically true as far as initial trial sales go. This is partly why you see so many varieties of a toothpaste brand, or a pain-relieving medicine or a pasta sauce, on store shelves. But the missing qualifier is that to ensure *repeat* sales your new products need to stay true to the core brand promise, and each product has to stand on its own merits. Each product must solve a different need or desire so as not to cannibalize the sales of the original. New items should not disappoint consumers whose trust you have earned and who expect you to deliver the same quality and experience. This qualifier may sound obvious, but it is often overlooked.

In my quest to swiftly expand our line, we rapidly added new flavors, topping out at sixteen varieties within a couple years. Even though we were only in a few hundred stores and were generating sales well under $1 million, I thought we'd grow revenues simply through increased offerings—no matter what they were! To remind me of my arrogance and betrayal of my consumers, I still keep in my office today a jar of our most bizarre entrant: a sweet-and-spicy Asian teriyaki pepper spread. This product bombed, and it should have been obvious to me that it would. Why would I think that a Mediterranean brand made in the Middle East by Arabs and Israelis would have any credibility to sell an esoteric Asian flavor? This variety had nothing to do with our brand, and it raised eyebrows among our loyal consumer base.

Worst of all, the quality of our new spreads was far lower than the originals. The teriyaki pepper spread was gelatinous and, while the xanthan gum it employed to bind the sauce was technically all natural, in my heart I knew it did not nearly approach the premium quality of our first products. Our sundried tomato spread was addictive and special (PeaceWorks still sells it under the MEDITALIA brand and it continues to be one of the best products I have ever tasted). This other product was, at best, tolerable.

In my rush to grow our product line, I had obviously lost sight of what my brand represented. At that point in my career, I did not understand the importance of keeping a brand's promise. In my gut I knew these added products did not belong in our lineup, but I was greedy, unsophisticated, and unfocused. I rationalized things by thinking, "What is the big deal if some people don't like this variety? They just won't buy that product again and will go back to the originals. What's the harm?"

What I didn't think about was that consumers had trusted the brand, and I had a responsibility to maintain that trust. When people tried the teriyaki pepper spread, at best it turned them off, at worst it offended and upset them. Though they may not have articulated it in so many words, they felt the brand had lost its way and their dislike of that one product reduced their trust in the overall brand. It shouldn't have come as any surprise (but it did then) that that one big misstep cost us loyal customers; many of them stopped buying all of our products—even the ones they had previously liked.

Over the coming months and years we experienced a steep decline in sales, which I attributed to the inconsistent quality of our products. The way I had screwed up and betrayed loyal consumers was seared into my mind. My lesson was to never again sacrifice quality to gain shelf space, never to take consumers for granted, and always to obsess about quality control and staying true to the brand. Anything we launched in the future had to be at least as good as the products we already had on the market.

WHY A CONSUMER PRODUCT SHOULD *NEVER* DISAPPOINT—AND HOW TO ENSURE THAT IT DOESN'T

Even if you think you know what your brand stands for, and even if you feel your product will meet expectations, consumers may or may not share your perspective. How do you test or guarantee that? There isn't one single consumer—there are millions, and each of us has different tastes and preferences.

Case in point: the curious case of Netflix. I am a longtime Netflix customer. My wife and I love their "queue"—the list of DVDs of blockbuster films you want to receive, and the order you want to receive them in, one by one. Getting one DVD at a time saves me from the paralysis and time wasted trying to make the "perfect" choice out of all the options available on cable or online. We organize our queue every so often, and then watch what we get in the mail. That's all we have until we return it and Netflix sends our next choice. Instant streaming is the future, but that future has not arrived. Very few major new releases are available on instant streaming.

Reed Hastings, CEO and founder of Netflix, also consumes

his product but his public comments and his strategic moves with Netflix suggest that he experiences it quite differently from some of us. In the summer of 2012, Netflix made a policy change. They divided the streaming and DVD business, giving customers a financial incentive to opt for streaming only. They increased the pricing structure for the DVD service, and deeply angered many loyal fans in the process. In the wake of the changes and consumer reaction, Netflix executives expressed surprise that anyone would want to hang on to the DVD service and not just migrate to instant streaming. Netflix stock suffered, customer satisfaction suffered, and eventually Netflix was forced to reverse part of its new policy.

From their statements, it seems Netflix decision-makers didn't seem to understand that the type of stuff they may have watched—documentaries, independent and foreign films—which were readily available instantly, was totally different from what many of their consumers looked for: new releases of top movies, which were only available on DVD. Netflix obsesses about consumer satisfaction. And Hastings deeply understands his product. Even in this scenario, they had a blind spot into what the Netflix experience was like for a significant portion of their consumers whose individual preferences may be hard to decipher.

All brands are susceptible to such danger. Even a founder-led brand (like Netflix) can lose a connection with how others interpret their brand. How do you prevent that from happening?

While many marketers favor focus groups—gathering consumers in a room to react to brand initiatives—I find them mostly ineffective. I'm skeptical of the concept because the focus group consumers you round up tend to tell you what they think you want to hear. Focus groups tend to be administered by third parties and I believe that having someone else interact with your consumers and gather the insights for you is like playing telephone—something is always lost in translation from one person to the next. You miss so many layers of subtlety— facial expressions you could only absorb directly, or contextual answers you may need to elicit. Most focus group marketers bias consumers by asking leading questions, even inadvertently. Then there is Henry Ford's quip on why he never asked consumers for advice about his cars: "If I had asked people what they wanted, they would have said faster horses." Consumers may not know how to solve for a need they may not even realize they have. And sometimes you need others to validate a good idea before consumers embrace it.

In the early years, we could not afford professional focus group consulting firms anyway. So we'd walk up and down our office building, knocking on every door and offering other companies' employees free pizza on their lunch break in exchange for one hour of their time. I noticed how easily influenced the group was by others, how difficult it was to remain unbiased and fresh in that context, and how wasteful the whole experience was.

Instead, I started walking into public places—a coffee shop, a supermarket, or the post office—and intercepting one person at a time, asking conflicting open-ended questions to avoid biasing consumers.

To this day, when I meet someone I don't know who comments on our brand, including sharing that they love KIND, I try to learn from them. I ask, "Why do you love KIND?" I do this not for the compliments but rather to really understand their vantage point. And in the rare instances when someone has the guts to tell me they don't like our products or are dissatisfied with a particular aspect of the brand, I try to also learn from them and get a deep sense of where they are coming from. Of course you can't be (and don't want to be) everything to everyone, but you want to understand what those gaps are. So when we are launching something new, I still try to go down to the post office or supermarket with some samples, share them, and as hard as it is to do, I try to really listen to the feedback.

Another way to learn about your most loyal consumers' preferences is by forming a kind of focus group in real time. We have an e-commerce membership program called KIND Advantage. You need to buy very high volumes of KIND to be part of it. Those that do, receive unexpected shipments of new prototypes or new finished products from time to time, along with a request for their feedback. Part of what makes this group particularly valuable is that they are putting their money where their mouth is. We are able to learn from actual purchasing behavior of this defined group of loyal consumers. People may be inclined to want to please you by saying they "like" something new you present to them. But they won't be so nice if they have to pay for it. Consulting our most loyal consumers has an important ancillary benefit: They sense they are a part of our decision-making process and that we appreciate them as leading members of our community.

When launching new products, we also pay extra money to create mock-up packages that look finished and contain actual product, and then we place them on store shelves to see if people will pick them up. Inside the product we include a note encouraging them to visit our website and provide us with feedback.

Placing a product on store shelves helps you spot issues with package design that may not have arisen in an office environment. Also, it is invaluable to observe whether a product elicits interest in an actual retail environment. But even that model has its limitations because you may not immediately know if, once sampled, your product will generate loyalty and reorders.

You will only fool or disappoint consumers once. But there are tens of millions of consumers to be confused. So if you launch an inferior product and see initial sales, you may be thinking, "Great, this is a hit." But if your quality standards or brand promise is inconsistent with your original great product, every time you sell that new product to unsuspecting consumers, you may be losing their repeat business. Inconsistency in a brand is like introducing a virus into your brand system; you may have no idea that it is slowly spreading through your brand body, disappointing one consumer after another. If their disappointment is high enough, they may well abandon your brand altogether. That is why tracking repeat sales is so important, even if so hard.

The practice of "A/B testing" has become very popular among tech and digital companies. The idea is to launch your app or other tech product very swiftly, and test and retest it constantly, changing it and reinventing it based on user feedback. That can work in the tech world, where consumers are getting Facebook, for example, for free and will tolerate this rejigging. But it is different at a consumer products company.

PUSH VS. PULL

My experiences with my brash growth in the Mediterranean spreads space as well as my much more organic growth at KIND have taught me how important it is to focus on growing in a sustainable way. In the consumer product arena, the wise mantra is "the pull is more important than the push": As important as it is to "push" a store or buyer to stock your product in the first place, getting consumers to pull your products off the shelf is the far more important transaction. The push for shelf space can be made based on personality or friendship or your salesmanship, but if you get on the shelves and the product doesn't move, you burn your relationship with the buyer and eventually your product will get pulled in another way: discontinued.

I attribute much of KIND's success to our obsession with quality and our commitment to ensure we are true to our brand—that we understand what we stand for, and deliver on that experience every time we connect with our community. The threshold for launching a product at KIND is thus extremely high: A new product must exceed expectations—it can never bank on the goodwill we earned from consumers; it has to add to that goodwill; it has to always be true to what our brand stands for, always deliver a surprised "Wow, this is better than I could have imagined." A great product idea that does not fit with what our brand stands for should be pursued by another brand—not by KIND. And an idea that is consistent with our brand concept but is not executed in a way that will deliver on the taste and healthful properties that our consumers rightfully expect will not be launched by KIND, no matter how neat the idea may seem in theory.

TRYING TO BE EVERYTHING
TO EVERYONE MAKES YOU NOTHING TO NO ONE

When starting PeaceWorks, I didn't understand that different sales channels serve different purposes, that quality trumps quantity, and that there is a life cycle to a product and its distribution. I didn't quite get that each and every single place where I sold had to be a resounding success and stand on its own in order to build sustainably large sales. Fundamentally, I didn't know that all products and services should have a properly tailored distribution migration strategy: launching your products in channels where consumers are more likely to be adventurous first adopters (say, health and specialty food stores in the case of an innovative natural product); and slowly expanding into larger environments as you build brand awareness and a loyal following through product trial, word of mouth, promotions, and traditional and social media coverage. Instead, I felt I needed to sell to every store I passed, from neighborhood convenience stores to Bloomingdale's and Macy's. I had this mindset that every store had to become my customer. I was so proud of my determination. But grit without focus and strategy can lead you to waste your time, effort, and money.

On one sales call back when I was getting started, I remember visiting a small convenience store on Eighty-Fourth and Broadway, begging the owner to try my spreads. Mr. Kim kept trying to explain his reluctance: "These products are not right for my shop. People come in here to buy essentials like bread or milk." I kept insisting, "But this sundried tomato spread is beyond delicious." I opened the jar, dipped a piece of baguette into the sundried tomato spread, and almost forced it into his mouth. He could not get rid of me. He kept walking around the aisles, stacking ketchup into the shelves. I shadowed him everywhere he went, even to the basement, explaining how special this product was. After two hours, I finally got him to order just one case—$28.20 worth of product. He did it just so I would go away. I was so proud of myself. "Daniel," I said to myself as I walked out with my chest up high, "you're going to win because you don't give up."

But every time I visited that convenience store, even a decade later, I counted every one of those dozen jars of sundried tomato spread still sitting on that shelf, accumulating dust, hurting my brand, and unfairly occupying that poor man's valuable retail real estate. I was embarrassed. I should have invested those two hours in my relationships with specialty stores, where my products were well-received and had at least a decent chance of selling.

I made a related mistake with what I thought were creative marketing programs that I designed to boost PeaceWorks sales. Because I was actually too successful at getting retailers to like me, I ended up selling some retailers too much product. I didn't factor in that if the product does not move off the store shelves swiftly, you are not doing anyone any favors—not yourself and not the retailer.

In one egregious example, I set up a preferred vendor program to reward stores that placed large orders. Any retailer purchasing sixty-four cases of my Mediterranean spreads—an $1,800 order at the time—also received a wire display rack that cost me about $200, two in-store product demos, and our commitment to mention them in any articles written about us. I did not realize I was doing my customers a terrible disservice.

Sixty-four cases was just too much of this specialty product and took too long to move off their shelves, creating uneven inventory management (the sundried tomato spread and basil pesto sold quickly, but the rest of the flavors barely moved). It also hurt my own business. I would create a wave of new sales with these programs, and incur the not insignificant costs of the racks and the time for the demonstrations; then months would go by with no reorders. My customers had too many jars of my spreads on their shelves, and they resented me for it. Fortunately, they knew I had good intentions. But they wouldn't order my bestsellers till they got rid of the dogs.

We carried our lack of focus to the extreme in the early years. Because I was so passionate about our model to promote coexistence through business, I rushed from our flagship efforts in the Middle East into efforts in conflict regions across several continents. I thought we could replicate the model with neighboring conflict-torn populations. In Indonesia, we manufactured Bali Spice, which sold sauces and noodles made through cooperation among Muslim, Christian, and Buddhist women, as well as coconut milk made by Sinhalese and Tamil workers in Sri Lanka. From my native Mexico, we had Azteca Trading Company, which sourced raw materials from the war-torn state of Chiapas to make a line of chipotle-based sauces in Texas. The number of mistakes I made with each of the above lines would require another few books. I didn't have the patience to focus on building one big success first.

PeaceWorks was (and still is) a good concept. But all this was too much for our five-person operation. It was insanely dumb, but, like many entrepreneurs who believe they can do it all, I didn't see that at the time. We couldn't pay attention to all those brands. When you're building a business, you want to focus and deliver excellence at what you do. This simply cannot be done when you are launching multiple ventures, dozens of new products, and selling everywhere and anywhere at the same time.

CELEBRATE FAILURE BY LEARNING FROM IT

All my mistakes from those days in the wilderness are responsible for KIND's success today. Trying to forget or hide your mistakes is a huge error. Rather, hold them near and dear to your heart. Wear them proudly. Big failures hold better lessons than any success—as long as you are in tune with yourself and are open to learning from them. I can trace every one of my accomplishments to earlier failures that I learned from.

I know that when you are experiencing failure, it's pretty damn painful. It is easy in retrospect to wax poetic about it. But in the moment, you don't think you will survive, let alone have the time to reflect on how valuable those lessons will be for you in the future. That said, this is the most important time to constructively criticize yourself and reflect on what you did wrong, as well as how you can do things differently in the future.

Even when you are succeeding, it is important that you be attuned to your mistakes and actively look for those failures. When things are going well, fast growth can hide a lot of weaknesses and deficiencies. There are companies that seem like juggernauts of excellence because they happen to be part of a fast-growing market. But when that market's growth slows, or when they get hit by a challenge, their weak culture or lack of internal strength may bring them down. It is easy to lead and seem like a superstar when your company and your brand are taking you places. What is really worth admiring, though, is when you hit a wall and your team's character is tested.

To build a culture of constant introspection and renewal, we at KIND encourage our team to engage in "start-up think"—to review all practices every year, and to reinvent systems or practices on an ongoing basis if necessary. Question every decision anew, think critically. If you are failing, you are forced to do this. Let those failures invigorate you with the knowledge that, once you know what you did wrong, you can now start doing it right. You are half of the way there. If you are not failing, are you aiming high enough? At KIND we embrace the "fail fast, succeed faster" approach and welcome risk-taking and experimentation (with the qualification that we do not roll out products unless we are confident they will outperform in their category). And if you are succeeding, do not let success get to your head. Force yourself to question assumptions—to use the AND way of thinking to see if you can improve on any and every facet of what you do. Let errors inform you and keep you grounded and keep reminding you that you are neither invincible nor a genius, and that you can always do better.

WHY FOCUS MATTERS

Business is like the game of Risk. If you expand your armies too quickly and try to conquer land after land, you disperse your forces and leave your borders vulnerable. Enemies can then invade and defeat you. Your zeal to build an empire can lead to your demise. Similarly, when you're launching new products, you first need to make sure you defend your original leading items—to establish your core and continue to win on that central offering. You want each new move to be strong: Your products need to stand on their own and prevail at every store where they compete. Otherwise, if you fail with new products, you'll also dilute your assets and expose yourself in the key areas where you had an opportunity to succeed. You'll be deploying resources and attention that are desperately needed to maintain and grow your market share in your core.

You can expand eventually, but you need to do so only once your flagship line is well cemented—or a competitor will come in and take away your market share. When you do expand, make sure you're not changing the value proposition, which can confuse and scare away your existing customers. And confirm that you have enough resources to push hard. It's a matter of playing offense and defense. Being passionate without a strategy won't help your business.

A few years after KIND's launch, a friend showed me compelling data that the fruit and nut bars I had created were tiny, as a category, compared to the slab bar segment, which at the time overwhelmingly dominated the space. He recommended we launch a range of slab bars. I actually considered it briefly, because we were still trying to decide the principles that would bind our product lines.

In evaluating this idea, I had to think about what KIND was going to stand for. Your brand gets defined by what you choose *not* to do as much as by what you choose to do. We could have gone in the direction of making a slab bar that contained fruit and nuts, and the common thread with our existing products would have been the use of fruits and nuts to make bars of a variety of types. The choice we made for our second line would be of extreme importance because consumers would connect the dots between the original and the new product line to infer the brand's common denominator. It was a very important decision.

After struggling with the question, making a slab bar didn't feel KIND to me, and we passed. It was a huge market and "opportunity" that we were "giving up." But KIND had been born out of the recognition that slab bars did not satisfy me and millions of other consumers. I wanted to be able to recognize the food I was putting into my mouth, to avoid processing our ingredients beyond recognition. I listened to my brand. And it told me, in my heart and in my gut, "That is not where you are meant to go."

Analyzing data is an important tool in strategy—more so for sales and category management, but it is also deeply embedded in new product development strategy. It is a dangerous tool, though. Data can tell you about others' trendlines—how other products are performing. But data lacks heart and soul. You need to look inside for that, and listen to your gut to understand if the "trend" fits with your brand and your unique value proposition. Data also doesn't predict tomorrow. More often than not, new product developers try to catch on to other brands' waves, only to learn that by the time they try to get on, the wave has dissipated and surfers are trying to catch a new one. If you decide what products to launch based on data only, you will most likely miss the big-picture opportunities. To really lead, you need to combine the left brain with the right brain— the scientific analysis with the artful sense of how to create magic within your brand.

Regardless of where we end up with new product-line innovation, defending our core products was and will forever be a crucial part of our strategy. That's why we continue to invest in KIND Fruit & Nut bars even as we've expanded into other areas. We continue to innovate with new flavors, to ensure consistency, to constantly strive to improve even on what we consider to be perfection, and to obsess about quality. Failure to do so would risk losing all the customers we've worked so hard to attract.

DOING IT RIGHT

Entrepreneurs who market consumer products crave a wide distribution network—being in as many stores as possible. But the productivity of each store matters far more, particularly in the early years when you have scarce resources to promote your product (or service).

When we launched KIND, we knew we had to start by investing our scarce resources at leading health food chains like Whole Foods. A Whole Foods store has a lot of traffic, and shoppers there are more likely to be adventurous and try new brands. We can sell hundreds of KIND bars in one single day at one Whole Foods store. In contrast, a convenience store or a pharmacy might sell a couple KIND bars a day on average.

If we were going to invest resources into letting people try KIND bars, say by having a team member cut up and hand out samples, our return on investment at the premium natural and specialty retailers was much higher. We learned it was almost impossible to overinvest in demos and sampling at these kinds of stores.

In contrast to our early efforts at PeaceWorks, when we were undisciplined and trying to be everywhere when we were not ready, now we were sharply focused on natural and gourmet stores. In addition to the national Whole Foods chain, specialty chains like Gelson's in the Los Angeles area, Mother's Market & Kitchen in Orange County, Draeger's and Andronico's in the Bay Area, Treasure Island Foods in Chicago, Fairway Market in New York City, Kings in New Jersey, PCC in Seattle, Central Market in Texas, and Sprouts Farmers Market and other upscale grocers across the nation were formidable partners. To this day, we find that we still have not hit the ceiling with these pioneering accounts. After years of assertive sampling, plenty of Whole Foods consumers have yet to try a KIND bar. We continue to do demos there and our sales continue to increase at our core accounts.

Paying attention to store productivity and investing most in the stores that perform best is as important for electronics, widgets, and diapers as it is for food products. You need to identify your core retail account or partner, where the sales per store will be significant, and which is the most natural fit for your product. It's important to figure out which store sells to your true consumer—the most frequent, most loyal buyer of your goods. You need to honor those accounts with a lot of TLC and support. My rule of thumb is that you're never doing enough. You can always service those accounts better, rather than trying to establish new links elsewhere. Your inclination as an entrepreneur may be always to pursue more stores, but odds are you have not done enough with your core partners. Remember to exhaust those existing opportunities because you're far more likely to get a return on your investment by doing so.

Once you're doing this well, define a migration strategy for sales. Look at the concentric circles of opportunity moving outward from your core customers—like ripples in a lake. In our case, KIND then progressed to upscale supermarkets like Lunds, Byerly's, Harris Teeter, and The Food Emporium.

The next step was regional grocery powerhouses like H-E-B, Wegmans, Fred Meyer, and King Soopers. We also started to get into the higher-end stores within national and semi-national chains like Kroger, Safeway, Publix, and Stop & Shop—targeting pockets of consumers willing to discover healthful new products. Each of these successes was exhilarating, but—crucially—we were also careful to pause to support each new partnership and opportunity before reaching for the next one. We made sure to prove ourselves and our products at each level of the testing process. We understood that if we were too aggressive and asked to get into all of a retailer's nationwide stores at once, we might not have enough sales per store to warrant the continuation of the relationship or have the chance to grow within that chain. We needed to focus on building a strong consumer base in tandem with the expansion of our distribution footprint.

I remember when Cecil Bogy, the buyer at Kroger, gave us a shot with two hundred Kroger stores. I challenged my team member Rami Leshem to go for more. But cooler heads prevailed; Rami and Cecil knew better than to dilute our focus and that we first needed to succeed at those stores. At that time, we were not ready to support a national launch. But by performing well at the best stores, we slowly expanded to more and more stores and eventually gained national distribution across their 2,600 stores.

Once we were in supermarkets around the country, and once loyal consumers were seeking us out and complaining that they couldn't find us, we moved into alternative channels of distribution: sporting goods stores, drugstores, coffee shops; convenience stores; airport, train-station, and travel retail stores like Hudson News; office-supply chains like Staples and other nongrocery retailers that would put us in the checkout aisle.

PATIENCE IS A VIRTUE

Only when you're operationally mature do you pursue clubs like Costco, BJ's, and Sam's, and retail giants like Target and Walmart. You don't want to be on those shelves too early and not be able to carry your weight in terms of generating the "pull" for your products from a critical mass of current and prospective consumers. Beyond the sales turns and performance against which you will be benchmarked, you also need to have well-developed internal systems to properly manage and service those accounts. Large retailers require data and tools and logistical sophistication that a small company may not have. You owe it to yourself and these larger accounts to be disciplined and engage with them only when you are ready to deliver logistical excellence. Our philosophy is that, wherever we go, we want to be that retailer's favorite supplier. That may mean sometimes you need to develop consumer loyalty and operational muscle before being ready to partner with a new account.

Lately, as the wellness category has become so coveted by retailers, even large players that historically preferred to wait to introduce proven products into their stores have considered investing in pioneering brands earlier. If a large retailer expresses interest in launching your products, this can represent a huge opportunity. But it is a high-stakes gamble because low awareness about your brand or new products will make it harder for you to generate the turnover that a large retailer needs to justify keeping your products on its shelves. If you lack the brand awareness, you need to make sure you have the market resources, distinctiveness, and retailer commitment to promote and sample the product and ensure sell-through. You also need to ensure you can manufacture and deliver in a timely basis. If you don't know your limitations and you press forward, the early entry can backfire: It can lead to the discontinuation of your products and to excess manufacturing capacity. And it can set your sales plans back by a few years, as retailers may hesitate to give you another shot after a bad experience.

The peril of not being ready to appear in major stores is a problem KIND knows all about. Around 2007, one Walmart buyer gave us a chance. She was a KIND consumer herself and really believed in our brand. She wanted us to succeed. Walmart is a prize account for consumer brands, but it's a challenging customer for a fledgling start-up to have, because it has world-class service standards and expectations from its vendors.

We debuted in one thousand Walmart stores. At the time, there was no defined nutritional bar aisle, so we found ourselves on a shelf next to candy bars like Snickers (which are made of very different ingredients and retail for a fraction of the price of a bar made from whole nuts and fruits). The larger challenge was that Walmart consumers did not have sufficient awareness of our product. And we also did not have enough knowledge, as a company, about how to handle an account as big as Walmart.

Our product tended to go missing from shelves, because we couldn't control the distribution correctly. We sold through a large distributor and had no idea how to monitor our placement. Our products too often got lost in the supply chain. The test failed within a year and KIND products were discontinued. It was quite a disappointing setback.

When I hired our president, John Leahy, in early 2010, I wanted to try Walmart again.

"We're not ready," John said. "We'll go after them when we're ready."

We spent the rest of that year and the next working on our internal systems, our distribution, and our tracking. We hired team members who had experience working with Walmart and who understood how their supplier ecosystem worked. In early 2012, we began making presentations to the company. By that point, KIND had enough brand clout; we were a very different company than we had been five years before. By April 2012, we gained distribution at Walmart.

We now sell four-packs, multipacks, individual KIND bars, and KIND Healthy Grains Clusters at Walmart, all at attractive prices for consumers. The arrangement has gone so well that John and our Walmart team were even invited to Bentonville for a day of meetings and tours, an unusual honor for a company that usually allots half-hour meetings even to important vendors. Because of our success with Walmart, we received a call from their sister company, Sam's Club, which became a customer as well. Eventually, we got to work with Walmart's senior management and develop a major strategic relationship.

We had a similar experience with Target. Several limited tests, beginning in 2011, did not go spectacularly, but we gave the relationship everything we had and took nothing for granted. John persuaded the company that we deserved a real shot so we could invest in them on a nationwide scale (by then, our awareness and momentum warranted no less). We began selling regularly at Target in September 2013 and gained traction quickly. They now feature all of our lines prominently. Our granola line is the bestseller in its category. They noticed, and they invited us to partner with them on their prestigious Made to Matter initiative, spotlighting socially conscious companies on the cutting edge. We are blessed to consider them a formidable partner.

John, who has been selling to the country's largest retailers for the last three decades, notes that know-how is what matters here. "Regardless of category or product type, you have to have the infrastructure to support these major accounts and you have to have the internal knowledge of their systems and their brand," he says.

Whatever beachhead you conquer, you have to be able to deliver more productive returns to the retailer, on a same-store basis, than competing brands. Then the retailers start helping you expand. You need to be disciplined and respectful—to your brand and to the retailers—and keep walking past the stores that are not right for you, or not ripe for a relationship. Learn to wait.

Often you're anxious and excited to expand your business, and you don't want to slow down. It's hard to be patient when you want everyone to buy your product. One rule of thumb KIND lives by is to do only that which we can do with absolute excellence, without cutting any corners. And a trick I use to conquer my own fear of closing off opportunities is to say to myself, "I am not saying 'no.' I am just saying, 'not now, not yet.'" If there was a store I wanted to target, but knew my company wasn't ready, I wrote it on a list of what was to come. I learned to be disciplined enough not to drop everything and go for it immediately.

We entrepreneurs tend to sense—falsely—that everything we do will succeed. It is this sense of invincibility that prompts us to take risks others may not, so it is an essential strength to have this naïve bravado to some degree. But it can also destroy us if not managed.

Michael Porter, a professor at Harvard Business School, said, "The essence of strategy is choosing what not to do." For entrepreneurs, at a minimum, they can tell themselves that strategy means choosing what to leave for tomorrow. Create a list of priorities for your creative ideas, marketing campaigns, or anything else you hope to do. You don't have to cross off any ideas; you just have to put them into the right order. Eventually, you may get to do them—if you do everything else on the list first.

FOCUS PAYS OFF, BUT NOT WITHOUT PAYING YOUR DUES

Because of our early focus and discipline in the mid-2000s, KIND was starting to generate buzz, both at trade shows and in our media coverage. Something special was clearly going on. People sensed that something magical was happening with us.

In 2007, at the main trade show of our industry, the Natural Products Expo West, the excitement around our booth was hard to contain. We could only afford a small booth back then—

ten feet by twenty feet—for both KIND and PeaceWorks prod-ucts, which at the time we were selling under one roof. To amplify our reach, we were living our brand's social mission by doing kind acts for others at the trade show, including surpris-ing people by giving free massages, and offering people rides to their cars in the convention center's parking lot.

On the show floor, KIND was talked about as *the* hot prod-uct in the space. In 2007 and 2008, we received awards for the best new product at the trade show. Applications to work with us started to pour in from people with industry experience.

We were excited. KIND was a fun place to work, and we were all having a great time building something vibrant. But it wasn't easy. Ironically, it was during this period when we were experiencing 100 percent growth (even if from a small base), that our cash challenges were the greatest.

Entrepreneurs often don't realize that faster growth can strap your cash. If you're growing very slowly, your cash needs might not be as difficult to meet, as long as you are profitable. But when you're doubling your sales, you need to increase your working capital to manufacture more inventory, to increase your allowance for accounts receivable (to collect cash that you are owed for sales you made on credit terms), to hire more people—and of course to invest in promoting your brand. Prof-itable companies can go out of business if they don't manage their cash properly.

This is how we ended up with a chronic cash flow problem. Focus pays off in the long term, but in the short term you still have to keep plugging along. We fought hard for every dollar we had. In addition to skipping my own salary on many occa-sions, I had to make sure we didn't pay too early for anything we owed. We paid right on time, and we ensured our customers paid us on time. The KIND operations team would get on the phone to remind our customers that they needed to send in that check for the product we had sold them. We managed our inventory tightly, because we couldn't afford to be out of stock, but we also couldn't afford to have too much product, as we barely had enough cash to finance our most essential inventory. We had a tiny marketing and sampling budget.

Most of the impetus for our growth came from the product and the packaging itself, and from eye-arresting in-store marketing tools like signage and displays. Out of necessity, we tracked every wire rack we gave to stores because we could not afford for our customers to throw them out; we needed to refill those racks. Once customers sold through product, we had to swiftly replenish them before competitors put their products on our displays. Our small office was like a war room. A large map of the country hung on the wall, with pins tracking all our wire racks across the nation. Different color pins signaled when we had last visited or called those stores. Every asset was essential.

We had no alternative but to lean hard on our entrepreneurial spirit and to be disciplined about our finances. It was a long time before we were able to breathe freely at KIND without worrying about every penny that came in. I consider it lucky that our focus and single-mindedness allowed us to get to that point at all. And even luckier that such circumstances engraved resourcefulness into our culture and character.

BEING TRUE TO MYSELF

Around this period, I met Michelle Lieberman, the woman who would become my wife. I had been living a bachelor life for many years, married to the company, singularly focused on the mission of KIND and on my efforts for peace in the Middle East.

We met at a friend's karaoke party in the Lower East Side in New York City in December of 2006. When I walked into the bar, the first thing I saw was a guy dressed as Elvis singing karaoke. I teased Michelle that she looked enchanting in contrast. Fortunately, I did not sing any songs that night, or I don't think she would have agreed to go out with me. She was a doctor and spoke Spanish: I thought we hit it off right away. Michelle took more convincing.

After we started dating, we went through a period she playfully and patiently dubbed the War Years, partly because of my preoccupation and sadness about the Hezbollah-Israel War, but also because I was at war with myself. I had gotten used to obsessing only about my professional pursuits, and I was not used to letting anyone in.

I needed to become more open to developing profound relationships. Part of that involved recognizing that I probably had a fear of commitment and a fear of letting people into my life. That was both because I was intimately involved with my job, and because I didn't want to get hurt.

Similar to my earlier entrepreneurial efforts, in my prior relationships, I was not focused. I would be best described as a serial dater—never really investing the time to get to know someone, and for them to get to know me. I had to own up to the fact that I was scared. I decided that I needed to give my relationship with Michelle a chance, to put everything I had into it. For me, this was another epiphany about focus, discipline, and truth. I had to focus on her, and I had to allow myself to focus on my personal life even while running flat out to manage KIND.

At the time, I was also working hard to mobilize a million Palestinian and Israeli citizens to demand immediate and continued negotiations to establish a two-state solution. In October 2007, a seminal event we worked really hard on had to be canceled at the last minute; I was devastated by the setback. Michelle's love, partnership, and unquestioning loyalty not only helped me overcome my despair, but also made me realize how blessed I was to have her as my partner by my side.

A few weeks later, I proposed.

THE BUSINESSPERSON AS ACTIONIST

Above all, focus means getting stuff done. A lot of people have great ideas but don't act on them. For me, the definition of an entrepreneur is someone who can combine innovation and ingenuity with the ability to execute that new idea.

Some people think that the central dichotomy in life is whether you're positive or negative about the issues that interest or concern you. There's a lot of attention paid to this question of whether it's better to have an optimistic or pessimistic lens. I think the better question to ask is whether you are going to do something about it or just let life pass you by. Are you an actionist?

Action, no less than creativity, is essential for an entrepreneur. While others may ask whether the glass is half full or half empty, an entrepreneur just fills up the glass. Determination is fundamental.

Entrepreneurship is hard work, and most people who start a venture understand that they will be working around the clock and doing anything that needs doing. Being an entrepreneur is also about figuring out what needs to be done, what problems need to be solved, and then finding solutions.

In many ways, *attitude is destiny*. If you determine that you're going to do something and have a positive attitude, you can find fulfillment in the pursuit itself. Trying is half the win already. If you don't try, you've lost from the outset. One thing that my dad taught me is that change is not a spectator sport. You have to actively participate in shaping the world you want to live in. This sense of responsibility has influenced all of my business ventures.

The same is true with the blocking and tackling of sales. There were retail accounts that took me years to get, but I would not relent; I would not stop until those outlets were carrying KIND bars. There are still goals today that I won't give up on. John Leahy, our president, has the same approach. Every year, he frames and hangs in his office a printout with the logos of the most challenging accounts that he is determined to conquer and win over. He doesn't decorate his office with his successes, which are many. He reminds himself, and our team, of what remains to be done. That focus allows us to pursue those goals that are truly important.

I saw Starbucks as an opportunity for KIND from day one. I called the switchboard and tried to find someone to send samples to, with no real traction. I then met a Starbucks director at a regional meeting of the World Economic Forum in Jordan. He became a friend and introduced me to the marketing team at Starbucks. Unfortunately, they were not responsive.

In 2008, I was introduced to the vice president in charge of Food for Starbucks. Starbucks had just conceived a campaign called Real Food, Simply Delicious to freshen up its food offerings. I sensed that the vice president was seriously interested in us, and I invested team members' time and money in compelling presentations to her, in late 2008 and early 2009.

We had very few resources and a skeleton team. My team argued that I was taking away resources from immediate marketing needs to go on a wild goose chase. They were arguably right. I had been trying for the Moby Dick accounts for quite a while. I always explained to my team that we needed to combine pragmatic, realistic goals with those big, audacious objectives that are hard to achieve but that would be very impactful if we did manage to achieve them. Eventually things started clicking. I was invited to fly to Seattle and had a positive meeting with the vice president and her team. I felt like that boy who has a crush on the prettiest girl in the class and, all of a sudden, she winks at him, and now he is waiting by the phone, hoping she will call him back.

WHERE TO FOCUS NEXT: BIG DECISIONS

My Starbucks crush coincided with a period that was pivotal for KIND in two ways.

First, we had started to ask ourselves: How are we going to innovate without destroying the brand? It had been several years since we pioneered fruit and nut bars in the United States. I felt the time had come for us to take our next step. And I realized that a brand's second act in many ways is the most important move in defining the values and principles that it will represent.

We had to decide what would be the common thread that defined KIND: Was it the use of dried fruit and nuts? Was it healthy snacking? All-natural foods? Were we a bar company? Or was it about products with nutritionally rich ingredients you could see and pronounce? We knew what a KIND Fruit & Nut bar was, but we had yet to clearly define the KIND brand. We needed to ask ourselves these serious questions. And we needed to come up with answers before expanding mindlessly in directions that we might regret.

Second, and of more immediate concern, our cash flow challenges were deepening. Even though the company was growing and profitable, I still often couldn't pay my own salary. I was getting married, children were just around the corner, and I was asking myself how I was going to provide for my family. I couldn't continue skipping my salary for months at a time. That forced me into a strategic discussion with myself. Should I sell a stake in the company to investors? Should I sell the company? Or hold on tight?

While I was debating my course of action, one of the largest food and beverage companies in the world knocked on our door.

CHAPTER 5

KEEPING IT SIMPLE

Practicing Restraint to Stay Grounded

My maternal grandfather, Don Marquitos Americus, used to say in Spanish: *"Un hombre demasiado digno para agacharse a recoger un quinto, no vale un quinto."* "He who is too proud to pick up a nickel from the ground is not worth a nickel."

Born Marcos Merikansky, he immigrated to Mexico from Lithuania early in the twentieth century to escape a pogrom. He started out selling religious trinkets like figurines of the Virgin Mary and eventually became a respected cattle rancher. (After being conscripted into the Cossack Army, he had become an excellent horseback rider.) He was about five feet tall but strong and tough; he seemed to be built of steel, even when I knew him in his seventies. What I best remember is his humility and kindness, how he always helped the farmers who worked with him, how he sat, ate, and slept next to them and treated them as family. If my grandmother bought him a new shirt, she might soon find one of his ranchmen wearing it: He gifted what he had.

What I learned from my grandfather—and from my mom and her siblings, who were influenced by his values as well—was the importance of modesty in business and life. He did not attribute his attainments to his own genius or even his own talent. He seemed to understand that hard work and skill are essential, but that success is greatly a function of luck and circumstance. My relatives had fled persecution; they worked enormously hard, but they considered themselves lucky (not entitled) to have survived and flourished.

No matter how great and innovative your ideas are, and how hard you work, some will succeed and others won't. You can't control exogenous events—recessions, stock market crashes or bubbles, wars, fads, the luck of good timing—nor should you take credit for them when they benefit you.

This isn't just because humility makes you more agreeable (although, of course, being nice is its own reward). If you don't take anything for granted, you are more likely to prevent catastrophic failures, and you are less likely to just coast when things are good. I try to remember, at all times, that my company is just steps away from failure. For me it is easy because I vividly recall the situations when we did almost go under. The quest for survival is a powerful driver to keep one motivated.

In some ways, the laurels of success can threaten one's clear judgment more than the thorns of failure. One must consciously practice restraint to stay grounded and resist the temptation to become arrogant. As I reflected about what it means to stay grounded as a human being, I also started studying what it means for products with human adjectives like KIND to stay grounded to nature. That led me to an insight that would set KIND on a very special course a decade before others had appreciated the latent need to reform manufacturing to deliver food products whose "ingredients you can see and pronounce."

PRODUCTS GROUNDED TO NATURE

Historically, the way food companies have tried to add value and charge more for their products is by adding processing steps. Instead of selling an apple, they move the fruit further and further from its natural form, to distinguish it further, ending up with a fruit pastry. Instead of whole grains as found in nature, you have processed cereal with added sugar. As Michael Pollan explains quite eloquently in his numerous books, industrial food manufacturers think elaborate processes will justify higher premiums. At KIND, we've tried to do the opposite: We try to *simplify* our products. Using only natural ingredients, we can achieve a shelf life of twelve to fifteen months in our fruit and nut bars, using a little honey as a natural preservative. We try to let food keep its soul.

Paradoxically, it's actually harder to make a minimally processed product. When you're trying to honor the integrity of the whole nuts and fruits, you have to treat them with a lot of respect, and they're fragile. You don't want to scrape your nuts. Removing even a little of their naturally protective skin speeds up the process through which they will go rancid. In contrast to a slab bar that is easy to control and weigh because the homogenous emulsion yields standardized lumps of paste, every single KIND bar is different. You can't standardize the weight of a

KIND bar as much: One whole nut may mean the bar weighs a couple of grams more. You can't charge the consumer for the extra product, even though it costs you more. But when your consumers try a KIND bar, it makes it all worthwhile.

The concept of getting closer to nature extends beyond food. Starting in the seventies and culminating in the early nineties, our consumer habits trended further and further away from the earth and from natural "ingredients"; society glorified synthetic fibers, technologically enhanced music, colors not readily found in nature (neon), artificial living, and marketing extravagance.

But almost every consumer trend goes in cycles, with each new one correcting something missing or overblown before. When the pendulum shifts too far in one direction, entrepreneurs can sense the swing and will seize opportunities. Ideally, you're not seeking to benefit from a temporary fad, but from a longer-term macro shift in consumer attitudes. After the excess and artificiality of the nineties, for example, consumers have increasingly craved more authenticity and simplicity from everything we buy, including food. The brands that scream too loudly of "improvements" have steadily given way to the ones that are more direct and transparent. In the food space, which for too long oscillated toward undecipherable overprocessed stuff, the search for simplicity hopefully will cement itself for the sake of our bodies.

In business, you have to assume that the extremes will be short-lived. Consider some of the recent manias in the food industry: The idea that fat is evil led to the low-fat rage. Then carbs were considered evil, leading to the low-carb craze. As I write, we're in the middle of a gluten-free trend—which KIND happens to benefit from—and shortsighted entrepreneurs have jumped on the bandwagon, marketing *naturally* gluten-free products like water, salsa, and candy as gluten free. Of course, anything that doesn't contain gluten—which can only come from wheat, barley, or rye—is by definition gluten free and consumers won't be fooled for long. And just because something is gluten free doesn't make it healthful. Sugar is gluten free. So what? All these exaggerated fads built on misinformation eventually face a backlash when consumers get educated, which they always do in the end.

SIMPLICITY IN NAMES

The frontline evidence of simplicity is a company's name. I initially came up with the name PeaceWorks Inc. to convey how the business of cooperation can create social and economic harmony. Working together can foster peace. Peace actually works and yields tangible benefits. I liked it as the name for the company, but for our products I felt we needed a brand that spoke to the essence of the food itself.

Recall Moshe & Ali's? The complete story is that, after much brainstorming, I had the "genius" idea to brand our Mediterranean spreads as "Moshe Pupik and Ali Mishmunken's World-Famous All-Natural Gourmet Foods." I purposely made the name a mouthful. I theorized that it was so long, silly, and unexpected that it would generate buzz. People would think it was "so funny" and "so charming." Yet when I started getting press coverage, one of the first radio interviewers could not even pronounce the name. Most wouldn't even try. People didn't have time or patience for such a complicated name. So we shortened the brand name to Moshe & Ali's. Eventually we renamed the brand MEDITALIA to evoke Mediterranean and Italian cuisine.

I similarly complicated things too much when describing the *types* of products we made: I felt we didn't fit an existing category label—we made spreads and pâtés that could also be used as sauces or condiments, after all—so I decided we should invent a new category name. We called our spreads "spraté," which combined the words "spread" and "pâté" to convey the meaning of a versatile multipurpose condiment you could use for anything: as an ingredient for cooking, as part of a salad dressing, on pasta, as a dip, as a condiment on sandwiches.

In retrospect, it's clear I did not have the resources or the staying power to create a whole new retail category and to educate consumers on the definition of and uses for a "spraté." I learned that it's important to be careful about how much you try to change consumer behavior. It's hard to retrain people with a new vocabulary when you are a $10,000 start-up trying to make peace in the Middle East. I was complicating things too much.

I learned that the seven-hundred-year-old theory of logic called Occam's razor applies to names and to virtually everything involved in running a company: The simplest answer is usually the best one, and should always be chosen when possible. It's in perfect accordance with the AND philosophy, because both force you to question your assumptions. Why do it that way? Why stick with the way it's always been done? Is there a simpler way? Keep asking questions until you come up with the best answer you can figure out, one that doesn't force you to choose between two options you consider essential. The call for simplicity does not mean avoiding a worthwhile path that will

entail hard work and difficult choices. It means not overcompli-
cating things when you don't have to.

Determined to learn from my Moshe & Ali's mistakes, we set
out to keep it simple when coming up with a brand for our fruit
and nut bars. We wanted it to be one word, ideally three to four
letters long. Something straightforward. Our director of marketing at the time, Sasha Hare, helped not just with the ideation
for our name but also for our logo; she recommended we find a
name that could have human traits and connotations. We went
back and forth for months and ran through a ton of ideas, some
of them quite silly, including Nirvana Now, All Good, Purely
Divine, Health Heaven, Joy Bar, and Go Bar Go! Eventually we
settled on KIND. It sounded fresh. The name itself embodied
not just our purpose and mission—to be KIND to our bodies,
our taste buds, and our world—but also our focus on simplicity.

OUR MINIMALISM ATTRACTS
A GLOBAL CONGLOMERATE

In 2007, the world economy began to show cracks; soon thereafter, we found ourselves in the global financial crisis of 2008.
This was an unsettling situation for a company that makes goods
people buy with discretionary income. It is an understatement
to say that I was anxious.

At the same time, our dogged focus and our aggressive drive
to keep things simple attracted attention. That autumn, one of
the top food conglomerates in the world approached us about
buying a controlling stake in KIND.

This was eye-opening for me. For well over a decade, I had

been trying as hard as I could just to survive another day and get consumers to notice us. Now, the CEO of one of the largest companies on the planet was calling me.

The CEO had been introduced to our products by a mutual friend, and was a serious fan. She made the time to meet me briefly, and tasked several of her company's top executives with getting to know our company. I developed a good relationship with them. They saw the brand and product as having a lot of promise and talked about wanting to buy a controlling stake. We shared a considerable amount of financial and other sensitive information as part of the due diligence process. They also asked a lot of questions that I had no answers to. It was clear we were much smaller than firms they were used to acquiring. We had, at the time, some $7 million in annual sales and were hoping to reach $15 million in the upcoming year. But they saw the KIND brand as a potential platform for all their health and wellness initiatives.

Ultimately, they decided they were not ready to acquire a controlling stake in our company. They felt there was too much risk because we did not have full control over our manufacturing. All our production was located in Australia at that point, and they perceived our manufacturing partner as unreliable.

Seeing the offer yanked away after we had shared a lot of information made me feel quite vulnerable. Then the conglomerate came back with another proposition: They would buy a small stake in KIND, some 20 percent, becoming a minority shareholder. I consulted with my attorney, the man who had been my roommate at Stanford Law and one of the brightest students in my class there: A. J. Weidhaas. A.J. had been my outside corporate counsel ever since I founded the company, and his expertise was in private equity transactions.

He explained that it's always a bad idea to sell a minority stake to a strategic buyer. (A strategic buyer is a company operating in the same field, who would be a competitor to other buyers, as opposed to a financial investor like a private equity fund.) Once you've sold a small stake, no other buyer in the same industry is likely to want to acquire you, because they'd wonder why the minority investor is not doing so themselves, given they have more access to information about the company. Essentially I'd be giving up a premium one normally gets when selling a controlling stake, and I would be limiting my options in the future.

All through our talks, the recession was closing in, the economy was slumping, and consumer confidence was declining rapidly—the worst possible conditions for a company that sold premium healthful foods. So I felt I was carrying a lot of risk.

To further add to the pressure to take the deal, Michelle and I were expecting our first child. We had married in March 2008, with celebrations in Texas and Mexico, and then went on a very short honeymoon to Thailand, sandwiched in between a food trade show in California and the Skoll Social Entrepreneurs conference in Oxford, England. We had stayed at a medieval dungeon that had been renovated into a hotel; our son was conceived in that prison cell! Newlywed and newly pregnant, we were extremely concerned about our future. We had little income; Michelle was still in the midst of her medical training for her specialty as a nephrologist, and I had a very modest salary that I sometimes had to skip. How would we support our new family? This offer would have provided me a level of financial security I had never ever dreamed was possible.

And yet, as I thought more about it, the deal did not feel right. Beyond the financial considerations, KIND was still a fledgling that needed more independent nurturing. I would be limiting my freedom of action by inviting a conglomerate as an investor, particularly at that stage, even if it was a best-in-class corporation. Every friend I consulted who had done a deal like this deeply regretted it. Every entrepreneur that I spoke to told me that I would be miserable running KIND as part of a gigantic corporation, with all the attendant increase in bureaucracy, daily focus on Wall Street earnings reports, and countless other concerns, rather than a singular focus on our long-term mission.

We declined the conglomerate's offer and ended the negotiations amicably in late spring of 2008.

FINDING VALUE IN SETBACKS

We often comment in the West that the Chinese word for "crisis" is made up of the characters for "danger" and "opportunity." But sometimes you are too close to see it. On a recent trip to China, I asked multiple people to write down the word for "crisis" and explain the characters to me. They all wrote it out for me, but none of them had considered the juxtaposition of its components until I pointed it out to them. They were so close to their own wisdom that they had never even registered it.

However you write it, the insight is absolutely true. Tough circumstances like having a major financing deal collapse force you to stay grounded, innovate, think hard, and use the AND philosophy. Having to fight for your survival is a strong motivator to move conventions and pretenses aside. You have to think: How am I going to harness the pain and anxiety of this loss to make me stronger? How am I going to embrace the challenge with humility and determination? How am I going to win?

The one great thing that came out of my protracted interactions with that conglomerate was that they helped expand my sense of what was possible with KIND. I had always thought that KIND was to be an umbrella brand for healthy foods. But until some of the conglomerate executives had helped me imagine a much bolder plan for our future, I had not visualized how far KIND could go. This was a pivotal moment for me in thinking about our trajectory. In particular, it was the first time I realized KIND could become *the* leading trusted brand in health and wellness. That helped me internalize how big the opportunity was, even as I struggled to decide the best way forward.

I had to come up with a road map quick. Michelle and I were expecting to have another mouth to feed by December 2008. And the world's financial picture continued to darken.

I started asking myself whether it made sense to sell any or all of the company. Should I take some chips off the table in order to feed my family? Should I take on a larger investment in KIND and grow the company faster? If so, what would I do differently? Should I sell the entire company and use some of the money to advance my personal mission of peacemaking? What were my priorities? And what was the smartest way to advance them?

I seriously asked myself if I should sell the company and focus exclusively on making peace in the Middle East through OneVoice, the nonprofit movement I conceived and continue to guide. My friend and board member Jim Hornthal convinced me to do both—to follow the AND philosophy—and to keep running KIND while also guiding OneVoice.

My general experience is that you can only truly do one thing well at a time, so I initially resisted Jim's advice. But he persuaded me that diplomats, philanthropists, and heads of industry would be more likely to listen to me as the CEO of a successful company than if I was solely a philanthropist who had sold a business. I spoke with friends who had sold their own companies to pursue social goals, and I realized that many regretted the lack of a business platform to drive positive social change. So I decided to continue running KIND and bring in minority investors to catalyze KIND's growth. The growth of the company would also afford me more ways to build bridges. It would be a platform to deepen my impact on the world.

Before I started the formal process of seeking minority investment partners, a prominent private equity firm came to us and said they were very interested in becoming our partner. This seemed like what we wanted anyway—it was good news— and we seriously considered doing a deal with them. They proposed taking a minority stake of 20–25 percent consisting of common shares, where all investors are treated the same. But after they conducted due diligence on KIND—gaining access to sensitive information and leaving us vulnerable to their scrutiny—they reneged on the terms we had agreed. They gave me an ultimatum, demanding 40 percent of the company and the issuance of preferred shares that would effectively give them extra dividends and windfalls above what the common shareholders would get. They also insisted on adding a lot of negative controls that would limit my ability to run the company as I deemed fit.

The ultimatum came while Michelle and I were on a week-end vacation in Santa Barbara. It was to be our last time away together before our baby was scheduled to arrive three months later. Unfortunately, I spent the weekend on the phone and on email, being threatened by the private equity firm. "We are walking away if you don't accept these [revised] terms," they insisted.

Michelle and I had a series of very difficult conversations that weekend. She was very worried: KIND was still doing well but we wondered if the recession would impact us. Lehman Brothers had just imploded. The deal would have involved a $10 million payment for my family, enabling me to stop worrying not only about having to make ends meet each week, but even about schools and colleges for our offspring. Additional funds would have flowed into the company to jump-start our brand expansion. Given the financial climate at the time, forgoing this deal could have meant I would find no other. The private equity firm was probably trying to take advantage of the global crisis. But it didn't matter. I felt it was dishonest for them to press to renegotiate at the last minute. I was stung and felt betrayed. I could not trust them, so I could not consider bringing them on as a partner. Michelle supported my decision.

With the collapse of this second deal, I found myself drawing on my inner resources to stay grounded. I reminded myself that KIND was a great company and that others would be fortunate to partner with us. I also reminded myself that I could not just sell out to a group I did not respect; this was about more than money. This internal dialogue helped me keep down the feelings of panic.

SMART MONEY

When it comes to investors, you can get money, or you can get smart money.

At a critical crossroads and while trying to educate myself about my options, I called the founder of Vitaminwater, Darius Bikoff, whom I had met through my old friends Andy and Melissa Komaroff. Darius had sold his business, Energy Brands Inc., to Coca-Cola the previous year, and I knew he would have valuable advice for me.

"Is it true that any private equity firm is going to require me to sell preferred shares?" I asked him. "What's your opinion?"

"No, it's not true," Darius told me. "You should do the deal with us instead." Darius offered to do a common stock deal as I wanted, where all parties are aligned because they have precisely the same upside and downside per share. He introduced me to VMG, a private equity firm that specialized in branded consumer goods in the health and wellness space, and to Mike Repole, who had been the president and driving force of his company. Darius, Mike, and VMG agreed to form a group to buy a minority stake in KIND consisting of common shares.

As I got to know them through negotiations, I came to feel comfortable that VMG would be straightforward with terms. Kara Cissell Roell and Mike Mauzé, the main VMG principals with whom I dealt, were tenacious negotiators, but they always kept their word and were always forthright. I thought they could be helpful partners, since they had expertise in areas that my team and I did not. They were also long-term oriented. They convinced me that they would work together to move

KIND forward and serve its mission as well as helping the business to grow. Here, perhaps, was the investment deal that would finally come to fruition.

Even though we only met late in the fall, both parties sprinted to complete the deal before the end of 2008. Our baby was due on December 22, 2008, so we had planned on concluding our negotiations and closing the deal on the nineteenth. The morning of the eighteenth, however, Michelle started experiencing contractions. She actually decided to finish her rounds at the hospital and proceed to the labor delivery room in a leisurely way. When I heard she had started labor, I suspended the negotiations and rushed over.

The experience was strangely grounding for me. There was not one part of me that wanted to continue to negotiate and miss a minute of the birth. I was so at peace. Everyone was very patient and respectful and did what they could to complete the closing documents in the interim, even as both sides worried the other would get cold feet.

On December 19 at 2:26 A.M., our son was born healthy, and we named him Roman, after my father. This event completely overshadowed for me any other financial or legal discussions, even if they would be determining the trajectory of my company for years to come. Once I came up for air, we closed the deal on December 22, 2008. Then I went back to enjoying baby Romy.

KIND sold about a third of the company to VMG and the founders of Vitaminwater, a transaction that valued the company at $45 million. I got great partners and a great structure. Had I sold to the conglomerate or to the other private equity firm, my financial upside and my ability to run the company would have been severely limited.

LEARNING TO LEARN FROM OTHERS

I had been running my business by myself for fifteen years, five years since the KIND launch and ten before that. I wanted a partner who could teach me, who could be a strategic counsel. Though it can be hard on the ego, it's important to recognize the enormous value in having someone teach you. You may always be the visionary, the brand guardian, but that vision can be enriched greatly by partners who help you polish, operationalize, and execute your goals.

Of course, I have sometimes found it difficult to take this advice. My investors strongly suggested I hire a head of finance once they came on board. Why would we need a head of finance? Why waste resources that could go into growing the business? I already had a loyal team member, Doris Rivera, who was doing an excellent job overseeing our books. Fortunately Doris and I quickly saw the gap between our capabilities and what we would soon need to be able to do, and I listened to the advice to allow VMG to improve our financial reporting and systems while working through the interview process for a senior vice president of finance. Dan Kruk was far and away our best candidate, and he has helped expand our finance team from three to around fifty people as we've grown over the last six years.

Dan's first order of business—as instructed by the board— was to complete an audit and create a budget. I had run the company for many years without either: I wrote every check myself, knew when every payment was made, and did not think we needed to waste money that could be invested in sales and marketing on audit fees. What I didn't realize was that the company had reached the point where we did need this financial rigor. At a certain stage, an entrepreneur can no longer serve as the central point for all functions. You need people better than you to lead on each front, including finance. You need to stop writing checks, and you need to institute stronger systems and controls. Above all, you need to start seeing finance (and operations, and all other departments) as possessing equal strategic importance as sales and marketing. Having an audit and budget in hand allowed Dan to build a strong financial foundation that contributed to our results and the impressive financial returns for KIND's investors.

As we used the investment money to ramp up our business, I was also persuaded that we needed a second-in-command—a partner to manage the day-to-day business of the company—to ensure the trains ran on time. I agreed to hire a president, and we conducted a long and difficult search. I finally found someone, and recommended this person to our board. The board approved the candidate.

Dan Kruk, however, didn't know that the search was over. As fate would have it, Dan's wife ran into an old friend at a high school basketball game and found out that her husband, John, a former colleague of Dan's from their work for Playtex, was looking for a new job opportunity. The message got back to both Dan and John from their wives that they should get together.

They met for breakfast to catch up on the four or five years since they had worked together. Once Dan found out that John had experience in the natural foods channel with his past employer, he felt John might be a good candidate for the president position. Dan thought that John's numerous years of experience in the grocery, mass, drug, and club channels would be helpful to KIND's expansion into those markets.

Dan sent me John's résumé. My initial reaction was that I had already made a decision and the board had approved our choice. But since I had not yet offered the position to the leading candidate, Dan convinced me to give John a chance, and I agreed to meet with John, thinking we might find a way to use him as a consultant. After meeting with him, I immediately changed my mind and asked John to meet our investors. The rest is history. John came to KIND in early 2010 and instantly became the yin to my yang. Our expertise and management styles complement each other and we have formed a solid team to oversee and guide KIND. KIND would not be where it is today without John's managerial skills.

BALANCING EXCESS VS. SCARCITY MINDSETS

There's a certain simplicity and blessing in having no money as a start-up. You're not wasteful. You learn to do things in the leanest possible way because you have no other option. You have to run your business like a Swiss watch, with enormous efficiency. Because you have no margin of error, if you're anything less than efficient, you'll run the business into the ground. You get really good at it because you are forced to. You have no option but to optimize for cash flow, because it's a matter of survival.

What you must avoid is starving your business of the growth capital it needs. If you're growing too fast, you might not have enough cash to feed or sustain your growth, even if you're making money. It's a very tricky balance.

Once you've proven the concept and your products are selling well, you need to add fuel. The easiest and cleanest way to do this is simply to sell your goods and bring in profits. But few entrepreneurs can launch a successful company with only their own revenue as seed capital. Most new ventures require up-front investment in order to educate customers about their unique selling proposition.

The question of when to bring in investors is a difficult one. Most entrepreneurs will pour their own savings into the company at first; that's what I did. Beyond that, if you can bootstrap and max out your credit cards, it's risky and stressful, but it helps you retain equity at the very beginning, when the cost of capital is highest because you don't have the sales to warrant a high valuation. If you can avoid raising capital when you are still testing the concept and optimizing your product or service, you will avoid diluting yourself.

But all this simplicity can get you into trouble when you overdo it. We discovered early on that there's a fine line between frugality and putting yourself in danger.

Once, on a sales swing through the Midwest back in our early years, Rami Leshem and I ended up in Cleveland. After a long day, we started looking for a hotel room. We did not realize that we were in a bad part of town. We found a room for $30 a night, but the place looked just a bit too sketchy even for us. Instead, we splurged and went across the street to a much fancier place that was $40 a night. We doubled up, sharing a room, as we were over budget.

It was the best $10 we ever spent. The following morning

around 5 A.M. we woke to a thunderous noise. Looking through the curtains, we saw that the hotel we had passed over was the scene of an active shoot-out with the police. Apparently it was being used as a crack house. We just got lucky that night.

We learned a lot about simplicity, efficiency, frugality, and their pros and cons during the years when the company had no choice but to operate as leanly as possible. Generally, you want to be careful not to live in excess, getting cocky and wasting resources. The opposite side of the coin is that when you're building a culture of resourcefulness you want to be careful that it doesn't lead to a scarcity mentality.

If you create a scarcity mindset, your team may not be capable of visualizing things that could or should be done. Indeed, controlling costs can lead to a starvation mentality within a business. You may end up bypassing great investment opportunities where, if you only invest a little bit of money, you'd get a great return. When your team is living with limitations, they may discount these opportunities.

One example of a scarcity mentality is our experience with sampling when KIND first started. While I was comfortable cutting KIND bars into pieces and giving bites out at demos, I saw sampling of full bars as a lavish expense. I loathed giving away our product for free, and I only did it when necessary to convince retail buyers to make a purchase. In 2008, our sampling budget was $800. By then we were already selling $13 million a year. But we felt we needed to control costs, and we thought that giving out full KIND bars as free samples to consumers would cannibalize our own revenues.

To be fair, at the time, we did not have the cash to spend on giving away product.

But we didn't recognize that every bar we gave out was an investment, not an expense. We didn't realize that nine out of ten consumers who try a KIND bar will become purchasers and recommend KIND to others. We could have grown faster by giving out KIND bars and getting more customers. After the VMG investment gave us enough cash to get a sampling program started, we were blown away by the rapid expansion of our customer base. (See page 295, Growth in Units Sold.)

The healthy middle ground between an excess and a scarcity mindset is what I call a *resourceful* mentality. The resourceful team member avoids waste but thinks creatively about how to get done whatever needs doing on the best terms possible. A person with this mindset asks, "What's the best way to grow? Which things do I need to do and how can I get them done at the lowest possible cost?"

STAYING GROUNDED

Money can change your perspective on everything if you let it: how you run your life, your business, your family. The important thing is to not let money change how you think and behave.

Consider office furniture as an example. If you are a start-up without cash, you have to be resourceful and find a way to get inexpensive or free furniture. We literally scavenged chairs and desks that had been jettisoned on the sidewalks of New York. These pieces of furniture adorned our offices for some twenty years, from my basement cubbyhole days when I started the company until very recently—and we only stopped using them when they gave out.

When you suddenly have millions in cash in your business account, you can afford to buy a nicer desk, or a nicer chair, just like you can afford to fly business class if you want to. On its own, the purchase of that chair (or five hundred of such chairs, as you grow) will not register on your financial radar. But that's not the only thing that matters.

Each of these actions—purchasing new office furniture or flying business class—sends signals to your team about your culture: what is valued and expected. People will model their actions after what you do as the leader. In the aggregate, all of these decisions to spend more make you into a more lethargic company as you steadily lose your hungry outlook. An accumulation of those decisions will impact the bottom line of any company, no matter how big.

Instead of, Can I afford it? or, Will it even impact my bottom line? the question has to be, Do I really need it? and Is it the right decision to advance my venture? If that old desk is making you less productive because the drawers are getting stuck, or if you need to project a more professional image and you can't have decrepit-looking furniture, then get new desks. An even better question is, Can I achieve the professional image I am seeking without spending as much?

We asked ourselves that question when we leased new offices in early 2014. After a period of rapid growth, we needed a space of about 37,000 square feet. We could have afforded to pay market rates for the lease and design. Instead, we chose to look for arbitrage opportunities by finding a sublease that fit our needs. We got rates that were 25–30 percent lower than the market average by finding an empty space that the tenant wanted to sublet, with seven years left on the lease. Our team was creative and resourceful in the design and achieved a really cool aesthetic without exceeding the rental agreement's construction allowance.

We followed the same approach with our furniture. The standard practice is that companies leave the old furniture and buy new. Most people assume that to make the office look nice enough, you have to start from scratch. Especially for Fortune 500 companies, which are making billions in profits, saving half a million dollars in furniture is not worth the hassle. (But an accumulation of decisions stemming from that mindset is what eventually makes such companies less lean.) We pounce on those opportunities.

In each of the last three subleases we took over, we moved every functioning piece of furniture from our old office. Then the former tenant left us most of their furniture, for free. We only needed to buy a tiny amount of furniture to completely furnish the vastly larger space. We could have afforded to buy all new furniture; it just wasn't a good use of funds to throw away good furniture, and it wasn't environmentally responsible to do so.

If you walk through our office you would not be able to tell the furniture is a conglomeration of pieces from here and there over twenty years. Our look is cutting-edge, even compared to offices where four times as much was spent to achieve the same aesthetic with new stuff. Instead of new furniture, we can spend money on any number of crucial business initiatives or share bigger bonuses with our team. Plus, herein was a cultural lesson that our team absorbed about how we do things the AND way: We got a great space *and* we were resourceful.

To get the look in our offices right required a culture of

thinking about and questioning assumptions. We had to carefully take inventory of all available pieces of furniture in the old and new locations then match and sort these against expected needs. A couple of our team members invested several hours thinking about which groups of chairs and desks worked in different clusters and sections so everything looked as though it had been deliberately designed to sit together. We had to care enough to exert an extra effort up front.

KEEP IT SCRAPPY

After an influx of investor money, some of the stress goes away. Suddenly you're able to sleep. You don't need to obsess about getting that last bill paid that very second. If you end up being a little bit over with your inventory, the company won't fall apart. But you can't allow yourself to think that way. You have to keep your vigilance in place and not be spoiled by your cash.

Scrappiness is a value you have to preserve. You need to take care when you bring in the money to help you finance your growth that you have built a culture of scrappiness that money can't destroy. Make sure you've created the financial mechanisms to prevent the money from making your team more lax.

The question is how to spend the money in the most effective way. We figured out by trial and error how to keep it simple, keep our values, and not let the money turn KIND into a different company.

In our case, we segregated the investment cash into a different account. It couldn't be tapped for unapproved working capital. I had to explicitly approve any allocation of our investment funds. In rare cases, it was justified for us to adjust our working capital formulas. For example, if you are required to hold extra days' worth of inventory because you are growing too fast and have several products whose sales are hard to forecast, it's unwise to be overly tight with inventory. But other than bona fide operational adjustments, we were strict about investing the new money only in areas that would support an acceleration of our growth, such as a deeper bench in our team or more assertive sales and marketing tools.

Fiscal prudence also applies to managing your incoming orders. There's such a thing as your customers ordering too much product. They might be diverting it. Or they simply might not know better. You want to think of the long term and ship only product you know will be used for the right channels and on the right time horizon. If something looks too good to be true, it probably is. In the late nineties, PeaceWorks had an incident where one of our customers was ordering a ton of product. We were not sophisticated enough to see the red flags. This was a company that had not ordered much previously, and the increase in their order was sudden. We shipped them everything they wanted, and before the payment period ended, they declared bankruptcy.

Evidently, we discovered later, when they knew they were going under, they made the calculated decision to order cases and cases of merchandise, which they could sell without having to pay for it. It was an unprincipled action on their part, but we could have prevented it if we weren't so greedy ourselves. We should have wondered what had prompted their dramatic uptick in orders. We learned our lesson.

Today, KIND has three systems in place to prevent this sort

of problem. We keep tabs on the health of our distributors and retailers, using monitoring agencies and our own data. We carefully allot "credit terms" and will ship on credit only an amount that we reasonably conclude they can sell through their channel. We also ensure they are paying us on time. If they're late on their payments, we stop shipping until they catch up.

WHEN IT'S TIME TO INVEST IN GROWTH

My investors were pleasantly surprised at how diligent I was with avoiding wasted resources. At the same time, they wondered whether I was too obsessed with controlling costs and not sufficiently focused on investing in growth. You can only cut your costs down to zero, theoretically. But the upside is infinite.

For reasons I explain later, I had spent the vast majority of 2006 to 2008 outside of the United States, working on peace in the Middle East. As part of the investment deal, I promised my private equity partners that I would focus the majority of my time on KIND after the transaction closed. I was in New York when the recession hit hard in January 2009. People were talking about a total meltdown of society. We missed our January and February sales goals, which was very rare. I was worried about investing so much money in marketing, which we had never done before, at a time when consumer spending seemed to be retrenching. I had never had the luxury of spending discretionary cash in acquiring new consumers through more aggressive marketing, and I wanted to be prudent about when to spend it to ensure we got a return on our investment. Frankly, I was a bit scared.

Mike Repole grounded me. "You already took some money out," he pointed out to me. "We agreed we would take some risks, so stop being scared and just go for it."

He was right. Now that I could provide for my family, I could take those risks. This was a difficult shift in direction. I was very reluctant to waste resources. That can sometimes translate into missed opportunities.

I followed Mike's advice and we stayed focused on the marketing plan, not pulling any punches. For the first time, we built a field marketing team dedicated to giving out samples of our products and letting people experience them during the optimal usage occasions—whether it was during snack time at the office, or when traveling on a plane, or commuting on a train, or during a cycling trip, and so on.

Initially I had seen samples as a cost center. The $800 we spent in 2008 was primarily for samples to retailers, not to consumers. I needed to start learning to be okay with spending money on the right investment. Sampling was a huge missing piece of my strategy. In retrospect it became obvious that sampling was an investment and not a cost.

In 2009, we expanded our sampling budget from $800 to $800,000. Given our products' high quality and taste, letting people taste them was the best way to build awareness. People had to try our products to know how delicious they were. Today, we invest over $20 million in field marketing and sampling programs every year.

Of course, even better than letting people try your products for free is when they are motivated to buy one and try it on their own. By the spring of 2009, our distribution was steadily expanding and our products were available in over 25,000 stores. Word of mouth was driving sales, as fans steadily raved about KIND to their friends. The most valuable location from a sampling and initial trial standpoint is at the "impulse" section—by the checkout counter. I hadn't lost my focus on the possibility of showcasing KIND near the 11,000 premium cash registers in Starbucks stores across the United States.

My conversations with the vice president in charge of Food at Starbucks had been progressing slowly but steadily. If the early conversations had constituted the crush on the prettiest girl in class, the following months had involved cautiously courting the relationship, steadily and persistently showing interest, without coming off as a stalker. Things moved slowly, when all of a sudden the stars aligned and Starbucks and KIND started dating. As they focused on their "Real Food, Simply Delicious" concept, senior management at Starbucks greenlighted the decision to sell KIND bars in Starbucks stores. This was a big deal because, until that point, Starbucks had not carried packaged foods from an outside brand. They carried biscotti, chocolates, and other confectionery items that were all under Starbucks' brand.

Once Starbucks decided to move forward, it was impressive to see how swiftly the gigantic organization could execute. We were asked if we could keep up with them and deliver product within sixty to ninety days. We pounced on the opportunity and made it a strategic priority to deliver to all their depots in a timely fashion. We supported their launch by gifting one KIND bar to each of their partners (team members are called partners at Starbucks; I gather they also shun the term "employee"). We also provided 86,000 bars, broken into four pieces each, to offer as samples to a few hundred thousand Starbucks consumers.

The natural foods community watched this step with fascination. Every food brand started knocking on Starbucks' door to see if they could also develop a supplier relationship with them. And whereas retailers traditionally are loath to learn that a competing retailer now carries KIND, Starbucks was seen as a tastemaker and other retailers welcomed the new distribution.

GROUNDED WITH PURPOSE

A major issue when a social enterprise accepts an investment is how its new partners will jibe with the company's social purpose. Before I closed our deal with VMG, I made the case to our prospective investment partners that the social mission helps the brand in a variety of indirect ways. And I explained that, regardless, the social mission is an immutable part of our enterprise and transcends the business justification. For us it was about maintaining KIND's soul.

Outside investment is a shot in the arm, energy and momentum to any company looking to grow. But another major challenge that tends to surface after significant outside financial investment is keeping humble as a person and as a business leader. How do you stay grounded amidst financial success? You suddenly have an infusion of money or you take an amount of money out to provide for your family that you never thought possible. How do you remind yourself of what you stand for and how you need to live your life?

The answer, as it had been before, is introspection. You need to talk to yourself. You need to remind yourself what your values are. It takes a conscious effort to maintain a sense of proportion, a sense of where you came from. You have to remind yourself that money is not your purpose, but a tool to support it. It helps me to see my own surplus money as belonging to society. I'm just the guardian entrusted to putting it to good use.

There's also the question of how this will affect your family. We want our children to learn from us. If I retire now, my children, who are still young, won't grow up seeing me working. What will that teach them? They weren't alive for the fifteen years I spent sweating up and down the streets, carrying boxes in and out of the basement, worrying whether I'd make it, and working at all hours with all my might to get there.

If I want to instill in them the values of charity, hard work, and entrepreneurship, Michelle and I agree that we have to stay grounded and keep working with the same spirit as before. It's important for our children to know there are limits to what we and they will spend, to know there are boundaries to what we will allow ourselves to do, to live in a world where we create an atmosphere of appropriate financial limitations and a sense of proportion.

APPROACHABILITY: LETTING OTHERS LAUGH AT YOU

A key part of staying grounded in a work environment is not taking yourself too seriously, and ensuring your team members don't see you as unapproachable. The more a company succeeds and grows, the more a founder runs the risk of being perceived as infallible or intimidating, particularly by more junior or newer team members. At KIND, we've created a culture where it's okay to criticize yourself, and for others to provide you blunt feedback. You are human, you make mistakes, and you need to rely on your team to let you know when you've messed up. The corollary to institutionalizing the idea that every team member's ideas are valued is to accept feedback. Be open to changing your mind when your team members' ideas are better than yours. Credit and honor others' individual and group contributions and ideas, rather than claiming them as your own.

My thick and confused Mexican Jewish accent keeps me humble. To make it worse, as someone who went to law school in the United States, I sometimes use legal-speak. Some tell me the combination is hilarious. I think my accent softens my passion and tones down any perceived negative intensity, especially when I'm talking about serious matters. The effect is to make people smile. "Who can blame this poor guy?" they think. "He sounds like Ricky Ricardo."

Because I wasn't raised in the United States, some of my idioms are also out of whack. For example, when we entered the assertive sampling phase to try to scale consumer awareness and purchases through product trial, I referred to it as the time to "just pour water." The correct English phrase is apparently "just add water." I've also been known to say "Don't throw the baby out the window with the bathtub" instead of "Don't throw the baby out with the bathwater" and more than once have mangled the separate idioms, "pound the pavement" and "hit the ground running," into "hit the pound running." I was likewise surprised to learn that "Don't be a backseat quarterback" didn't make sense to my team, and that having a look "under the skirt" in terms of evaluating a new business opportunity could be interpreted rather differently! I joke that instead of idioms, I use idiotisms. My team teasingly calls them Daniel-isms. I celebrate my stupidity and don't take myself too seriously. That's my personality. But it also benefits my style of leadership to use self-deprecating humor.

THE CASE FOR PARANOIA

Staying grounded and humble also means never getting cocky and always staying alert to business threats. Sometimes, someone really is out to get you. In business it's always crucial to keep your antennae up. You need to retain the humility to remember your company is not invincible. Nothing is static in business: you are either gaining or losing market share. As Intel founder Andy Grove wrote in his 1999 book of the same name, "Only the paranoid survive." You should always feel vulnerable and exposed.

In our case, a healthy dose of paranoia was justified. Around 2009 and 2010, KIND's success was starting to give rise to a swelling tide of copycats. We needed to figure out how, if at all, to respond to this. We knew we had to use the infusion of money from our private equity investors to be creative. Our challenge was this: How could we continue out-innovating all the imitators and stay ahead of the pack?

CHAPTER 6

ORIGINALITY

Unlocking the Ability to Think Boundlessly

Once KIND Fruit & Nut bars gained traction, we began carving out a new competitive space within the nutritional bar category. Because of our products' uniqueness, there were no true competitors on the market. Consumers who wanted a whole nut and fruit bar came to our shelves. Our marketing work was centered inside the stores—"in the trenches," as we say—and emphasized the quality of our ingredients. We built case-stack displays of our products at the end of the store aisle and sought to place racks and temporary displays near the checkout area. Other snack bar companies mainly watched from the sidelines.

Then, a few years later, companies large and small started launching products to try to compete in the new subcategory we had created. They emulated our ingredient combinations, our use of whole nuts and fruits, and our use of clear wrappers. But somehow none seemed to register in consumers' minds.

Whether the imitators came from a leading retailer, a major manufacturer, or a small start-up, we were blessed that consumers stuck by us.

In 2011, yet another competitor launched a fruit and nut bar designed to mimic KIND. This new entrant also claimed their bars had 60 percent less sugar than the leading fruit and nut bars.

There are three ways to lower the sugar in a whole nut bar: use less fruit; use fillers; or replace the honey-based binder with artificial ingredients. This company was using a combination of tactics, using sugar alcohols like maltitol or sorbitol that can cause bloating and feel and taste artificial, as well as relying heavily on processed ingredients in lieu of nuts. To further bolster their comparative claims, they pitted the nutritional information from the "leading" bars that contained fruit against one of their bars that contained no fruit. In other words, they were not comparing apples to apples. Had they compared their bar to our Nut Delight (which contains no fruit and also no maltitol and sorbitol), the sugar content would have been practically the same.

The competitor's flagship product promoted itself as "zero sugar" and "all natural." But we knew that you can't make a zero-sugar snack bar from all-natural ingredients. Real food has some sugar. Nuts naturally contain a little sugar. Fruits contain sugar (even breast milk does). But like a plethora of companies that were trying to make money on America's obesity epidemic and consumers' fears about it, this company was trumpeting silver bullets that contained "zero sugar" by making products with artificial compounds.

Limiting sugar intake is something consumers are increasingly mindful of, and for good reason. And at the same time, a lot of articles were describing sugar as "the" evil to avoid at all costs, creating exaggerated fears and obsessions to avoid any sugar intake, even if part of a nutritionally rich product.

We were faced with a serious dilemma. Was the absolute fear of "sugar" something that would harm us? Should we launch a line with "natural sugar alcohols" like erythritol and cut our sugar count in ways similar to our competitors? Should we introduce a zero-sugar product?

Early on at KIND, I had made a commitment never to have sugar as the first ingredient in our products. At the same time, KIND was built around respect for ingredients found in nature. We would no longer be able to say we used "ingredients you can see and pronounce" if we added sugar alcohols or other compounds to deliver on the "zero sugar" fad. This betrayal of our values would alienate our customers. I came to the realization that it would not be true to our brand to substitute artificial ingredients. We would continue to deliver wholesome solutions by focusing on real food, not lab food. We did not want KIND to become a functional diet product. We wanted to remain a healthy snack that is part of a healthful lifestyle.

We weren't prepared to compromise, so we decided that we had to design a new product that would let us compete in an honest and transparent fashion and address the valid consumer concern of reducing sugar content. It took us a year, but in 2012 we launched our KIND Nuts & Spices line. These bars had less sugar because we removed the fruit and replaced it with spices to boost the flavor. We worked incessantly to bind our nuts with the minimum amount of honey and glucose. We reduced the sugar in our dark chocolate coating. This way we were able to deliver only five grams of sugar or less per bar while keeping our brand promise.

Rather than go to the mat with our "zero sugar" competitors, we decided to change the conversation. Naming the new line Nuts & Spices allowed us to refocus consumers' attention on what our bars do have (nutritionally rich nuts and spices) while being true to our brand. This decision allowed us to play to our strength, which is ingredients you can see and pronounce, instead of positioning our products as diet foods.

The strategy of letting our ingredients be the heroes paid off for us. Our KIND Dark Chocolate Nuts & Sea Salt bar, which debuted in this line, is the #1 best-performing bar in the entire nutritional bar category on a same-store basis, according to Nielsen and IRI data.

By staying true to our principles and thinking with AND, we leveraged our competitors' actions to strengthen instead of weaken us. In retrospect, I find this episode a perfect example of the need for innovation that is still true to a brand promise. We were appropriately apprehensive about our rivals' actions, but we used competitive threats as opportunities to reaffirm our company's values. This strategy not only helped us define even more clearly who we were and what we stood for, but it helped us out-innovate and outflank the competition.

INNOVATION THAT STAYS ON BRAND

An added benefit of staying on brand with the introduction of KIND Nuts & Spices is that we didn't unwittingly undermine our original line. It may seem quite simple in retrospect, but there are many recent examples of brands that have failed to protect their core products when introducing new lines: Consumers saw the marketing for the new lines as evidence that the brand's original products had been superseded, and they stopped buying those core products. For example, you may have a beverage that has 240 calories. When you introduce a new ten- or zero-calorie version, you inadvertently highlight the high calorie count of your original product. Brands that are most vulnerable here probably started with a problematic feature, but all brands can damage themselves if they are not careful when they launch new lines.

When you're starting to innovate past your core product, you constantly have to remind yourself what your brand stands for. You run the risk of confusing consumers by giving them conflicting messages. This is the time to evaluate what your brand means to consumers and what you want it to represent. It's a tough question: Who are you as a company? The key, before you expand, is to know the answer.

To innovate is to do something that is truly different and disruptive, that takes you into an area where you have not been before. But effective innovation must stay on brand and make sense to those who know what to expect from you. There has to be a common thread, a consistency, an underlying premise or set of values, so that there's credibility to your efforts.

You can transcend your origins but you need what marketers call brand permission to succeed. That means that you need to get the consumer to sign off on the direction your new products are moving your brand. If you're a candy bar maker, will a consumer trust you to make healthy snacks? Probably not; you'd be well advised to start a new brand because your candy brand has negative brand equity in the space of healthful eating. If you have a sugary beverage brand that's fun and irreverent, everybody assumes your ingredients are artificial. Trying to make a natural version of your product may actually hurt your parent brand because it's going to create friction. People won't believe your new product is natural, and they'll question why you felt the need to create it. Maybe your core consumer may not care about wellness-promoting drinks since they're choosing to buy a fun soft drink.

Sometimes companies stop understanding what their brand represents as they grow bigger. A gigantic conglomerate often hires an entry-level brand manager who inherits a small brand and wants to make a mark. This can have disastrous results for the brand.

Consider Balance bars. Two decades ago, the Balance nutritional bar was launched with a unique value proposition, promising a balanced "meal" of 30 percent protein, 40 percent carbohydrates, and 30 percent dietary fat. This formula was linked to a popular diet at the time, and immediately gained traction with consumers.

While the company was guided by its founders and stayed focused on its mission, it grew to more than $100 million in sales from 1992 to 1999 before being acquired by Kraft in January 2000.

Then the well-respected brand lost its way. Over the next ten years, every time a trend appeared in the nutritional bar space, the Balance-Kraft team seemed to want to pounce on it. When organic felt like it had legs, they created an organic version of Balance bars. When KIND pioneered whole nut and fruit bars, they created Balance bare. Among the dozen trend-driven variants were Balance CarbWell, Balance Organic, and Balance

100-calorie bars, each launched to capitalize on fads sweeping the country.

The strategy made no sense. The original Balance bars were functional products. Their whole brand was about achieving balanced meals through a specific formula and appealed to a particular consumer segment that coveted that functional feature. All of a sudden, the newly anointed brand manager looked at sales trends and tried to follow brands that were growing faster. The brand shepherd did not consider whether consumers would trust Balance to make an organic bar. But the Balance brand had no brand permission to go to some of those places. Plus, every time the company launched a new product, it implicitly provoked friction, questions, and confusion about the original product. The consumer was left to wonder if the changes meant that the original was obsolete. At Balance, I believe that the brand manager didn't stop to think, "How can I credibly defend and grow my core?"

Consequently, Balance faltered; by the time that Kraft off-loaded the company in 2009, Balance had lost its leadership position and credibility. Kraft sold the brand at a loss to a private equity firm.

Whether you're a small company or a division of a large one, if you have been given the responsibility to grow a brand, the first thing you must do is understand what that brand stands for. This is not an easy exercise. Different people see brands differently, and brands evolve. But it's important to comprehend why people are buying your products and what they expect from you.

Someone once told me: "A brand is a promise. And a great brand is a promise well kept."

KIND'S SECOND ACT

Once KIND Fruit & Nut bars had been on the market for five years, we felt it was time for us to start expanding beyond our original category, balancing the natural tension between authentic innovation and authentic branding.

Normally when you're innovating, as U.S. Ambassador Thomas Pickering once told me, it is wise to move just one square over on the checkerboard. You are more likely to understand the adjacent spaces and your consumer is more likely to see the logical progression of your brand.

Our common thread could have been making "bars," expanding beyond nutritional bars and adding granola bars to our assortment. Or the use of "nuts and fruit" could have been our common denominator, moving into fruit and nut trail mixes. But we felt if we stayed in bars as our second act, people would know us as a bar company; and if we launched a fruit and nut trail mix, we'd be seen as a fruit and nut company.

We took the risky strategic step of moving a couple of squares over—beyond fruits and nuts, and beyond bars—because we wanted to send the message that KIND transcends those boundaries. We concluded our most distinctive value proposition was using healthful ingredients that were minimally processed.

And thus, in October 2011 we introduced KIND Healthy Grains Clusters, a granola-like product that can be eaten as a snack on the go or with milk or yogurt in a bowl. We wanted to signal to the consumer that the common denominator of KIND products is nutritionally rich ingredients that you can see and pronounce. We felt we had a responsibility to live up to the potential of this concept *and* to forge a new path at the same time.

Because of my experience with the teriyaki pepper spread and other early debacles, I also knew we could not even think about selling a product that wasn't 100 percent as good in every way as our core bars. With KIND Healthy Grains Clusters, we felt we had a great product that distinguished itself and provided a different value proposition from other granolas. It introduced the use of five super-grains, as opposed to just oats: millet, amaranth, quinoa, and buckwheat, plus gluten-free oats. We made the product in versatile clusters. We were confident that the clusters could represent the KIND brand, and we were proud to bring them to market.

To get real-world feedback, we took the expensive step of creating small runs of Clusters in real packaging ("live" product in fully designed and produced packaging). This experiment cost us tens of thousands of dollars, which for a small company was a big investment. We tested the products in stores to see how consumers reacted. We internally insisted that the new products would need to exceed the store's minimum sales thresholds if we were to actually launch them in the marketplace. Rather than promoting the granola with ads or signage, we let it stand on the shelves by itself, to make sure it could win on its own merits.

The Healthy Grains Clusters took off rapidly. Inside each bag from the test batches, we included an invitation for feedback. The results were clear: Consumers loved it and let us know that they understood that the product was much more nutritionally rich than the other granolas for sale at the time. It was gluten free, non-GMO, tasted delicious, and was nutrient dense. We officially launched the line in collaboration with Whole Foods, which partnered with us to showcase the product and celebrate its innovative features and great taste. Three months later we rolled out the line across the nation. KIND Healthy Grains Clusters is one of the fastest-growing product lines in the granola category, garnering over 10 percent of all granola sales after two years on the market. At one major retailer, the line represents upwards of 40 percent of total granola sales.

Despite our obsession with quality, we did falter along the way. Early on, we received some customer complaints, which was a fairly new experience for us: We sell tens of millions of bars per month and get a handful of complaints. We try to tend to every single one of them, both to make things right with any consumer we disappointed, and to see if we can identify broader lessons for constant improvement. But all of a sudden, we were receiving over one hundred complaints for every million Clusters we sold, which, while modest perhaps for an average company, was quite unusual for us. Tony Celentano, the head of our consumer relations team, flagged the problem as soon as these dissatisfied customer reports started to come in. In November 2012 we received a record 202 complaints per million on the Clusters, and it really alarmed me.

It became clear that a couple of the ingredients we were using—buckwheat and amaranth—were more fragile than we had understood (they go stale quite easily). These complaints prompted us to check on the freshness and quality from our suppliers and to perfect the conditions for storing these ingredients at our end. Our team dove into the issue at headquarters while Bob Rhodes, our head of manufacturing, and Brian Lutter, our lead on the Healthy Grains production team, camped out at the factory for weeks, sacrificing many weekends with family to swiftly correct the issue. Within five weeks we had instituted a number of changes to optimize freshness. Today, we log fewer than 0.35 complaints per million Clusters units sold.

Two hundred and two complaints per million might not seem like a very big number. But for every person who takes the time to complain, there may be thousands that just give up on your brand. Every single one of those consumers is a human being that we had let down. At least for those who reached out to us, we could sincerely apologize and send them replacement product. But it broke my heart that perhaps thousands of others were disappointed and lost to us.

Complaints are a rare opportunity to get feedback and do something about it. Listening to your consumers and creating systems to ensure that you incorporate their feedback is extraordinarily important. We love the overwhelming praise we get from consumers—including unsolicited testimonials about how someone lost weight, or how a KIND act made someone's day, or how delicious our products are. But because we don't want criticism to get lost amidst all the love, we instituted a system where our weekly feedback reports must first list any and all complaints. A dozen team leaders review these reports on a weekly basis to ensure their respective departments are acting on them.

INNOVATION: YOUR SECRET WEAPON

No matter your business, you want to make sure you have a product or a service that distinguishes you from the crowd. A central part of American culture is celebrating original products and ideas that make this world a little better.

In the consumer products world, there is a pejorative term

for items that are not innovative: me-too items. Me-too items proliferate a few years after a trend takes hold and/or one company puts out an innovative and winning product. You see this again and again if you look at any recent food-industry trend: the coconut-water craze, the low-carb craze, the gluten-free craze. But you also see it across other industries, from apparel to digital apps.

From the retail buyer's perspective, why should they give shelf space to a derivative item? The me-too item is not doing anything for the category or bringing in new shoppers. Without offering consumers something new, it's just going to cannibalize sales in the category. The whole idea of blindly copying a product is also bad for the company doing the copying. Consumers don't really go for the umpteenth brand of coconut water or gluten-free granola and supermarkets don't have the shelf space to hold them all. Consumers don't have any reason to trust the #5 or the #20 brand, unless they provide a differentiating proposition. Lower-performing brands eventually get discontinued from the shelves. If you're not playing to win, my theory is, don't even play. Pick a different game where you have a chance to lead.

The AND philosophy thrusts innovation and creativity. Innovation is what makes our world go round. It's the key to a venture's success. And it's an equalizing factor. You don't need to be the largest company out there. If you are the most creative, you can level the playing field (or, as I once said to my team in my semi-intelligible Mex-English, "The leveling field is your creativity"). This is why start-ups and entrepreneurial companies—innovative by design—often win against big corporations.

QUESTIONING THE WAY THINGS ARE

Every morning, millions of men wake up, get dressed in suits, and put on a tie. They spend their whole day at work with a piece of cloth wrapped around their necks and hanging down to their stomachs. They accept as a given that this is normal business attire. The vast majority of them will go through their entire adult lives without ever questioning why they wear this thing around their necks, or how this fashion even came about.

Why does it make sense that this long piece of cloth should represent elegance or professionalism? How did this custom get started? Certainly when we observe "strange" customs from other cultures—like the large wooden rings that some African tribes use to elongate their necks—we marvel at their foreignness or oddness. But we take for granted that our own customs are perfectly normal.

The most credible explanation for the origin of ties that I have found is that in the early seventeenth century, Croatian militias visiting Paris marveled at a Parisian fashion of wearing colored scarves around their necks. They adopted these as their uniform, wearing neck scarves "à la croate," which then morphed into the "cravat" or modern-day necktie. But there's no logical reason why, five centuries later, we should still follow this fashion, when our society has had no compunction about tossing out so many of the other customs that were accepted back then. We live our entire lives taking so much for granted, and we tend to accept as givens many assumptions that are ripe for a challenge.

It is in the daily routines of our business and personal lives that so many opportunities for creating value exist. The more entrenched the practice or custom, the more that it's possible it may no longer be relevant. Critical thinking can help us question whether it is still (or ever was) an optimal way to do things. The AND way of thinking and methodology can help you quickly analyze those underlying assumptions and question whether they are valid, or whether you can introduce a better way to do things.

I spend a lot of time thinking about the assumptions behind any decision I make, and evaluating whether other options are available or need to be created. It is not a decisive style of leadership, and it can paralyze an organization if it is not complemented by swift and decisive leadership, which in KIND's case is provided by our president, John Leahy, whose mantra is "speed to market." But this contemplation can unlock value for important strategic opportunities.

There's a way to incorporate rigorous thinking into our lives. You can also teach your team to run a formal brainstorming process in which you think with AND. Over the years I believe we have become good at doing both at KIND. There's still a long way to go; on a scale of 1–100, I think we're at 10.

You have to ask yourself continually: "What are the underlying assumptions that are limiting me?" Sometimes those assumptions will be valid, but that's how you have to start. You just need to make it a practice to talk to yourself. We're so busy that we tend not to even find that time.

Whether it's lying in bed before you sleep, or consciously choosing not to make phone calls while you're commuting to work, give yourself time to mull over whatever you're dealing with. I happen to use showers as a venue for unstructured thinking and for talking to myself.

One of the biggest dangers of smartphones and other digital devices is that we don't get a chance to talk to ourselves as much. We're constantly getting stimulation, reviewing email, voicemail, and social media. We don't give ourselves the time to let our minds go where they want to go. You need to block out time. If you can, structure your work life to have one hour during which you let your brain go every day.

THINKING BOUNDLESSLY

And what are you supposed to do during these free-form think breaks? When there's an issue you want to solve, use this time to play with it. Frame the question differently. Try breaking it down into smaller pieces and then just start tackling it that way. Set this as a dedicated agenda for yourself: What am I going to think about as I'm showering, or walking down the street?

Or maybe there is no burning question with which you are grappling. Letting your brain wander and meander can be healthy and lead to great ideas. First you need to empty your mind of trivial concerns, and let it fill itself up with whatever comes to you. Let your thoughts wander in any direction your consciousness takes you. You're creating space for ideas to come to you.

A lot of the best ideas—including business opportunities or creative ways to confront social problems, or just ways to make your life more fulfilling—can come from a totally unstructured process in which you let ideas flow freely through your mind.

Surprisingly, as far as I know, this is not something that we are taught as kids or as adults. If anything, we chastise kids for drifting off and we prescribe them medications to help them stay focused. Creative brainstorming and conscious drifting should be encouraged. American creativity and ingenuity has propelled our success. Fostering it should be at the center of our educational system.

As a child, I had a lot of time to myself. I spent most of my afternoons doing what today would be referred to as unstructured "free play." I wasn't overscheduled with activities, quite the opposite. The garden behind my bedroom was a theater where all sorts of different worlds were created every day. And at night, before I fell asleep, I spent a lot of time daydreaming that I was a magician with supernatural powers, which I deployed to thrust Arabs and Israelis to make peace. The power to dream—to imagine new paths that challenge conventional wisdom—was exhilarating.

BRAINSTORMED IDEAS: A CAMEL IN NEW YORK CITY

In 1996, when PeaceWorks finally had some distribution of our Mediterranean spreads in New York City, we decided to do a splashy launch event. We timed it to coincide with a meeting of our advisory board, a slate of luminaries who were coming in to discuss business strategy.

At the time I had two recent college grads working with me. We sat down to brainstorm ideas on how to best promote the brand. One of them threw out a silly idea, suggesting that we have a camel walk down the streets of New York to generate attention and garner media mentions. New Yorkers get used to seeing the most bizarre sights on the street, and it's difficult to jolt them out of their reveries. We thought we could get people to notice us with a camel.

At first, we dismissed the idea as ridiculous and kept brainstorming. When we came back to analyze our options at the end of the exercise, we revisited it again.

"That camel thing is so irreverent and so insane, maybe it could work," I said.

We decided to try it out. The first place we called had already rented out their camel for the day. I didn't realize there was an active market for renting camels in Manhattan! We eventually found someone who could rent us a camel for $1,000.

To go along with the camel, we needed actors to play Moshe and Ali, the mascots of our brand. We couldn't afford professional actors so I walked up to Spanish Harlem and spoke in my native Spanish with two nice guys from the Dominican Republic who were standing on a street corner. I convinced them to take the job for $150 each. One dressed as Ali, the magician, with a robe and Arab headdress. The other, who had a beautiful full beard, which we made white with talcum powder, wore a chef's outfit and a big white hat.

The invitations were fancy printed ones, tucked inside pita bread for extra effect. We were breaking all the rules because we had nothing to lose and no reputation to protect.

We asked Ben Cohen, who was a member of our advisory board, if he would lead the camel toward a restaurant to which we had invited a hundred people, all food industry names. He agreed to do it, and he wore a shirt that said, "Moshe & Ali's: Cooperation Never Tasted So Good." Every time Ben tried to give someone a sample, the camel snatched it from his hands. So there was Ben Cohen, of Ben & Jerry's fame, walking down the cobblestone streets of TriBeCa as a camel ate from his hand.

This stunt won us a ton of press coverage. We were in *The New York Times,* and that evening I turned on the TV and discovered we were on Fox's *Minute,* the local news channel's minute-long roundup of the day's news. That was a big thing for me. Sales inquiries followed.

None of this would have happened if we had shunned the crazy ideas up front.

KIND'S BRAINSTORMING PROCESS

At KIND, we have a practical process for brainstorming and filtering new ideas. First, we carefully think about the ultimate goal we are trying to achieve, and make sure we are not confusing that goal with tactical objectives. Second, we exhaustively list all the assets and tools at our disposal. Third, we start ideating. We allow ourselves the use of existing assets and tools, as well as our stated goals, to help trigger ideas, but we remind ourselves that these are not there to limit us but to get the creative juices flowing.

It is vital to separate the creative brainstorming process from the analytical evaluation process that will follow it. During the ideation process, we don't allow any filters to stand in the way. For example, we never allow cost considerations or other practical constraints like manufacturing efficiencies to be up-front filters on our creative process. We remind ourselves not to criticize any contribution, nor to start analyzing why it may not work. The words "no," "that won't work," "let's be realistic," "that makes no sense" and all other put-downs are banished from this phase.

Once we've exhausted all creative ideas, we list the appropriate filtering criteria: feasibility, cost, expected impact on the intended audience, adherence to the brand, time, likelihood of success, the ratio of inputs to execute relative to intended outputs, and so on.

We use the filters to prioritize the ideas that best accomplish the goals. Typically, after we complete this process and come up with a broad concept, we then repeat the process and start brainstorming with greater specificity within the concept or idea that we chose. It is not uncommon for us to go through three to four rounds of brainstorming with increasing focus to yield the best idea.

WHY YOU NEED FILTERS

You need to be comfortable brainstorming and daydreaming, but thinking critically, about yourself and about your ideas, is a vital corollary. Allow yourself to be naïve when you come up with ideas. Then use filters to protect yourself from your own naïveté.

Sometimes you may not be able to recognize which ideas won't work. This is where you have to rely on your team and your advisers. In the early days of my business, I was lucky enough to have my team talk me out of one of my more impractical ideas. I wanted to launch a PeaceWorks café in New York City where patrons could invite homeless people to dine at their tables. The concept centered around allowing diners to meet the homeless and have conversations that would lead to a better understanding of what they endure—to foster empathy.

My team pointed out that, although my heart was in the right place, there was no way this would work, practically. How many customers would want to pay money to sit down to eat next to a stranger, let alone a homeless person? And how would we find homeless people who wanted to have dinner in such a patronizing situation? It was doomed to fail. Idealism is a good thing, but too much of it can be self-defeating.

That's also why boards and investors are a valuable filter to help test your ideas. One friend of mine, Martín Varsavsky, is a successful serial entrepreneur who has started over fourteen ventures, and created billions of dollars in value. Yet he won't start a new business without attracting outside investors. I once asked him why. "Because their participation validates my idea and decreases the risk that I am deluding myself," he explained. "If I can't convince others to put their money behind a new concept," he added, "it probably is not worth my investing my own."

That's not to say that you always need to take no for an answer. I am not as disciplined as Martín, and I certainly believe in the courageous inventor who challenges all naysayers. But there is something to be said for Martín's filtering process. You have to look at why people are saying no to your ideas. The rule of thumb is to not override your board, but sometimes you can if you are able to answer the vast majority of their questions in a serious way. Without some creativity and naïveté—and the ability to listen to your gut and challenge skeptics—you won't be truly innovative.

THE VALUE OF WACKINESS

When brainstorming, every idea must be jotted down and cele-brated. Every new idea can then be a springboard to others. Un-less you are coming up with wacky and silly ideas, you are not truly testing your assumptions.

Some of our wackiest moments can lead to valuable break-throughs. After months of calling the buyer of Stew Leonard's, a specialty foods institution, I realized I needed to come up with something creative to get him to call me back. As I left my ump-teenth voicemail, I randomly offered to wash his car if he tried my products and they didn't sell. "That is the first time someone has offered something like that," he chuckled when he finally returned my call and gave me a shot.

I learned the value of wacky ideas in Japan, where I spent the summer after my college graduation working at Japan Counsel-ors, a company that advised American clients on how to gain more market share in Japan. I was in charge of translating and editing their "English" materials and teaching English to their Japanese employees. To this day I wonder what happens when some of those staffers show up speaking English with a thick Mexican intonation.

My Japanese-American boss taught me a lot about Japanese culture and about public relations. Japan Counselors was known for its hilarious stunts: They orchestrated a public contest for the loudest screamer, sponsored by Halls Mentho-Lyptus cough drops, and one for the most exotic beard, sponsored by Schick razors.

My favorite was when they ran a campaign, sponsored by

Raid insecticide, to find the biggest cockroach in the country; one room of the office held a collection of the most horrifying cockroaches that readers had mailed in. The crazier their campaigns, the more media coverage they would get. The job opened my eyes to the power of media and creativity to help you tell your story.

Naïveté is important to creativity. Sometimes it's better not to know that a plan is impossible, impractical, or otherwise unfeasible. Without these mental limitations, you can get around the problems and find a way to make your idea possible. After all, if something is immediately obvious, then others are probably doing it already.

An illustration of the triumph of creative thinking over practicality was our marketing effort at the Natural Products Expo West, our industry's biggest trade show. KIND attends this show every year, and these days we have a big presence, but when we first started out we had only one small booth.

When you're small, you have to think of guerrilla marketing hacks. What we did was convince the entire community to become our partners in the marketing effort. The idea was to get people to wear T-shirts with the KIND logo at the expo. We made up thousands of shirts and gave them out to everyone we could, on the condition that they wear the shirts to the trade show. We came up with fun challenges, like scavenger hunts, for show attendees. Participants had to try KIND products and do a kind act for someone else, and if they collected enough stamps, they would win a T-shirt and be entered to win other prizes, including the opportunity to make a Big KIND Act of their dreams come true. We also gave out logo bags for people to collect all the samples and materials they accumulated as they walked the show floor. So even when we were tiny, our presence was felt, partly because of our disruptive products and compelling brand, but also because of our guerrilla marketing efforts.

This worked frighteningly well and became a tradition. Every year, thousands of avid fans flood the convention hall wearing our gear and acting as KIND billboards.

I can't overestimate the value of crazy ideas to my work. All our best ideas were considered bizarre at the time: a bar made from whole nuts and fruit; transparent wrappers; the idea of bringing Arabs and Israelis together through commerce. My thesis adviser thought I was bonkers when I suggested economic cooperation between Israelis and Arabs. Every one of the major things I've done started out as a crazy thought. Only once we pulled it off did it start seeming obvious in retrospect.

UNLEASHING PERSPECTIVES

After many years of questioning assumptions, my team teases me about my method of relentless probing into a particular issue; they call it the Mexican Inquisition. It's my way of being the devil's advocate for every challenge. Team members who don't know me well may think I'm arguing for a particular perspective. In fact, I'm just trying to get at the truth by questioning all sides and uncovering any false assumptions, to discover where the juiciest opportunities for adding value lie. The ideal is to build a culture of healthy discussion where everyone is comfortable challenging my or anyone else's ideas without ever feeling or making someone else feel that the questioning is a personal attack.

We try to foster an authentic culture that celebrates everyone's contributions. To do that, I constantly highlight situations where I was wrong and point out how my team members changed my mind or had a better idea that I initially rejected. For example, when Facebook was on the rise, my marketing-team members Erica Bliss Pattni and Elle Lanning insisted that we should more prominently recruit fans to join our Facebook page. My initial instinct was "Why should we be building some-body else's network? Why don't we just build it on our own website? Why put our future in somebody else's hands?"

I was wrong about this. In our efforts to build the KIND Movement, I discovered that Facebook authentication—validation of your identity from your community—added enormous value that we couldn't manufacture on our own. Today, you can join the KIND Movement either by authenticating an email, or through your Facebook account.

CRITICAL REINVENTION

One always thinks about new product development and marketing campaigns as the areas ripe for innovation. Companies often underestimate how important thinking outside the box and questioning assumptions can also be for day-to-day operations. That's particularly true because these are processes that your company has followed for years. People become accustomed to doing things the same way every day. Many changes in technology or society or even in your own business may warrant new ways of doing things but you will not realize it unless you take the time to evaluate those practices.

Critical *reinvention*—which builds on the permanent start-up culture that I've described—is as important as original invention and innovation in a company. Our objective at KIND is to continuously question every aspect of our operations so no obsolete practices get carried over through inertia. We've instituted a practice of reviewing what has worked and what hasn't worked in every department for the prior six months. This helps everybody constantly question our strategy and tactics and recalibrate their efforts based on earnest analysis.

A good example of process innovation is how we launched our online sales. Back when we founded KIND, online sales of food products were practically nonexistent. Some food brands' websites had e-commerce engines, but they were more of a curiosity than a real driver of sales.

While I was somewhat skeptical of how far online sales could go with perishable food products, I was completely convinced that online sales of shelf-stable foods, particularly ones that were not too expensive to ship—a function of cost relative to weight and volume—would dramatically increase. Most important, I knew by then that KIND was the type of product that became a habit. People who tried KIND bars would repeat purchases at a frequent rate. Our most loyal consumers ate a couple KIND bars a day, and many ate a handful a week. Enabling them to receive shipments automatically would be efficient for them and would help us ensure they continued to integrate our products into their lifestyle.

I initially faced a lot of opposition from board members whose perspective I deeply respected. Mike Repole, who had built Vitaminwater in the off-line world, felt I was wasting my time and company resources trying to chase online sales that he thought could never be more than 1 percent of our business.

I persevered. I wanted to create a platform that would make it easy for our most loyal consumers to receive automatic orders with a customizable degree of frequency. KIND Advantage offers the ability to get product in bulk from our website, KindSnacks.com, at significantly lower prices than the suggested retail. It provides free shipping. We're constantly innovating to offer more flexibility, including rotating flavor choices, the ability to send gifts to friends, and incentives for introducing new customers into the KIND community. Most important, at least for me, is that KIND Advantage members receive free products from us as a surprise. We occasionally send them shipments of our newest products at no cost to thank them for their loyalty. We rely on them for feedback and consider them our most important KIND ambassadors.

Our perseverance paid off, and online sales—through our own website and through third-party purveyors on the web— became a key channel for us. For the last few years, online has greatly outpaced our strong overall growth and now represents close to 10 percent of our sales. Today, Amazon is one of our top twenty customers, and "KIND" is consistently among the top ten most frequently searched terms for food on Amazon over the past two years, according to executives there.

THE ORIGINS AND ORIGINALITY
OF KIND'S TRANSPARENT WRAPPERS

I am often asked how we elected to pack our products in see-through wrappers. Why had no one used clear packaging for nutritional bars or healthy snack bars in the United States at the time? What were the assumptions underlying the status quo, and how did we come to realize they no longer applied to KIND?

CHAPTER 7

TRANSPARENCY AND AUTHENTICITY

The Value of Open Communication

How did it come to be that we introduced transparent wrappers in the nutritional bar space? In retrospect the decision is obvious: to showcase the artisanal look of whole nut and fruit bars. What surprises me is that the answer was not obvious when we were assessing the issue. We debated at length. The conventional wisdom at the time was that highly stylized opaque foil with vibrant colors would eclipse actual products. "Real ingredients can't compete with marketers' idealized renditions of food," I was told. In some countries like Australia, clear wrappers were in use. But they cost more, and the available options did not protect the ingredients as well as foil. In the United States, where all major snack bar manufacturers made slab bars, often coated with a flavored compound (not products that would sell themselves on their looks), nobody had yet bothered to invest in the technology for transparent packaging that could also keep products fresh.

We decided to challenge the false assumption that no one wanted to see the bar itself. We sensed that consumers would find our use of whole and nutritionally rich ingredients particularly attractive.

And so we developed technology to create the right barrier properties in the wrapper, to prevent oxidation and to seal in the correct amount of moisture. This involved working with packaging specialists and tweaking their established manufacturing processes. We continued to optimize and explore improved packaging options over many years.

We also challenged conventional wisdom about what the printed packaging should look like. If we were doing all of this to celebrate our whole nuts and dried fruits, then we needed to create minimalist designs, deferential to the protagonists: the raw materials. We went through multiple iterations of proposed designs, and rejected bursts of energy, a sense of motion derived from the graphics, or extra personality created by icons, seals, symbols, and texture. Every line mattered. When you design a package, by definition you face an infinite number of choices. Because of our minimalist aesthetic, what choices we made had to be very carefully thought out.

In line with a *straightforward* brand, we decided that all the shapes in our packaging should be straight. No curves. No circles. Indeed, if you visit our website or explore our packaging, you will seldom find any circles or curves.

TRANSPARENCY ACROSS ALL TOUCH POINTS

Transparency and authenticity may be the values most associated with KIND by our consumers, largely because of our clear wrappers (literally transparent). But those who know us best can sense that transparency and authenticity are central to all we do. We convey these values through our products' names, our minimalist design, and our marketing. Less visibly, we foster open communication with our team and our strategic partners, own up to our errors, and handle transitions in lieu of "firing" people. Adopting a culture of authenticity carries some risks, but overall it makes us far stronger.

We really strive to ensure authenticity in all our marketing. For example, we shun stylized and romanticized images of the product in our packaging. My gut feeling is that consumers have been conditioned to mistrust images purporting to show what the product inside the box will look like, because they always end up being disappointed. We thus avoid images wherever possible. In the rare cases where we feel we need to show images of our product in display cases, we use actual pictures of our products in their wrappers and we make a concerted effort to choose images so true to life that consumers will feel they got what they saw.

In the same vein, we use straightforward names and avoid gimmicky choices, even if we have to resist the creative urge. For example, our product featuring chocolate, nuts, and cherries is called Dark Chocolate Cherry Cashew instead of Black Forest Cake Supreme or any other such concoction. People nowadays take this for granted, but it was bit of a daring choice in 2004, because competitors used inventive marketing names that evoked desserts or other indulgences. We wanted consumers to know precisely what they were getting when choosing our products.

There are some disadvantages to being so direct. Competitors can more easily try to copy our product names, because they are tougher to protect legally. Perhaps Crandelicious Almondini could have been trademarked but Cranberry Almond cannot. Still, overwhelmingly, our choice to be so frank has been received as a breath of fresh air; consumers seem to be tired of spin and obfuscation. It doesn't work for all brands—it may make a different brand seem boring or trite. But it works for our brand: KIND consistently gets the most awards and the highest praise in the food industry, from nutritionists, doctors, chefs, and tastemakers alike. And we continue to grow organically, based on the unsurpassed loyalty of our consumers. Consumers often give us feedback that our value proposition—simplicity, minimal processing, lack of artificial ingredients, straightforward marketing that avoids gimmicks and deception—feels and is authentic.

This level of transparency corresponds with one of my own personality traits—unusual bluntness and frankness when I communicate. This too has its pros and cons (as I am told!), but I pride myself on creating a culture that is transparent and rewards open communication both among our team members and with our trading partners and consumers. I think our community appreciates it. I think it hits a chord in the marketplace.

WHY AUTHENTICITY MATTERS

Authenticity is also about accepting who and what you are, and having the sense of self not to portray yourself as something else. If you are authentic, you learn to move past the urge to be different things to different people. It's crucial to be transparent about your strengths and weaknesses, and to accept your mistakes. Always showcase your top selling points in marketing, but don't try to run away from characteristics that are part of you. Being true to yourself—for a leader as much as for a brand—will make it easier for others to understand what you represent and to respect you.

Authenticity does not mean perfection, but people will choose an authentic brand with some limitations over a fake brand proclaiming flawlessness. Authenticity is an ongoing quest: As we grow we strive to be extra vigilant about honoring truth, transparency, and authenticity.

Authenticity is the value that helps consumers *believe* your brand promise. The more authentic it is, the further your brand can be heard without having to scream so loud.

Consider brands that command your respect. These are brands with a defined and credible identity. If you see a new product in their line, you immediately know what attributes to expect, even if the new product has a new flavor or competes in a different category.

AVOIDING EXAGGERATION AND DECEPTION

When you're dealing with social causes, you need to be particularly humble about how you position your community efforts. We try our hardest to be transparent and authentic in how we talk about our social mission at KIND. I am shocked when people say, "If you buy this product, you will save a child's life." It's manipulative and oversimplified to claim that one consumer's purchase of a nutritional bar or a sweater will save someone's life.

When we were starting out, one of my team members suggested we say, "By buying this jar of sundried tomato spread, you will make peace bloom in the Middle East." My response was, "We can't say that. It's disingenuous." I explained that we could be factual and explain PeaceWorks products involve economic cooperation among neighbors in conflict regions. But you really want to avoid overstating your case and suggesting you are solving an intractable conflict by getting people to buy your products. Hyperbole is all too prevalent, and it hurts those who are trying to do things properly. Consumers aren't that naïve, and when the claim proves false, they lose faith not only in that company, but in other companies that are trying to take modest steps in the right direction. When it comes to establishing credibility, it is better to under-promise and over-deliver.

The companies that have gained traction in the one-for-one space seem to understand the importance of not overstating claims and of being transparent and authentic. The Toms shoe company has created a whole movement around one-for-one donations, with every pair of shoes consumers buy spurring a donation of another pair to someone in need. It's not our business model, but to the best of my knowledge they've been careful to be objective and specific. The economics clearly work within the purchase price of a pair of shoes. Warby Parker, which sells eyeglasses, is doing something similar. They can afford to sponsor a donation of a pair of glasses within the retail price of their eyewear, and they do excellent work at balancing their modest and sincere mission with aesthetic excellence and competitively priced products.

Years ago, we thought about launching a direct-correlation model where each purchase of a KIND bar would feed someone who was hungry. We liked the concept, and we thought we could give away a meal or a nutritional kit for each bar we sold. We would not have said we were "saving lives." But even with a more humble, less overblown way of expressing the claim, the economics weren't viable. Nutritional packets cost about twenty-nine cents each. Proper meals cost more. To insert that cost into the price of every bar, after adding retailer and distributor margins, your bar would need to cost an extra $1 compared to your competitors' products.

TRUTH IN ADVERTISING VS. SHALLOW MARKETING

Exaggeration and deception in the food industry have jaded many consumers. But that provides an opportunity to companies that commit to being transparent and authentic.

Consider the variety of ways in which companies portray their products visually. Most consumers don't trust the images of products on advertisements because they know everything has been retouched. Most of us know that a TV dinner looks more like astronaut food than the attractively photographed feast on the package.

Authenticity also extends to claims companies make about what they are selling. The Greek-yogurt craze illustrates this point. This type of strained yogurt, widespread in Greece and Turkey, became popular in the United States for good reason. With wholesome, nutrient-dense ingredients, it has incredible nutritional properties.

Some brands have tried to jump on the Greek-yogurt bandwagon by selling products with a coating that is flavored as Greek yogurt but has little to do with actual Greek yogurt. This sweet coating doesn't have probiotic properties or protein; it's basically just sugar. But that hasn't stopped unethical marketers from trying to dupe consumers by boasting their candy or bar is made with "Greek Yogurt." Some also boast about protein content (Greek yogurt is a good source of protein), but don't explain that their protein is not derived from Greek yogurt (since it's actually *not* Greek yogurt they are using) but rather from other processed ingredients that they add later, like soy protein isolate. Their packaging strives to get the consumer to make a connection between Greek yogurt and a health product—a "health halo" as it is called—by using Greek-yogurt-flavored compound, where in fact they are selling sugar-laden products with no real nutritional value, and then adding supplements.

Since 2004, KIND has sold some bars with yogurt coating. When the Greek-yogurt craze hit the market, several yogurt-compound suppliers recommended that we ride the wave by buying the Greek-yogurt-flavored compound and touting our products as "Greek yogurt," as other bar manufacturers did. I wish I could say we immediately dismissed the option, but this is a competitive marketplace. We felt pressured, and we actually discussed the idea. Fortunately, we rejected that path. I explained "it's going to be a short-term victory that leads to a long-term decline in our brand's credibility."

For a while, some of my team members thought we were missing a great opportunity because the brands riding the "Greek yogurt" wave were gaining a lot of distribution. But, within two years, the brand most prominently touting its bars as made with "Greek yogurt" declined precipitously in market share.

Consumers are pretty sophisticated. You can fool them once. But over time they have an uncanny ability to sort through most of the deceptive claims. Candy manufacturers may remove artificial colors. Some may offer "organic" candy. But most consumers realize that a product whose primary ingredient is sugar is just going to deliver empty calories, even if it has natural colors or its sweetener is organic brown rice syrup.

My experience is that the food manufacturing community is overwhelmingly made up of good people trying to do the right thing. Large companies usually have strict legal standards because they are under a microscope and they are careful not to get in trouble. Most entrepreneurs start their companies with a sincere desire to nourish their communities. But in the competitive heat of the battle, executives under pressure to distinguish themselves sometimes push the boundaries too far and make inflated health claims rather than making authenticity their mantra. Sooner or later, consumers lose trust in them.

All companies—like all human beings—make mistakes. What's important is to take responsibility for any errors and try your best to rectify them and prevent them from happening again. I recall an incident in which we made a technical error because we were unaware of a Food and Drug Administration definition that affected one of our labels. Fortunately we received a letter from a loyal consumer alerting us to the problem. We researched the issue and realized our consumer was right. We worked swiftly to correct the wrapper and reached back to the consumer to thank him.

TRANSPARENCY AND FAIRNESS IN THE MARKETPLACE

You are supposed to stay objective and unemotional in business. I find this challenging. For me, doing things in a fair way is an integral part of how I find peace. I think it's shallow and narrow to focus only on your short-term business interests. You have to create a culture of values that leads to enduring loyalty between you and your team, and your suppliers—an expectation that you're going to treat them well and they will also treat you that way. You set that reputation and expectation and it helps you in the long term.

My model for how an executive should operate transparently was my dad. When I was about thirteen, I accompanied him on a business trip to Laredo, Texas. I was a little bored, so I went into an adjacent warehouse, found a forklift, and started driving it around the building. I drove faster and faster, taking sharper turns. Then I lost control and rammed the forklift into a pillar of TV equipment.

My dad disciplined me by talking with me as an adult. He was frank about his expectations and his disappointment. It probably would have been easier to scold me or send me back to the hotel room, or ban me from watching TV, but he held me to a higher standard. He pushed me to recognize my errors and to be more introspective, to grow up and take responsibility. I was so ashamed at having let him down that I did try to be more mature, at least for the rest of the day.

I was the type of kid who got bored in class and told jokes that made the students *and* the teachers laugh. Even so, my parents often were called in by the principal to discuss my lack of discipline. I expected to be grounded after these conversations, which is what happened to my friends when they got in trouble, but instead, my parents would sit me down in my dad's study, with his huge mahogany desk and his large imposing figure sitting behind it. My mom would ask me to explain what happened. They would sit and wait for my explanation, which forced me to communicate and acknowledge my mistakes and figure things out for myself. The psychological pressure of this was far greater than if I had just been castigated and told I couldn't watch TV. In the short term, I kept making mistakes, so perhaps their approach didn't work exactly as they had intended. But looking back, I think it built character and taught me about how to relate to myself and to be more up front with others—far more than I could have realized back then.

I have carried these lessons with me and do my best to apply them in business. In the realm of supplier relations, we also follow unconventional rules in our efforts to be authentic and fair. We not only share lots of information with our strategic partners and suppliers; we actually consult with them on critical decisions that will impact them, particularly if our decisions will impact them adversely. We want our suppliers to be able to plan around our changes, and we try to phase in new practices to minimize the harm to those suppliers and partners. This is not because we are saints. By behaving this way we know that our trading partners will also value us and be equally transparent with us.

We are tenacious negotiators, but we often surprise service providers with bonuses when they exceed expectations. We worked with a consultant from Denver on a peculiar quality improvement issue. He hit it out of the park. We sent him a surprise bonus that was higher than the actual fee we had contracted with him; he never had to worry about negotiating his terms with us. He knew we'd take care of him in a fair and generous way, and all his engagements with us showed particular poise.

We also strive to be fair with competitors. However, when someone infringes on our trademark and creates confusion in the marketplace, we fight back because we consider that unjust, both to us and to consumers. As our brand has gained strength, we have unfortunately faced many competitors' attempts to emulate our designs and even our brand name, KIND. We've been forced to spend millions of dollars defending our trademarks. But beyond the issue of justice, it is vital for us to ensure that we control our destiny. We can obsess about quality and authenticity all we want, but if consumers are duped into believing an inferior product is ours, they may associate their disappointment in that other product with us.

In one instance, one competitor created packaging that was strikingly and confusingly similar to ours. During discovery, we confirmed this was not a coincidence. The designer had been instructed to purchase KIND wrappers and boxes and expressly directed to achieve a "similar window shape and coloring to

Kind." In another instance, we had to defend against a maker of vitamin supplements that used the KIND brand name and added the mottos "kind to your body" and "kind to our world." An acquaintance that was confused emailed me that he normally didn't buy "scammy diet pills" but "when I saw KIND it closed the deal for me since I trust your brand." He concluded by writing, "Of course, I reached for your vitamins knowing that if my hair falls out I'll know whom to call." In this case, I was able to point out to him that we had no relation to that brand—and had prevailed upon that company to change their packaging and ensure they distance their branding from ours. But how many unsuspecting consumers were lured into believing they were buying something from us? Companies that want to be transparent with consumers need to make a concerted effort to respect the trademarks of others.

A DIFFERENT KIND OF COMPACT WITH YOUR TEAM

It's a cliché to say that your people are your most important asset. Finding and keeping team members that fit our culture and work ethic is crucial. Training team members and inculcating our culture—which is pretty different from that of other companies—takes time. We are all working as hard as we can, we're expanding rapidly, and we simply don't have the time to go looking for new people to replace good team members. Once we've invested time in someone, we try as hard as we can to be loyal to them and to do whatever it takes to make them happy working with us.

Not everybody is going to stay, and when people are not exerting their best efforts, you have to let them go. But whether they're unhappy and they decide to leave, or we decide it's better that they leave, we all try to manage the transition in a humane, adult fashion.

I hate the term "firing"—as well as today's corporate culture of swift, cold departures that goes with it. The thought that someone who gave precious time out of their life to a corporation is suddenly given a box in which to pack their belongings and then escorted out of the building is offensive and almost always unnecessary. The prevalent system for leaving a company or organization is unnecessarily inefficient, traumatic, and impersonal. There are much better ways to approach a departure.

I have tried to cultivate a culture in which, other than in cases of serious, deliberate misconduct, nobody is just summarily terminated with two weeks' notice (or no notice). Instead, they are given coaching to try to redress shortcomings. Frequently, after such coaching, team members are better able to contribute to the company and are happier about staying—and they continue on with us.

On the flip side, our expectation is that team members won't just give notice and leave within two weeks. Instead, if a team member feels, for personal or professional reasons, that he or she needs to move on, we hope to have an early and open discussion to explore options. If leaving is the final choice, we work together on a changeover plan to ensure that the team member interviews, hires, and trains his or her replacement, while initiating a smooth transition into their next phase in life: If they plan to search for another job, they can start doing so openly while at KIND so long as they do not neglect their other duties.

We uphold an honor code under which team members do not search for jobs under the radar, without first sharing their intent to do so with the CEO or their manager. While this is taboo at most companies, where you would never dare to tell your boss you were looking for a new job, we find it works well.

This transparent arrangement has upsides for both the company and the team member. We have frequent and open conversations about professional growth, promotions, and responsibilities with team members who are searching for new challenges. We also reward those who ensure a smooth transition, by providing them positive references, access to our contact networks, and, where warranted, a financial package that recognizes their commitment to excellence till the last day of their tenure. Importantly, we continue to invest in our team members' professional growth even if they advise us they may be leaving in one or two years. One's instinct is to start circumventing a colleague who you know is not going to be around in the future. But that attitude causes people to withhold information about their plans. With both parties feeling a sense of responsibility and partnership, it is so much easier to invest in your team and empower them more quickly, without feeling threatened that a sudden departure will leave a hole in the organization.

This alternative to surreptitious interviews and surprise firings requires a culture that welcomes engagement about team members' interests and goals, in which you don't chastise but actually encourage people to openly discuss their career options with their manager. Team members need to have realistic expectations. Executives are expected to act as a friend and coach to those reporting to them, thinking about how to grow each team member within the organization if at all possible.

The result is that we do a lot more hiring from within than

most companies. Team members expand their expertise and roles much faster, there are more opportunities for advancement, and the company also grows more quickly and organically.

Of course this is not a perfect system, and not every team member abides by it. It is particularly hard to get senior managers with extensive experience in the "real" world to follow the KIND philosophy in this context. Senior managers who join us from the outside are initially quite skeptical of this approach. But we've created an ethos that works for the most part and makes us proud of our team-member retention and transitions.

THE ASSISTANT LADDER

To keep your team members motivated and empowered, it's crucial to keep training them with new skills or roles that advance them within the company, while making sure you expand the team as needed to bring in expertise. I tend to favor raw skill over years of experience when hiring my assistants. They bring a burning passion to excel, but they are also impatient to grow. So my goal is to groom them to then take on other responsibilities at KIND. I can only do this if they train their replacements to ensure a smooth transition that doesn't require me to teach the new assistants what they need to know about me and how I operate.

Consider the different career paths that some of my assistants have had. I had one assistant, Darya Shaikh, who developed an interest in the sociopolitical work of OneVoice. She came to me and suggested that she move over to work for OneVoice. We found a spot for her there. Over the course of several months, she hired, trained, and transitioned her replacement. Darya stayed at OneVoice, received a series of promotions, and, ten years later, she became the executive director.

The replacement Darya found for the assistant position was Kim Walker. When Kim decided she wanted to apply to graduate school a couple years later, she let me know a year in advance. I wrote her letters of recommendation. Before she left for school, she trained Adeena Schlussel (now Cohen). This allowed Kim not only to learn how to train and manage a new team member, but also to add to her résumé experience with having someone report to her.

Adeena had been my assistant for two years when she started exploring other options within KIND. She gravitated toward advancing our social mission, which at the time was embedded within the marketing team. The expectation is that you have to find someone better than yourself to replace you, and when Adeena was offered a role to advance the KIND Movement, she first hired and trained Julianna Storch. Adeena ensured she overlapped with Julianna for several months so that when Julianna started nothing would fall through the cracks; the transition was seamless, and I did not need to teach her anything. Because Adeena was still in the building, Julianna could reach out to her if there was a historical issue she needed some background on.

Even though Julianna had only recently graduated from college, she mastered the job as my assistant at a time when the demands on our executive office were growing exponentially. Eighteen months after she joined the company, it was clear that she would benefit from an expanded role that gave her more responsibility. We created a new position for her as my chief of staff. This allowed her to hire Rebecca Halpern as our assistant. Julianna's responsibilities are steadily increasing as she takes more and more leadership and helps leverage me further. It catapults her onto a higher career path, while we start to invest in Rebecca's professional growth also. If we had a different culture or hiring practices at KIND, I might have had to start from scratch each time someone left the executive assistant job and in so doing, no doubt I would have lost precious time and focus from my own job. It also enriches the company—and team members' institutional memory of it—that these sharp minds stayed with KIND.

WORK-LIFE ISSUES THE KIND WAY

Like any entrepreneur whose company is intertwined with his life, I work all the time: in the office, out of the office, on weekends, whenever I am awake (and frequently when others are sleeping). But especially since my first son was born, I try to set limits on when I will be in the office. I leave by 6:20 P.M. whenever possible so I can play with my children and help tuck them into bed. Of course, as soon as they are asleep, I'm often back on my laptop at home, but it's important to me to prioritize spending time with them and Michelle. Family, to me, is everything. My family is the reason I am building KIND, and they are the reason I am trying to do my small part to make this a better world.

At KIND, I try to understand when people have to make their own choices about the amount of work that's doable for their family life. I consider this enlightened self-interest. As a society, we're not going to build the best possible world if children are not getting attention and love, and parents are being torn apart by conflicting family and work demands.

We think our team members are best in class, and it makes sense for us to help them be happy; our investment in that happiness cements their interest in and enthusiasm for the company in return. For instance, one of our top marketing people decided to move away from New York City because of her husband's job. The role she was in couldn't be done remotely, but we helped her find a new role within the company that would allow her both to telecommute and to visit the office occasionally. In consultation with her, we named her the vice president of shopper marketing, responsible for customizing programs for our retailers' consumers. She does this job from her new location and travels once a week, either to see customers or to visit headquarters.

Similarly, Darya, the executive director of OneVoice, recently had a baby. She decided that, after returning from maternity leave, she would prefer a more flexible schedule, which necessarily came with less responsibility. She crafted a job as OneVoice's director of social entrepreneurship, and helped train her executive director replacement.

As your enterprise grows, this philosophy of open communication gets more challenging. You don't know everyone as intimately, and you're working against the American corporate culture of keeping things to yourself. Some people don't trust that you really are going to protect them until the last day they leave. It saddens me greatly when that fear leads them to announce an abrupt departure to another job.

Sticking to these principles for managing people takes active leadership. A few years ago, we had a mid-level team member whose performance would have gotten him or her dismissed at other firms. I'll call him Edmond. He was difficult to manage and found interpersonal dynamics in our office to be a challenge. In meetings, Edmond droned on. He took way too long to explain his work. He made lots of mistakes in analyzing data.

But John and I recognized that Edmond was extraordinarily creative, and was able to see solutions to problems that others couldn't. He was a good person and had the company's best interests at heart. Our principles of loyalty dictated that we should try to find a role that might suit him.

Because we wanted to keep him, both of us set aside time to coach him. Then we engineered his move to a different position that played to his strengths, without making him responsible for tasks that were tougher for him. Edmond eventually started generating excellent results. Both he and his manager added enormous value to KIND.

OPEN COMMUNICATION AND OPEN MINDS— PARTICULARLY WHEN THINGS ARE NOT WORKING

Not every story has a happy ending. When it's necessary to let someone go, it's best handled gently. We recently parted ways with a senior manager who was relatively new to the company. Everyone agreed that he didn't fit into our organization, but we arranged a short transition period, which allowed him to keep his company phone for a reasonable amount of time. We made sure other team members knew that we respected this former team member and appreciated his integrity.

Sometimes, the fault is at the top. Several years ago, a team member who we will call Edwina had been with us for a few years and was on track to lose her job. Her attention to detail was not good, and it was harming our business. Her manager gave Edwina the news that she was being terminated. Unfortunately, the manager had her escorted from the building immediately, carrying her belongings, in front of the whole office. Her colleagues saw Edwina leave and knew what was happening. It was precisely the kind of demoralizing, dramatic departure we try to avoid.

I had been traveling the day of this incident, but when I found out about it, I was terribly embarrassed, as well as worried about the effect on the morale of the rest of the team. I called Edwina to apologize for the way she had been treated. I also made sure that she was able to exercise her stock options and gave her a loan to do so, as she had not been provided fair notice or fair treatment. Edwina was not meant to stay at KIND—she was not able to perform to the necessary standards. But she was a wonderful human being with the best intentions, so why should we have treated her like a criminal and walked her out in shame?

I then called a team meeting to let everyone know that this is not how we treat people, even when we all agree that they will have to move on. I made sure that the manager understood his mistake clearly. I urged him to put himself in the shoes of the person losing their job and to be more empathetic.

WHEN LOYALTY FAILS: A CAUTIONARY TALE

This policy of loyalty to our team members, and willingness to work with them when they face performance roadblocks, can occasionally backfire.

The first hint that this might be happening at KIND was a few years ago, when one of our long-standing team members who we will call Kevin came back from a Las Vegas trade show. Kevin's expense report indicated that he had spent the whole week working there, but when other team members pointed out that he had put in a daylong appearance at the trade show and then vanished for the rest of the week, I called him on the discrepancy. He said he had been working hard, was stressed out, and needed a break. After a warning, I let the matter drop.

In retrospect, I should have seen this as a red flag that someone I considered a trusted colleague was taking liberties on company time and at company expense. But this conflicted with the policy I've had for many years of treating our team members as adults who can and should make their own decisions about how best to achieve their business goals. What I didn't realize was that this wasn't a case of a staffer slacking off one week and making it up with extra effort the next. It was the start of something bigger and more insidious.

Soon after, John, our president, alerted me that Kevin had been charging the company credit card to go on personal trips, taking extended vacations and reporting them as work, and showing erratic behavior. I needed to deal with this situation, but I was struggling with how to respond. I thought I had to balance my loyalty to my original team members with the need to provide John with the tools to ensure accountability. And Kevin was at the helm of an ongoing project that we urgently needed completed. I was convinced he was the only person in the organization who knew enough about this area of operations to handle it, other than myself. (This turned out not to be true. In fact, as I later learned, Kevin had been phoning it in for months, and team members reporting to him were already doing most of his work.) So I was indulging him, undermining my president, and setting a terrible precedent for leadership.

Then Kevin came to me to ask if he could move to the other side of the country. This came as a surprise, because the job he was doing was crucial to our development and it could only be done from headquarters in New York. There really wasn't any way for him to telecommute, or even to fly back and forth, while keeping this particular job. But he insisted on the move, which he said was for personal reasons.

After some discussion with Kevin, we offered him what we considered an extremely fair offer: a six-month transition period out of the company, during which he would live in the city he had chosen and help train his replacement. He could keep his stock options in the company, which he would have lost had he quit (since then, we have instituted a policy to buy back all shares from team members who depart). This would be a major dislocation for the company, forcing us to start over with a new executive at an important time in our development. But since we believe in helping people find the career path that's best for them, even if it's not with us, we felt we were acting in a way that was consistent with our principles.

I expected that Kevin would be happy with this offer, since it allowed him to move and start looking for a new position in his new city. But he reacted angrily, accusing me of treating him poorly. The outsized negative reaction perplexed me.

I asked if we could meet and discuss the offer, but he said he wasn't going to be at work for the rest of the day. John's view was that something was going on and that we should fire him immediately. I wasn't sure. I went into Kevin's office—something I would ordinarily never do if he was not present—and realized that he had already cleaned it out. All his personal effects were gone; the place was bare. Clearly he hadn't planned to return to work, either that day or at all. He was not considering our offer.

I was getting increasingly concerned. I called our IT team and asked them to take a look at Kevin's computer. It had been wiped, with all the data and emails deleted. Now we knew he had something to hide. But what was it?

Working through the night, the team was able to retrieve emails he had (incongruously) sent on company email. We realized that not only had he been actively looking for another job for some time, in secret, but also that he had already had interviews with several of our competitors. In fact, the emails indicated, he was on his way to the West Coast to meet with a rival that had made concerted efforts to copy our products.

The worst part: The emails revealed that Kevin had offered to bring with him data about our products, our customers, and our processes. This was confidential information he had only been able to access because of his high-level position at KIND.

I was devastated as I read the emails in which my colleague, to whom I had been so loyal, talked about handing over our trade secrets—the knowledge our team had developed over ten years of hard work—to our competitors. It's one thing to seek out another job; it's quite another to steal information and try to sell it to rival companies when you leave.

The next few days were hard. I was finally able to reach Kevin by phone after he ducked my calls, and I pointed out, as calmly as I could, that he had signed both a nondisclosure and a non-compete agreement. He said glibly that his lawyer told him they wouldn't hold up in the state he would soon call home, where such documents typically have less force. I'm an attorney myself, although I don't practice, and I knew this wasn't true; we're a New York–based company and New York state laws applied to this contract. But he believed his lawyer's advice and was continuing to meet with the other company.

We weren't able to convince Kevin to stop shopping our data, so it was time to go to court. Our lawyers filed for an injunction, and a judge issued a temporary restraining order that prohibited him from using our stolen data in any way while the lawsuit proceeded.

Now we had to serve him with the papers. If you've seen a TV legal procedural, you have seen—more or less—what this looks like: The person is handed an envelope and told, "You've been served." Until the papers are physically delivered, the person can always claim they didn't know about the judge's order. In the meantime he could share sensitive data and cause us irreparable harm.

We sent our lawyers and investigators to Kevin's home, but he wasn't there. We tried every address we had for him, as well as any place we thought he might be. No luck. A week and a half had passed since I discovered his empty office.

After a lot of detective work to figure out where he was, our lawyers arranged for a private investigator to try to intercept

Kevin as he came off a flight from the Caribbean and serve him with the papers right there. If Kevin slipped through our dragnet at the airport, we would have no idea where to find him next.

It was a long wait. Then the phone rang. The lawyer was calling to say that our team had successfully served the papers.

That was just the beginning of the suit. The case was so stark that the judge turned the temporary restraining order into a permanent injunction, but the process involved months of distractions and grief.

During the lawsuit, we were able to conduct document discovery on the rival company where Kevin had been interviewing. We read emails between their executives that showed they were delirious over the prospect of getting some of this information. The restraining order prevented the transfer of data.

The incident was extraordinarily dispiriting to me. Even though Kevin deserved the headaches he brought upon himself, including his own legal bills and all the embarrassment and aggravation, I felt bad for him. I had considered him a friend. I still get a sad feeling when I think of that episode.

To feel sympathy for someone who has betrayed you could be interpreted as a sign of weakness. "Why should you have any feelings toward him?" one might ask. "Isn't that the reason why he took advantage of you in the first place?" I certainly learned to be more attuned to situations where someone might be abusing our trust. And nobody who knows me would doubt that I have the fortitude to defend my family and my team's interests. But I do not doubt for one second that the culture of loyalty and transparency that we have built at KIND is overwhelmingly reciprocated and is directly responsible for the loyalty and transparency that we get in return.

Furthermore, I don't perceive the ability to empathize—even with someone who has wronged you—as a weakness; instead I see it as a strength. It is normal to retrench and doubt others particularly when we feel under attack. But too often we overdo it and end up acting more aggressively than warranted. Lack of empathy can lead to misunderstandings, lost opportunities, and burned bridges. In a business environment, that can destroy value. In geopolitical situations, it can result in lives lost. I've learned how powerful empathy can be, and how important it is to have the courage to use it, particularly when we feel most vulnerable. Part of what motivated me to create KIND and the KIND Movement are moments of courage and compassion that my dad witnessed during one of the darkest periods in humanity. My dad felt the duty to transmit the importance of kindness to me. I will explain why.

CHAPTER 8

EMPATHY

Channeling the Ability to Connect and Create Community

Being the son of a Holocaust survivor marks you and makes you acutely conscious of our human frailty. My burning commitment to build bridges stems from a survival instinct: to prevent what happened to my dad from happening again to other human beings. Part of the reason I exist today is that my grandfather and my father were always kind to people, treating all with respect. And amid the worst evil, some risked their lives to reciprocate.

The birth of KIND and its social mission were stirred by this history. KIND sprang forth at one of the saddest times in my life—an episode of grief that paradoxically coincided with a period of great personal and professional growth for me.

The year we conceived the KIND brand, 2003, started like any other year. I had just gotten back from a surprise trip to see my parents in Mexico, where our whole family had gathered for a rare reunion in Puerto Vallarta.

I rarely took time off, and my parents were not expecting me to join them on vacation. I surprised them at the airport. I asked a tour guide to lend me his jacket, his cap, and his tour placard, and I went over to my mom and dad, offering them a tour with a disguised voice. At first they didn't even recognize me in the guide's uniform. Then my dad got choked up at the surprise.

It was a time of great stress for me. I was spending a lot of time thinking about the healthy snack bar we were designing, which still did not have a brand name. Our cash challenges at that point were enormous. I could not pay myself a salary. We had to discontinue an important line because the manufacturer, which we didn't control, had changed the formula to add artificial ingredients to his product. So our financial situation was tenuous in the extreme. And I was preoccupied with the launch of the OneVoice Movement. I was having difficulty sleeping because I felt guilty that I was not doing enough to counteract all the violence and hatred propagating in the Middle East.

That week in Mexico with my family was a welcome respite. I remember reading the book *Perfume* on a boat ride out in the clear blue waters of Banderas Bay and discussing it with my dad. I remember hugging my dad and fighting with my siblings over who would get to hug him. He was a large man, like a teddy bear.

I came back just after the New Year and immediately reimmersed myself in the company's challenges. It was a few days later on January 8, 2003, when Doris Rivera, at the time our director of operations, walked into my office crying.

I was worried something terrible had happened to Doris. Then she told me that my mom had just called her, and she had some bad news: My dad had died. My immediate reaction was that she was wrong, that it wasn't possible. I told her she must have misunderstood. I called my mom and when she told me herself that my dad had passed away that morning, I began arguing with her: "Are you sure? Did you try to give him CPR? There must be something we can do. Call the doctors. Call the ambulance. Have you tried everything?" I felt we needed to change the facts. It's part of my personality never to accept adversity, and I insisted that this too could be changed.

At some point, I realized that my dad was not coming back. I started crying. Then, all while trying to cope with the devastating loss of the man I most loved and admired in the world, a switch inside me flipped. My obsession immediately turned to following my dad's standing instructions to look over the family. I started rifling through my files, looking for papers that my dad had given me, thinking about my responsibilities now that he was gone. I went into crisis-management mode, trying to exert some control over the situation.

I didn't know what to do with PeaceWorks and OneVoice when I left that day for the funeral in California. I deputized Doris and Rami, my head of sales, to be in charge of the company. I left prepared to be gone for months, which ended up being the case. I needed to be with my family, to help my mom, to take care of my dad's affairs.

My friend Dari Shalon happened to be with me at the office when Doris gave me the news. He drove me to the airport. I'm not sure how I would have functioned without him by my side, helping me pack and get on the plane.

In the Jewish tradition there are rites of mourning that have developed over thousands of years. The first week you observe shivah: my siblings, my mom, and I stayed in my parents' home in Los Angeles for the entire week, without leaving the house, covering all mirrors, the men not shaving our faces. Three times a day we recited the mourners' prayer, the Kaddish.

ONEVOICE IS BORN

Coincidentally, I was scheduled to give a talk about OneVoice to five hundred people in Los Angeles on January 15 at the Wilshire Boulevard Temple. Having been cocooned with my family for a whole week, I did not feel capable of standing up in front of an audience to talk about my work. I felt completely paralyzed by the loss of my father.

The talk was supposed to be on the day the shivah ended. We held the ceremony to end the shivah at the temple, an hour before the event. The ceremony was a small family affair with only two dozen close family members. Rabbi Harvey Fields asked every one of us to go around the table and share some memories or lessons that we remembered from my dad. The overarching theme was my dad's kindness and generosity toward others—how he always made people smile and have a better day. When everyone was finished, he looked at us and said, "You cannot say that your father is gone. He's here with us." It was hard for me to describe, but since I had arrived in L.A., I felt I was carrying my dad inside me. When I went to sleep or when I closed my eyes and looked inside, I felt his presence, not as a dream, but in a surreal way that was tangible. I felt an emotional imperative to carry on his legacy and aspire to adopt his attributes. Rabbi Fields took me aside and said, "Daniel, I know this is difficult. But I think your father would have wanted you to proceed with the OneVoice talk tonight."

The previous fall, my parents had come to see me talk about this concept of OneVoice. At the time most people thought it was a crazy idea to build a grassroots movement of Israeli and Palestinian moderates, let alone for a confused Mexican Jew based in the United States to kindle the effort. While my parents initially felt it was a far-fetched idea (and were still wondering when I would go back to being a nice Jewish lawyer), they were proud of my effort and began seeing the possibilities. Imam Feisal Abdul Rauf, a prominent Muslim leader, had introduced me to Edgar Bronfman, Sr., the head of the World Jewish Congress at the time. Both had agreed to join our advisory board, and the IBM Foundation had agreed to support us. OneVoice was starting to gain momentum, and the talk I was giving in L.A. had been in the works for six months. My friend and cofounder Mohammad Darawshe had flown in from the Arab village of Iksal in Israel to help me with the launch efforts.

Giving that talk was one of the hardest things I've ever done in my life. I had never had trouble speaking publicly, but that day I had an anxiety attack before going onstage. I stood in the bathroom looking at the mirror, my face unshaven for seven days, with my heart accelerating and my body sweating. I felt dizzy. Fortunately, Mohammad was there to help carry the day.

The following night, I had to speak at a second OneVoice event at the home of Danny DeVito and Rhea Perlman, to a crowd that included a few dozen other celebrities, directors, and producers. Months before, when I was invited by Rhea and my friend Joel Fields to speak before all these famous people, I had been excited, but that day I was there in spite of myself, to fulfill my responsibility.

For the next couple of years, the majority of my time was

spent in the Middle East, California, and Texas, with only sporadic visits to New York. My siblings, my mom, and I spent a lot of time together. My brother and I were helping settle my dad's affairs in California and Texas. In the Middle East, Mohammad and I were getting OneVoice off the ground, opening offices in Tel Aviv and Ramallah, hiring a team, building a board, raising money.

Any logical entrepreneur would not have done things the way I did them. My company was barely surviving. Launching a new line is always hard enough, and yet I was doing it remotely. I would fly in, work with my team on the KIND launch, and then fly out again. I kept up by email and phone. These were the cards I'd been dealt. I felt a duty to my father both to carry out all my family obligations, and, in his memory, to build the OneVoice Movement so we could advance and achieve peace.

The year he died, I had a lot of time to think about my dad because, for the first time in my life, I was attending services at a synagogue twice a day. Consistent with the Jewish tradition of mourning, when a family member passes away, you recite Kaddish three times a day over the course of a year. (The afternoon and evening services are scheduled back-to-back.) At first, not having been brought up as a religious Jew, I did not see the point of doing this. I told my rabbi, who was Orthodox, that I just couldn't connect with Hebrew prayers and didn't understand them: "Why would God care about me exalting him? Isn't that self-aggrandizing of human beings to think that it's important for us to praise God?" It felt hollow and self-important.

The rabbi told me, "Do me one favor, Daniel. Try it for a

month and if it doesn't seem right to you, we'll talk." My dad really respected Rabbi Scheinberg, and even though my father was not a religious man, I knew that he had observed Kaddish for my grandfather when he died, so I decided to try it. I also received a book from the rabbi, *Pirkei Avot,* "The Ethics of our Fathers," with moral maxims to reflect on and live by.

Two thousand three was among the hardest years of my life. My dad was my best friend, my mentor, my hero. Wearing a beard for the first month, in line with the Jewish mourning tradition, I felt like a foreigner in my own body. I felt people looked at me and related to me differently, perhaps because of my own emotional vulnerabilities. It was a big commitment, wherever I was in the world, to say Kaddish three times a day. I did this in Davos, Switzerland, at the World Economic Forum, in different parts of the Middle East, and around the United States. And yet it was a year of enormous personal growth. The Kaddish prayers opened me up in ways that I had never experienced before. It was my meditation on how to become a better human being, how to do things differently to make this a better world, and how to honor my dad's memory and let him live inside me and through me.

KIND IS BORN

In April 2003, my team member Sasha Hare, our director of marketing and new product development, was brainstorming with me about the brand name for the healthy fruit and nut snack bar we were going to make. We batted ideas back and forth over email as I traveled, with occasional in-person meetings.

From all our brainstorming, the name KIND resonated the most. It had a human attribute that we connected to what became our motto: "Do the KIND Thing for your body, your taste buds, & your world." It was about not sacrificing taste or health or our social responsibility to make this world a little kinder.

The name KIND particularly spoke to me because my dad's essence, the reason he had survived the Holocaust, and the way he had lived afterward were all connected to compassion. His entire story, as I started looking back, was a string of kindness. He treated everyone as an equal, whether a bank teller or the bank president. With waitresses, flight attendants, or anyone who was not in a friendly mood, my dad made a point of getting them to smile. Others were also kind to him, including, crucially, his enemies, who had helped him survive. His life taught me that kindness and empathy are the foundations on which humanity will stand or fall.

EMPATHY FROM MY HERITAGE

I was born in 1968 in Mexico City. My three siblings and I—my older sister Ileana, my younger sister Tammy, and my younger brother Sioma—grew up in the sheltered Jewish community there, which numbered about 50,000. Our parents, while not religious, were active in Jewish organizations. They cared passionately about raising their children to be part of the larger world around us, not just the insular Jewish community.

My mom, Sonia, stayed home to raise us. She was raised in Tampico, Tamaulipas, a cattle-ranching region where her family was one of only a handful of Jewish families. The family loves to joke that when my grandfather Marcos docked in the port of Veracruz when he immigrated from Poland, he thought he had landed in the United States and only years later did my grandfather discover that he had been learning Spanish instead of English and that he was living in Mexico, not in the United States.

My mom was the outgoing, friendly bridge-builder of our family. Having been raised in a predominantly Catholic country, among people who had seldom (if ever) met a Jew, she had an extra sensibility about her responsibility to be an ambassador of the Jewish people. She would make friends with the taxi driver and the fruit merchant. When we went to the movies, my "uncle" Jordan, a dear family friend, would offer popcorn and candy to the people sitting around us even if they were strangers, a custom my parents adopted and I still follow.

My father, Roman, was born in 1930 in Riga, Latvia, and raised in Kovno, Lithuania, where my grandfather, Sioma, had a small business making corsets. My grandmother, Rosa, told me a story about my father that sums up his ability to empathize and his kindness. When he was four or five years old, a poor child knocked on the door of the family home in Lithuania. It was a cold winter night, and the child was asking for food. My father went into the kitchen to make the other child a sandwich. As he piled onto the sandwich everything that he himself would want to eat, my grandmother told him to hurry, because the child wouldn't wait, but would go beg somewhere else. When my father returned to the front door with the sandwich, the child was gone. He ran out into the street, barefoot in the snow and without a coat, to find the other boy and give him the food.

As they grew up and war approached, my father and his older

brother, Larry, frequently got into scrapes with local kids who would shout anti-Semitic taunts and otherwise bother the Jewish kids. When the Nazis invaded Lithuania, life for the Jews quickly worsened. My dad was nine years old when the war started, and his brother Larry was fourteen.

They were living in an apartment building, where the porter was a Lithuanian who was often drunk. As the German occupation took hold, food quickly became scarce in Kovno. One night, the porter said to my father, "I know you're hungry, so come with me and I'll show you where you can get food." My father followed him down to the street. There lay the body of a dead man. "This man is Jewish," said the porter. "You can cut him up and eat him if you want to."

"That," my father said later, "is when the cruelty started." I was nine when he told me this story. My mom interrupted him to say, "Roman, he's only nine years old, don't tell him about this." He said, "Daniel only needs to hear it; I had to live it."

Massive pogroms swept Lithuania as the German occupation took hold. A huge percentage of the Jews were killed at the time, mainly by Lithuanian paramilitaries but also by the Nazis.

One day, the porter took Germans dressed in military uniforms into my father's apartment. They harassed and threatened to shoot my family; then they took my grandmother into another room. My dad was too young to understand what may have happened when she came out crying. He remembered that they eventually pushed everyone out of the apartment into the garden downstairs and said, "We are going to shoot you." The porter then whispered something to the soldiers, and they walked away. The porter told my family to go upstairs. Then he came up and said, "Open up."

In an interview my cousin Serge Bluds recorded with my dad about this incident, here was my dad's recollection of what the porter then said to my grandfather:

> "Lubetzky, I want you to know that to every apartment of this building I brought the Germans and I made them kill every Jew here. Except you. And to you, I let you live because you were a person who always would offer me your hand, shake my hand . . . you would give me a little bottle of vodka, would talk to me like a decent person, and this is why I don't want you to die, because you are a good man."

Then my dad continued, "This was a very important lesson to me at the time. To remember that even such an animal like this guy recognized that someone was humane to him and it paid off to be humane and not be, you know, with your nose in the air."

The porter then commanded my family to leave the apartment before he changed his mind.

As horrible as the incident was, it was not lost on my father (or on me) that my grandfather's thoughtfulness toward others had spared his family.

My father, his family, and the remaining Kovno Jews, some 40,000, were herded into ghettos, where they were kept under horrible and humiliating conditions. Those who survived were sent to a nearby concentration camp, which produced tinder from the local forests to feed German tanks during wartime gas shortages. That was where my father and his family ended up.

Just before the Nazis left Lithuania to the Soviets, in 1944, they loaded many of the camp's prisoners, including my family, onto the infamous cattle cars and shipped them by rail back to Germany, where even worse camps awaited them. At one point, the overcrowded train stopped and the Nazis took all the women off with no warning, including my grandmother. She had no time to say goodbye to her husband and sons.

My father, his brother, and my grandfather continued on to the Dachau concentration camp, where starving inmates were kept in subhuman conditions and forced into slave labor, building an underground airport the Germans had designed in the hopes of evading Allied bombs. Despite their suffering, the three were able to stay together, and my father credited my grandfather with helping him survive. Once, my grandfather was able to barter for a pair of shoes, without which my father felt he would have died. Another time, my father almost fainted under the weight of a keg of explosive chemicals that he was required to carry. My grandfather quickly helped him keep it steady.

Many years later, I watched the movie *Life Is Beautiful,* which made me feel uneasy about the moments of joy and humor that the characters experienced despite the horrors of the Holocaust. I called my father and asked him, "It never crossed my mind, but was it possible that people could share a laugh or tell a joke in the midst of all that suffering?"

"It was essential," my dad told me. "Particularly because of the darkness, your grandfather's sense of humor is what kept me and many others alive." My dad explained that my grandfather told jokes to the inmates to keep them in good spirits. He even tried to pierce into the humanity of the German guards by telling them jokes and stories.

Amidst the worst circumstances, the human spirit also shows itself. My father never forgot a German soldier who took risks by throwing at my dad's feet a rotten potato that provided him the sustenance to go on. Although he could have gotten in trouble for helping a prisoner, that soldier risked his own safety to feed my dad. My dad always said that potato—that fleeting moment of kindness—helped him stay alive.

Just before the end of the war, in 1945, the Nazis marched the prisoners in my family's section of Dachau out of the concentration camp and toward the nearby mountains. It was freezing, they had no food or warm clothing, and the prisoners were in very poor health. As they stumbled down a steep ravine, a snowstorm overtook the group, and my father found himself huddled with his brother and father under a thick blanket of snow. When the storm stopped, they emerged to find the Nazi guards gone. For the first time in years, they were free. The group straggled back out of the mountains and into a village in search of food.

Suddenly, they saw tanks approaching. Afraid it was the Nazis, they were relieved to discover American soldiers, who liberated them. I've always been grateful to American servicemen because if it wasn't for them I wouldn't be around. Countless Americans sacrificed their lives to stop Hitler and save people they had never met.

After the war ended, my uncle, who was about twenty years old by then, joined the U.S. Army as a translator in Berlin and helped start a reunification program for survivors who were trying to reconnect with their missing family members. He also discovered that my grandmother had survived the war as well.

She had gone back to Lithuania after her own liberation from the concentration camps to search for her missing family, not knowing that they were in Germany. She was unable to get across the border between the Soviet-controlled and U.S.-controlled areas because the border guards discovered that the cousin with whom she was traveling had hidden some money in his clothing. She was sent to prison for a year and reemerged after Soviet rule had taken firm hold of the region. Trapped, she supported herself as a piano teacher, trying repeatedly to get out of the USSR. It took her until 1955 to obtain a visa to travel from Lithuania to Mexico, where she was finally reunited with her husband and sons after twelve years.

After the Allies found them near Dachau, my father and grandfather were sent to recuperate at St. Ottilien, a German sanatorium that the Allies had taken over. They spent a year recovering there. At one point one of the other patients started threatening my grandfather and my father took a knife and started screaming at the crazed man to get away. My grandfather told my father, "Roman, you cannot let them turn you into an animal. You have to remain a human being and stay above them." It's as the celebrated Rabbi Hillel said: "In a place where there is no humanity, strive thou to be human." That quote is embossed on my office wall.

After a short stay in France to await visas, my father and my grandfather went to Mexico, where two of his uncles and an aunt had emigrated before the war; later, my uncle Larry joined them. My dad was sixteen and spoke Russian, German, Yiddish, and some other Slavic languages. He taught himself Spanish and English by watching movies and reading books. He educated himself by buying used encyclopedias and reading them cover to cover. With only a third-grade education—after the German occupation, he never went to school again—he was one of the most erudite men I ever encountered. Eventually he spoke nine languages.

In Mexico, the family had little money, and my father started off working multiple shifts at factories. But he felt incredibly lucky to be alive, and he always tried to help others. He used to give money to a blind man he saw begging on the street. Then once, he noticed that the beggar got into a fancy car and drove away. When my dad told me this story, I asked him if he was upset to be the victim of a con artist. "I'd rather make the mistake of giving to someone who doesn't need it than run the risk of not giving a hand to someone who does," he said.

My dad had the rare strength of being able to recall that dreadful chapter of his life without letting it embitter him. He lived a life that was fulfilled, optimistic, and positive, and, as much as it emotionally drained him, he frequently spoke about his Holocaust experiences, so that we may never permit such tragedies to befall humanity again.

After some time in Mexico, he started working in a jewelry shop and learned that trade. Then he and his father opened their own small jewelry shop and traveled to Switzerland. My grandfather and my dad spoke Swiss German quite well and were able to get a business started. They began getting the concessions to represent some of the best watch brands in the duty-free channel and in Mexico, starting with Bulova and then Cartier, Audemars Piguet, and Rolex.

Many years later, my dad partnered with four other Holocaust survivors to build one of the most successful chains of duty-free stores along the U.S.-Mexican border, called International Bonded Warehouses. The company later went through several mergers and was acquired by Duty Free International and since then by several other companies.

THE MAGIC POWER OF KINDNESS

My dad was on to something with his focus on kindness. Many scientific studies show that people are happier when they are kind to one another. Kindness is a magical power, what we at KIND call a net-happiness aggregator: both the person doing the kinding and the person being kinded are better off (at KIND, we use "kinding" as a noun to describe an act of kindness, and "kinded" as a verb—i.e., "what a nice kinding," "he kinded someone," "you've been kinded").

As we developed KIND, we sought ways to advance our business and social missions at once. Relying on the power of kindness is a sensitive undertaking. The challenge for the KIND Movement, as we named our collaborative effort with our community, is to inspire people to be kind more often without tainting the selflessness and wonder that come when people have no ulterior motive to their kind acts. Our goal with the movement is to inspire kindness in an authentic and effective way. Telling someone, "Be kind to one another and win a KIND bar" or "Be kind and enter for a chance to win a trip to Las Vegas" would destroy the purity and magic of the act. The impetus to be kind has to be its own motivator.

We've evolved in how we think about and how we execute this mission. In the beginning, for example, we would surprise people by having our KIND ambassadors do kind acts for others. We held umbrellas to walk people to taxis or to their destinations when it was raining. We carried people's groceries to their cars.

These are all kind enough actions, and our team still occasionally performs them, but they also are quite transactional. They're clearly driven by us trying to please our consumers and, in that sense, they still live in the realm of self-interested behavior. There is nothing wrong with that, but there's nothing magical about it either. It's how brands have behaved for centuries. The lightbulb came on when we realized that our community could be challenged to join us in our journey to inspire kindness.

We made our community the protagonist in true acts of kindness. The best analogy is President Kennedy's dictum: "Ask not what your country can do for you; ask what you can do for your country." People want to be authentically inspired. People want to do the kind thing. The vast majority of our consumers are blessed with the ability and power to do the kind thing for others. We realized that both KIND and our consumers would get more fulfillment from unleashing kindness toward those who really needed it than from our consumers receiving another little pat on the back. Once we had that idea and that insight, bringing it to life took several years and is still an ongoing but invigorating process.

The first efforts to transform the KIND Movement into a shared undertaking with our community started in 2008. At that time, a bright young team member named Natalie Gourvitch had just finished an internship with OneVoice, where she had worked closely with me on an effort to get one million Israeli and Palestinian citizens to sign a petition for rekindling peace negotiations. She joined KIND to help me build a network of KIND ambassadors, part-time team members out in the field, in different cities, whose primary task was to give out samples of KIND bars and to surprise people with kind acts.

I shared with Natalie the idea of us initiating chains of kindness by giving people a black plastic card with a unique code that would enable them to join this secret society of people doing kindnesses to one another. We would do a kind act—giving them a free KIND bar, buying a coffee for them, or carrying their groceries—and then hand out these black cards with a cryptic invitation, a web address and a code, and no other explanation. We brought this program to life later that year.

My hope was that people would be intrigued, go to our website, and discover that they were now part of this secret society of good. The card enabled them to register how they were KINDED and then to pass on the card to somebody else along with a kind act, with a hope that they would continue this chain of kindness. From the website, you would be able to monitor where your card had been.

What we liked about this program was that we were letting new people try KIND bars and that we were taking the cold commercial transaction of sampling and elevating it into a special moment. It was advancing our business and our social mission at the same time. We would initiate a chain of kindness by giving someone a bar, and frame it in a much warmer way that inspired them to pass it on: We just KINDED you; now go do a kind act for someone else.

As we designed the process, there were two questions I posed to Natalie: "How do you ask your community to lead the way in helping inspire kindness, rather than us doing kind acts to them? And how can we do it in an authentic way, so the purity of the act is preserved?"

Natalie and I worked hard on giving life to this platform, and we succeeded. For a handful of people, with few resources, working out of a small loft in New York's Chelsea neighborhood, it was fun to create an experiment in which some of these cards traveled all the way to Mexico, England, and even India.

There were limitations to our approach. First, I underestimated how hard it is to get people to go from their off-line lives to the online world and take the time to register themselves. Second, I compounded that problem by making this card so secret that you needed to be pretty curious to see what it was all about. Third, you could only track your own chain and see where your own card had gone. If your card had a short life, the experience was underwhelming. The best chains made it eight or nine stops along the way, but it was so easy to break the chain if only one person didn't follow it up. There was no network effect, no exponential aspect.

In its next iteration, we decided to open up the system so that you could track not just your own chain, but all other chains of kindness. Anybody could visit the website and explore the different chains that had traveled around the world. You could choose to see the longest chain, or look for chains near you, and read what acts of kindness each person had logged. While it was neat and cool and fun, it was more of an experiment than a way of life. You needed to be lucky enough to be included in the chain and then you could only participate once. It was not designed for repeat participation. And again, if one person didn't pass it on, the whole chain died.

In the third iteration of these black plastic cards, we opened up the platform to enable anyone to initiate a chain of kindness by printing their own new card from the website. What's more, we created an incentive for people to participate that we felt would not destroy the purity of the kind act. We created a contest with prizes of $5,000; $10,000; and $25,000 for the charity that inspired the most kind acts. You could support your preferred charity by creating a new code, linking it to your cause, and then logging kind acts that you performed in its honor.

At that point, we felt we had finally figured out how to maintain the purity of the kind act and that we'd created the right incentives, because we were motivating people to support a charity, not us and not themselves. Some of my team members suggested that we should encourage people to buy KIND products to win. I immediately rejected that idea, because it would destroy the integrity of the process.

The problem was, in their zeal to raise funds for a charity they cared about, a lot of people did not respect the honor code of doing kind acts that were sincere and earnest. We achieved quantity, but the quality of those kind acts was far lower than we would have liked. We would see dozens of entries from a single person: "I opened the door for my brother," "I gave my brother a glass of water," "I closed the door for my brother." People were trying to game the system.

We quickly learned that we needed to authenticate participants in a more reliable way and to allow each person only one vote per round. We also needed to be enormously careful about how to create incentives, even for philanthropic causes. We wanted charities to get their community to support them, but we wanted to make sure every one of those people felt the power of true kindness without seeing it as a transaction.

The last thing I didn't love about the cards was that after doing a kind act, you needed to then pass the card on. Sometimes it was fine, but on many occasions it felt awkward or false. If you were at a fancy restaurant and sent over a free drink to a stranger along with a KIND card, it could be cute and clever and acceptable. But if you were helping a homeless person with a sandwich, it would be uncomfortable and inappropriate for you to ask them to pass it on.

My team argued many times that the cards weren't serving their purpose.

"We can't make it too confusing or complicated to get people to engage with the KIND brand," Erica Pattni, our then vice president of marketing, told me. "The consumer is self-interested, busy, and inundated with marketing. We need to accept that and create programming that gives a clear, valuable payoff."

"I would rather stretch consumers to reach outside their comfort zone," I said. "I believe that people will 'Do the KIND Thing' for the sake of humanity if we create a meaningful reason to do so."

"The cards are cool, but they're just a little clunky for people to embrace, and they're not scalable," Erica said.

"You guys in marketing have a warped sense of humanity," I said teasingly. "You should be more optimistic in your expectations of people."

The tension here, as Erica pointed out, was between idealism (me) and realism (the rest of my team). I wanted the program to be pure, which—I had to concede—led to ineffective engagement. But too much pragmatism would have made the program indistinguishable from other brands, which also would have defeated the purpose.

The next (and present) iteration of the program, #kindawesome cards, was a big breakthrough and works completely differently. Adeena Cohen, my former assistant, came up with the idea.

These are cards we hand out to someone that we notice doing a kind act—for us or for someone else. Their purpose is to celebrate and recognize kindness. If I'm with my four children and a lady cedes her taxicab to us (which happens all the time) I hand her a #kindawesome card. If I'm on the subway and I notice that someone stands up to let an elderly lady or pregnant woman take a seat, I approach the person who stood up and hand him a card. I say, "That was kindawesome of you, and in appreciation of your kindawesomeness, you can go to this website and enter this code," as I point to the information on the back of the card. If and when they go to the website and enter their code, we mail them a packet with a handful of KIND bars in appreciation of their kindness, along with another #kindawesome card for them to give to someone they spot Doing the Kind Thing.

When I see pregnant women, I actually stop them to explain the concept of the #kindawesome cards to them. If they haven't run away or called a police officer by the time I get a chance to explain, I then recruit them as our KIND ambassadors. I hand each pregnant woman ten to twenty #kindawesome cards so that the next time someone gives her a seat or honors her, she can recognize their act of kindness.

What's magical about these cards is that we're not interrupting the KIND act at the moment it happens. Only after the pure act of kindness is complete do we then celebrate the person. Friends are constantly asking me if they can have some to hand out themselves. We're exploring ways to disseminate them widely to all our KIND ambassadors and our most loyal kindaholics and friends, including through digital means.

If used properly, #kindawesome cards are a very effective

business and social tool for us. In the ideal scenario, in the next iteration of the program, millions in our community will earn KIND points from Doing the KIND Thing (performing or spotting KIND acts; sharing, wearing, or consuming KIND products). They will redeem those points in the form of #kindawesome cards that they can hand out to friends and strangers worth celebrating. Many may not have even tried KIND bars. The way in which they are introduced to our brand and our product is at such a beautiful point in their lives, when they are celebrated for doing something nice.

We also feel great about the business advantage of having KIND bars be the currency with which we pat people on the back. We feel that we're honoring the kind moment in a tactful and elegant way, and with a healthy snack that does the kind thing for their body and their taste buds. The costs are not insignificant, particularly when you add packaging and shipping costs. But is there a more impactful way to invest marketing dollars? Can traditional advertising approximate the human warmth we can create by merging our business and social objectives—celebrating KIND people by letting them try our products and share KIND with others?

KIND CAUSES

Separate from the #kindawesome cards, we have another platform that we've created to advance kindness, online and off, since 2011. Shortly after we had been disappointed with the quality of entries from our prior black-card contest, we wanted to find a way to support Big KIND Acts and inspire the community to help us perform them.

On the first Tuesday of the month—KIND Tuesday—we began inviting our community to do a signature kind act, for example, to write a note of thanks to a woman who inspired them. If enough of them reported doing that small kind act, it would trigger a Big KIND Act from us, on behalf of the community, for those who need it most—for example, to deliver comfort kits to women undergoing treatment for breast cancer. The community would join together to create this kind act. Without enough small kind acts, the Big KIND Act would not be activated.

Initially, only one hundred people had to commit to do a kind act to trigger the larger event. One of our first missions was giving a cold beverage to a person working outside during the summer. The success triggered more significant projects: One month KIND team members and volunteers cleaned up a beach; another month we handed out hundreds of pairs of shoes to poor children. One time we asked people to lend a helping hand to a parent. When enough of them did so, we donated diapers and baby care items to new families at shelters across the country.

For the first few months, excitement built throughout our community. Sign-ups were increasing, and we could see that the program was energizing people to do good. Then in June, we announced our Big KIND Act for the month, partnering with the Capital Area Food Bank in Washington, D.C., to provide wholesome after-school meals and nutrition education to thousands of children. To activate this pledge, 1,200 people had to do a small kind act—to give an orange to someone who provided them with nourishment. We worked hard to spread the word about the mission and we watched the numbers tick up on the website as the deadline approached, checking every ten minutes.

The number of people who accepted the mission reached 1,048. For the first time, we had failed.

My marketing team was concerned about us sharing negative news with our community. Elle Lanning, then our director of communications, said, "Daniel, this is a feel-good brand. Why depress people and chastise them by telling them that they didn't reach our goal? Why penalize those who need it most? It's not the way to engage with a brand."

I understood what she and Erica were advocating: You don't normally let failures hit your community. I explained to my team that this was actually a phenomenal opportunity for us to instill in our community the idea that they had the power to do good, and they also held the responsibility. If we seriously wanted to create a community where our members were the protagonists, they had the understand that, and let the chips fall where they may.

We crafted an email where we took responsibility for not doing enough to get more community members engaged. It was quite clear that we were serious. If our members did not pledge and trigger those KIND acts, the Big KIND Acts were not going to happen.

From: KIND Healthy Snacks
Sent: Wednesday, June 8, 2011, 9:49 A.M.
Subject: We failed.

We were unable to reach our Do the KIND Thing threshold, so this month, the Big KIND Act will not become a reality. But—we are optimistic that with your participation, next month we'll make it happen!

Please make sure you accept next month's KINDING Mission and click below on the "Tell Your Friends" button to encourage people you know to join the KIND Movement. If we all do just one small KIND act, we will make next month's Big KIND Act a success.

Let's make it a KIND comeback!

Behind the scenes, because we didn't want to harm those in need, we decided to proceed with the donation we had planned to make, but we did not announce it. That decision was my team's doing; my original plan was to roll over the challenge and make the donation the following month—if our community rose up to partner with us.

The disappointment rallied our community to help us trigger a KIND act the following month, when the Big KIND Act was to work with the Military Friends Foundation to host homecoming celebrations for the troops and donate half a million bars to service members. This time, our team left nothing to chance, and we worked hard to draw more people into the cause. We needed 1,200 people to accept that month's mission: to write a thank-you note to someone who protects you. We had 30,744 people join the mission. Accountability worked, and our community rose up in the face of failure. We proved that bestowing your community with true responsibility leads to deeper engagement.

After several adjustments, we launched what today is called KIND Causes. Now, anyone can upload their ideas to make the world a little kinder. Each month, members log in and vote for the project of their choice. The way they vote is by pledging to do a KIND act. The cause that garners the most support receives a grant and our team's support to make their idea a reality. Our goal with this platform is to eventually take it to the next level by building a KIND exchange. Not only will we sponsor one project a month, but also there will be thousands of beautiful projects that our community can support.

We continue to do nice things for people just because it makes the world a happier place. One popular project, our Flower Wall, has become part of our sampling program in a way that surprises and delights people. We hand out KIND products along with a fresh flower, which we ask the person to pass along to someone else. Now two people are happy.

Another way in which we try to inspire kindness and build the movement is by allowing our own team members to lead efforts for changing their own communities. In October 2012, Hurricane Sandy hit the East Coast and pounded New York City. We galvanized our team and our community to roll up their sleeves in devastated areas. Our team members were out there picking up debris and handing out tens of thousands of KIND bars to people who were affected by the disaster and to first responders. Spouses and friends joined in. One team member's husband rode a bike loaded down with supplies including batteries, candles, and KIND bars for those affected in hard-hit Staten Island. "Residents were touched by the outpouring of support," wrote team member Katie Reimer Nahoum in an email to me later that day. "I couldn't be more proud of our KIND team."

People ask me, "How is KIND a movement?" We talk about how we aspire to be not just a great brand and product, but also a movement, a community, a state of mind. That might sound like marketing hoopla, but it's true.

Since I founded KIND, I certainly have found that Doing the KIND Thing is ever present in my consciousness. I find myself more aware about opportunities to surprise strangers with touches of kindness, and about the meaning and satisfaction it gives to me to make someone's day. I constantly strive to be better, and I strive to be kinder to other human beings. Nearly every day, I recognize again that being a nice person is a better way to live. I am human, and I make mistakes, act rashly, and get upset at times. But KIND makes me better. I'm conscious of my role as KIND's founder and CEO and my responsibility to hold myself to the highest possible standard of ethics and human behavior. Fellow team members often share feeling the same way. If this great energy and mindset can be a tool for others in our community, just imagine how powerful KIND as a brand and platform for change will become. If millions or tens of millions of human beings identify themselves as part of the KIND Movement, if they enjoy their role as catalysts for greater kindness, and derive similar satisfaction and meaning, we will unleash a transformative force for social impact.

Eventually, my dream is for the phrase "Do the KIND Thing" to enter the public lexicon, so that whenever someone says, "Do the . . ." everyone will think, "KIND Thing." I hope this will encourage people to think about doing kind acts.

That's how we move from being a brand and a product and a company to being a community, a movement, and a state of mind. In our ideal world, in the morning a person eats KIND Healthy Grains Clusters with their yogurt, in the afternoon she snacks on a KIND Dark Chocolate Nuts & Sea Salt bar, and in the evening she spots a person doing a kind act and gives that person a #kindawesome card. Or she sees someone who needs some help, and because she's living the kind way, she feels that extra push to help that person. I aim for people to see both KIND and kindness as part of their identity.

EMPATHY IN MANAGEMENT AND BUSINESS

Kindness and empathy also help you to build a culture inside an organization. One of the things that team members in any company are most concerned about is whether they sense that managers truly care about them and their professional growth. Does the company empathize with them and care about them as people?

I'd like to think that at KIND we really stand out for that. It's increasingly difficult as you build a company to make sure every one of your team members sees his or herself as part of a family. I can no longer preserve our approach by having a strong bond with ten people, because KIND is much larger now. Our culture and values are the only way to transmit who we are as we grow. A lot of what I invest my time on lately is inculcating that spirit.

You can see this culture in our KINDOs program—our version of "kudos." Every month, each team member gets to celebrate a colleague for doing things the KIND way. Here is a recent example: One team member applauded the KIND campus ambassador who showed up to help when he moved his daughter into her college dorm, not only handing out KIND bars to the students and families but also pitching in to carry heavy luggage up the stairs. "His help, great personality, and kindness really gave the day a boost that it needed and everyone was talking about what a KIND gesture that was, far after he left."

Even though people do not traditionally think of it as a business skill, empathy can actually create enormous value, and lack of empathy can destroy value. As I shared earlier, the human impulse to adopt a defensive posture when we get hurt or threatened is understandable. As we grow older, many of us adopt reflexively cynical approaches to people and business. Assuming the worst in others can take you down a terrible path. If you react harshly, the other party interprets your aggression as bad faith rather than caution, and before you know it, overreactions have doomed potential partnerships and fruitful relations. When trying to strike a deal or prevent it from going sour, being able to put yourself in the other side's shoes can help you reach better decisions.

It is possible that in an adversarial relationship you need to show the other party that you won't cave to bullying or injustice. But you risk overshooting if you react emotionally (although it is difficult not to in those circumstances). If you are able to operate from a position of strength, it is important to also show empathy, and even to signal generosity. Often just explicitly acknowledging how the other side must see things can help them open up to see your side, and can help both parties reestablish good faith efforts to negotiate a fair outcome. More often than not in these circumstances, issues of honor and dignity end up driving dynamics more than the economics of a transaction. Empathy is thus key to achieve constructive outcomes.

The stakes are even higher when, instead of a business opportunity, one is dealing with regional conflict. I have observed how mistrust between Israelis and Palestinians prolongs and deepens hatred. Violence begets violence. And even when one side may be forced and justified to defend itself, the consequences of aggression invariably boomerang to harm both. Just as kindness is a net happiness aggregator, belligerence increases pain and darkness in society. When our vulnerability is greatest, mustering the strength to extend an open hand can at times lead to historic breakthroughs.

CAN YOU TEACH EMPATHY?

Some people are born with this ability to feel others' pain and the related desire to help. Others learn it.

I learned early to see all people as equals and to treat them with kindness. Sometimes, acting on these ideas made me look silly. I could not have been more clueless when I started at Robert E. Lee High School, just after I arrived in San Antonio. I had no idea that there were different cliques and subgroups in the school's byzantine social hierarchy. Coming from a private Jewish school in Mexico City where everyone was just like me, I had trouble decoding the social cues. I was friendly with the debate kids and the drama kids. One day I would sit with the jocks at lunch, the next day with the New Age punks, and then with the Mexican American kids.

I probably should not have delegated my fashion choices to my cousin Eddy, who, unlike me, was a careful and fancy dresser—but perhaps too much into the latest trend. We went to the mall and bought parachute pants with zippers down the sides and pockets everywhere. Eddy got us Michael Jackson–style fluorescent red leather jackets. Another day we would wear Levi's jeans or preppy Ralph Lauren polo shirts.

One day, a girl named Amber, on whom I had a crush (in spite of her multiple piercings, and punk-shaved multicolored hair), took me aside and said, "Daniel, you have to define yourself. You can't be all of these things. You have to choose one."

"I can't fit into a cubbyhole," I told her.

"You mean you refuse to be pigeonholed?" she said. "That's why you should take my advice, because you can barely speak English! Choose one group." But I continued to befuddle all the other teenagers by declining to conform to stereotypes. At Trinity University, I joined every club and organization—I felt like the protagonist in the movie *Rushmore*.

I had a similar experience later on, at Stanford Law School. Stanford had a beautiful campus and an atmosphere that encouraged people to compete with themselves rather than one another.

People there were kind for the sake of being kind. During my three years at Stanford, I only found myself in one contrasting situation. I used to host dinners for my fellow students every week at the ultra-chic Casa Lubetzky (my tiny apartment), serving the only dish I knew how to make: teriyaki chicken. Once a student stopped me and asked, "What is your angle? Why are you being nice to people?"

I was taken aback. I didn't understand why he was perplexed; I just wanted to have fun and bring people together. Looking back, I realized that not everybody had my orientation toward being nice to people. It was an insight that made me think later that KIND could help open minds to the power of kindness enriching your life and that of others. You can be happier by being nice to one another.

Building bridges between people is especially important today, both within companies and throughout the larger world, given all the challenges we will face in the coming years. I'm concerned about our ability to work together as a society. These days, as I travel around New York City on the subway, particularly in bad weather when the subway gets very crowded, I get scared as I observe how we can become so aggressive toward one another. There's no emergency; no one is starving or dying of thirst; we're all just waiting for the train. It may be cramped, or hot, or slow. Yet people sometimes act in a mean and cold way that's quite concerning. What will happen when we face real problems as a society?

Over the next couple of decades, humanity will encounter huge strains on our planet and our people: climate change, water and food scarcity, pandemics, nuclear proliferation, terrorism. The only way we can win against those challenges is to recognize that we have to fight on the same side.

It has always struck me as troubling that there is no common curriculum or agreement on what the community of nations should teach all children about our shared values. For a few years now, I have been designing a project that would educate kids across the globe about the values they share with their fellow human beings, even in nations or ethnic groups that their parents consider enemies.

I am beginning to gather leading experts to compile this universal values curriculum to be used in school districts across the world. We hope to partner with technology companies and global organizations to assemble a coalition that will provide free educational tools and incentives for schools to adopt the program. The idea is that a boy in Pakistan will be able to discover what he has in common with a girl in the United States. My vision is eventually to build a global movement of citizens who are proud of their own heritage as well as of our shared human values.

Only by building this consciousness do I think humanity has a shot at surviving the twenty-first century.

Many friends in the West have shared with me their concern about terrorism and fundamentalism. Knowing the work I do, they ask me, "How are we going to get Wahhabis in Saudi Arabia to change their ways? Why do wealthy Arabs fund ISIS, the 'Islamic State' terrorist group? How will we stop Hezbollah and Iran from supporting Assad's butchering of tens of thousands in Syria?"

I am not a pacifist. I recognize that the use of force is necessary to stop totalitarian aggression and abuse. After all, I would not be here if it wasn't for the United States' intervention in World War II. But beyond the use of military force when absolutely needed, what role can education play to prevent future conflicts?

Trying to force-feed another culture with your own values and sense of superiority will never work. We have a better chance if we recognize that every person in the world wants to be understood. By building a platform rooted in dignity, equality, and respect, where all kids can share what they feel they have in common with others, I hope that Muslims, Christians, Jews, Buddhists, Hindus, atheists, and others will join the dialogue and help one another discover our commonalities as a human race.

Because I was raised in such a sheltered environment, I comprehend how isolated we humans often are from one another. Sometimes these misunderstandings can be funny. I grew up not realizing that the language we spoke at home mixed Yiddish and Spanish, until a Christian playmate asked me what the word *tuchas* was (it means "butt" in Yiddish, which he didn't speak, and I was so insulated I thought it was Spanish). I also used *pishar* as a verb to mean "to go to the bathroom," combining the Spanish and Yiddish words into one, a turn of phrase my children still use.

But sometimes what you're learning are prejudices that can cause enormous harm if you don't understand the humanity of others. If your parents teach you intolerance and hatred during your childhood, what you get is bigotry, xenophobia, and war.

My friends challenge me on my naïveté: "Daniel, don't you know that the people who have the greatest hatred and ignorance of the other side don't want to be engaged with a curriculum on shared values?" I recognize how hard a road it will be to bring them into the conversation. But are we going to give up and not try? We cannot afford to just stand idle.

CHAPTER 9

TRUST

Learning to Let Others Lead

Every year, KIND attends the Natural Products Expo West, the world's biggest trade show of its kind. In 2013, it was held at the Anaheim Convention Center in California, and we were one of 1,800 companies exhibiting there. We were busy on the floor showing off our Fruit & Nut bars and KIND Healthy Grains Clusters granola, and launching some new extensions to the KIND Nuts & Spices line. We were also engaged in our usual guerrilla marketing tactics, handing out 6,000 T-shirts and bags to attendees who committed to Do the KIND Thing. Looking at the sea of KIND T-shirts, it felt like one in ten of the people on the show floor was part of the KIND Movement.

But the real action was two floors above the convention floor, where we had rented a room and quietly invited a dozen of our largest and most loyal retail accounts, including Whole Foods, Wegmans, Amazon, and H-E-B, for back-to-back presentations. These buyers, sworn to secrecy, would get an exclusive sneak peek at our new KIND Healthy Grains Bars. Our team had decorated the room with KIND T-shirts, floor racks, point-of-purchase displays, and a beautiful array of all our products. They even had branded napkins to match the décor.

This private approach to launching a new product was not our usual strategy (we usually did big public announcements on the floor) but we were breaking into a new category—granola bars—and we didn't want to tip our hand to the competition. Due to our premium ingredients, our new bars would necessarily be priced higher than most granola bars. We knew our major competitors could lower their prices even more, in a bid to keep customers buying their products instead of ours. We didn't want to give them that opportunity at the critical moment of our launch. Secrecy was therefore critical.

The night before the meetings, I was a little nervous. I intended to make the presentations myself. A lot was riding on this launch, and as the founder, I felt I could speak best to the product's features. I was in my hotel room, trying to prepare on my laptop, with all the lights off so my oldest child, four-year-old Romy, could sleep curled up in bed with his stuffed rabbit. It was his first time accompanying me on a business trip; I planned to take him on his first visit to Disneyland after the trade show.

Kroger, the nation's largest grocery chain, joined us for the first meeting. Their delegation consisted of five senior executives, including Cecil Bogy, our longtime buyer, who had been the first person to give Rami and me a shot many years before. Over the last year, Kroger had been impressed enough with our performance that Mary Ellen Adcock, the vice president for natural foods there, had invited us to join an internal natural-products task force. She asked John Cowan, the senior executive in charge of coordinating natural foods strategy with her, to attend this meeting.

Just as I was about to start speaking, John Leahy rose to welcome everyone and began to lead the meeting. "Thank you from the bottom of our hearts for accepting our private invitation," he said. "The purpose of this meeting is to give you a peek under the cover of an amazing new product line in yet another completely new category."

Only at that moment did I realize I should have checked in with John on what role he wanted me to play. While by that point I seldom participated in sales meetings, I had assumed that I was asked to be there to lead. Instead, I was suddenly conscious that John had a lot more experience, that he was the one who had put these meetings together, and that I should step back and follow his cue.

John was folksy and friendly, establishing a rapport with the visiting executives. He told the buyers his objective was to create something special for the launch, and he introduced our "sizzle reel," a video illustrating the passion and spirit both we and our customers have for our brand.

Then he coordinated presentations from the half-dozen KIND team members in the room, who discussed the product and the data behind the launch. Our marketing executives spoke eloquently about the brand, the new product's features, and our promotional strategy. We even had a nutritionist talk about the health benefits of the five super-grains in our KIND Healthy Grains Bars: gluten-free oats, amaranth, quinoa, millet, and buckwheat. Our sales team reviewed our performance at Kroger.

Then our category management director, Jon "Izzy" Israelite, explained that KIND was "on fire," growing six times faster than other leading brands. "Our success is driven by our loyal customers," he said. "Eighty-eight percent of consumers who try KIND repeat the purchase and refer friends." Izzy pointed out that the gluten-free food trend was sweeping the grocery store: In the latest twenty-four-week period, 23 percent of dollars sold in the energy bars segment were from gluten-free products, as were 15 percent of dollars spent on granola cereal. But for granola bars, the figure was just 4 percent. "We have uncovered a major opportunity as no mainstream national brand is currently offering gluten-free granola bars," Izzy told the buyers.

The meeting went off like a symphony, with every instrument playing perfectly. The only comment I added was to explain how obsessed I had been with achieving the right texture in a category characterized by overly dry or mushy granola bars. Our defining attribute, I explained, is a texture that is both chewy and crunchy, which makes a big difference in the sensory experience. Otherwise, I observed my team. Watching all of them working together was like witnessing art being made.

I was proud to see that they could speak with such authority and insight about the new product. They presented as well as I could have—in many regards better—while conveying confidence and professionalism.

On the spot the Kroger team authorized the entire line for all their stores and asked to partner with KIND in promoting them. It was a stark contrast to our earlier days, when it took us five years to get KIND into the first 180 of Kroger's specialty stores and several years longer to reach all 3,500 of their stores. The Kroger team later said it was one of the best meetings they had ever attended.

When the meeting ended, I left the room to take stock of what had just happened and headed to the men's bathroom. I was so shell-shocked that I walked into the women's restroom by mistake.

TRUSTING OTHERS TO LEAD

Every retailer we met that day bought the entire new line. We had never experienced such a fast uptake. It became clear over the course of that day that trust was the key element in our proceedings. We trusted these loyal customers enough to offer them an exclusive peek and a chance at partnership. They trusted the data and substance of our presentation, just as they had grown to trust the integrity of our products over the years. The KIND team trusted one another with different segments of the presentation. Most of all, I learned an important lesson about stepping back and trusting my team to lead.

KIND had grown from a core team of dedicated, overworked generalists doing several jobs at once to a large, professional organization with specialists who had either come in from outside or had been groomed internally to grow in a focused area about which they're passionate. Case in point: Rodrigo Zuloaga, now the head of new product development at KIND, was our entire marketing department in the early days, as well as the person in charge of e-commerce and trademark law; today those jobs are performed by more than three hundred team members.

With that growth has come an evolution in my role. Whereas I was once the founder, leader, salesman, box-packer, deliveryman, and collections officer all at once, I now need to retrench myself and empower my team to lead. My main role now that KIND has five hundred team members is to provide a vision, to inspire and to coach the team—to nurture the culture I have created. The best way for me to impact the company is to transmit our core values and way of thinking.

Indeed, before the series of private presentations and before the trade show doors had even opened that morning, I had gathered with our forty-person show team downstairs at our main convention booth to rally everyone to live by our values. Some were long-standing team members; others were at their first day on the job. With everyone in a circle around the black displays showcasing our products, wearing KIND gear, I reminded the team that we have to maintain our humility and tenacity.

"You have to treat every customer with the same gratitude, energy, and appreciation as if they are the largest customer in the country," I said. As much as our products "sell themselves," I encouraged the team to engage with every passerby and strive to educate them about our products.

To maintain our entrepreneurial spirit, we have to create a culture in which everyone remembers that every order, big or small—and every interaction, every moment—will define what our company is today and what it will become tomorrow. The moment you sit back as your customers are walking past your booth will haunt you five years from now when you realize, "That was the turning point when we took our first step toward mediocrity."

If you can inculcate in your team that every moment means everything, you can then step back to let them lead.

ENSURING MY TEAM TRUSTS ME

Looking around the booth that day, I also realized that some of my team members had never met me before. When we were a fifteen-person organization, and each of those people knew me well, I would say exactly what I thought, often including constructive criticism. But when interacting with a team member for the first time, and given that I might not see him or her again for six months or a year, I am aware that I have to be extraordinarily careful, lest their first interaction with the CEO be construed as intimidating or demotivating. It goes against my instinct, but, unless I know the team member intimately, I've learned to provide any constructive criticism about them to their supervisor so that it will be relayed in proper context as part of an overall review. The process may be inefficient, but it also permits our senior team members to lead their own teams.

As we grow, I also realize the importance of building bonds of trust with my senior executives. If they know that I am loyal to them and want them to succeed, then they won't be afraid to contradict me and voice their opinions, and also won't be offended if I debate with them when I disagree. When people in a big company do not trust that the CEO (or the person they report to) has their backs and welcomes and cherishes criticism and fresh opinions, they may be afraid to take risks, to make mistakes, or to confront a policy that they disagree with. This can create a Kremlin-like atmosphere in which intimidation stifles hearty debate. Similarly, they may feel they are being threatened when you disagree with their point of view.

John Leahy and I have a spectacular relationship because we

know we are there for each other. We are clear about each of our roles and responsibilities: He manages the day-to-day, while I'm the keeper of the brand and its evolution. We are very comfortable debating an issue and know criticism or disagreements are never personal. In instances where I have not achieved that relationship with others, or when a team member feels they need to compete with me or they feel I am not rooting for them, productivity suffers because of that lack of trust.

ASKING FOR ADVICE AND LISTENING TO IT

In group meetings, my instinct is just to lead. I tend to dominate the conversation. One of the areas I am working on is standing back and allowing my management team to take over. Learning how to contract your power and personality is of incredible importance. Unless you create that space, your management team cannot fill it up. Particularly at these group meetings, I've noticed that if I share my perspective, some may no longer want to argue for a different path. So I increasingly try to listen first, and I also play devil's advocate to ensure we are debating all sides of an issue.

I don't always have the right answer, and I have to seek counsel. In the food business, it's important to remember that you are not always designing products for your own personal tastes. This holds true for other industries as well; it's dangerous to consider yourself a focus group of one.

When I first started PeaceWorks, I was considering which Mediterranean spreads to import. I was in love with the sun-dried tomato spread, which had sparked my enthusiasm for the business, and I liked an olive tapenade that my Israeli manufacturer, Yoel, sent me to sample. But I wasn't convinced that his basil pesto would do well. I was twenty-five; my tastes weren't all that sophisticated. At the time, pesto tasted like grass to me. Yoel begged me to include it, so I ended up ordering five hundred cases of the sundried tomato spread, five hundred cases of the olive tapenade, and one hundred cases of the basil pesto to indulge him.

Yoel's sense of the market was clearly more fine-tuned than mine, because the pesto was the runaway customer favorite and still outsells both sundried tomato and olive four to one. The lesson I learned was not to listen only to my own taste buds and views, but also to seek and heed input from others.

At about the same time, I realized that I need to ask for help from more experienced executives.

I needed a sounding board so I decided to put together a group of advisers I could trust to guide me. This board had no fiduciary or legal duties (LLCs and small, privately held corporations are not required to have a board of independent directors); their job was simply to help me figure out my strategy at important decision points. I had no money to pay them, and they were all doing it primarily because they believed in my mission to foster peace between Arabs and Israelis. I wanted to give them a bit of upside potential, so I awarded them each a modest number of stock options. For some advisory board members who chose to exercise those options later, these grants worked out quite well financially, but at the time there was no guarantee that they would ever see any money.

To assemble the board, I thought carefully about the different areas in which I would need advice. I needed a legal mind; a strategic expert; and gurus in finance, the food industry, and other areas. I also asked my dad to serve on the board. In addition to being an entrepreneur, he helped me with personal moral support. He was someone who was there for me at all times.

I had left both the law firm of Sullivan & Cromwell and the consulting firm McKinsey & Company without burning my bridges, so Richard Urowsky from Sullivan and Jacques Antebi from McKinsey both agreed to serve as my advisers.

A series of serendipitous events led me to Ben Cohen, the co-founder of Ben & Jerry's, the wildly successful ice-cream company based in Vermont. After an article about PeaceWorks' efforts ran in *The Philadelphia Inquirer,* I received a phone call from Judy Wicks, a restaurateur who ran the popular White Dog Cafe—near University of Pennsylvania Law School—which specialized in sustainable and local food. Judy asked if I would come and give a talk about my work at a dinner she was hosting. When the event was over, she suggested introducing me to Ben, who was a friend of hers. I was starstruck; Ben was the godfather of social entrepreneurship (even though the term had not yet been coined).

I called Ben and offered to fly to meet him. Instead, he agreed to stop by my New York City "office." He walked down the basement stairs, passed through the trash compactor room, and entered my windowless storeroom stacked with product. We sat on a pair of folding chairs in between the piles of boxes, where he spent several hours grilling me to see if I knew what I was doing. He could see that I did not know much, but that I was a quick study. On the spot, he accepted my offer to join the advisory board. He clearly was doing it only to help me, not because he thought he could gain anything. He appreciated the sincerity of what we were doing and was generous with his time.

BALANCING EGOS

My board member, friend, and mentor, Fred Schaufeld once told me that an even bigger driver of human motivation than financial gain or greed is just raw ego. Over the years, I have come to see the wisdom of his point. We all have egos. We all want recognition for our contributions. We all want to be respected. It's normal to have those feelings. The quest for recognition and respect often does trump financial incentives.

Because it is such a potent force, balancing your ego and being mindful of others' egos is an important skill set. Ego in and of itself is not bad. A healthy ego can provide you with the self-confidence to pursue your dreams. And insecurity can be a motivator to achieve more. But too much ego can turn you arrogant. And too little ego can hamper your ability to be self-critical.

The more you succeed, the more that success can get to your head. As people praise you and start venerating you, you run the risk of taking it all to heart. The truth is, everyone in your team shares in your success or failure. Your inability to recognize them and their contributions can cause resentment, demotivation, and attrition. It can make them lose trust in you.

Shortly after inviting a couple of new board members to join KIND, I found myself trying to impress them. I dominated the meeting and tried to answer every one of the questions, rather than letting John and my other senior team leaders shine. I was trying to prove that I was on top of things and I had thought through the issues. But why did I need to prove that? Everyone around the room was rooting for KIND and for me. I reflected that night and wrote to all of them to acknowledge my error and apologize. I needed to trust that they trusted me and were not expecting me to prove myself. I needed to reciprocate by letting my team lead. That in turn deepened our mutual trust.

Besides being the right thing to do, celebrating your team is a smart business practice. It will motivate them at least as much as money and make them more loyal to your venture. Similarly, you should never let your own ego or insecurities intimidate you into not hiring people who are more talented than you at what they do. This seems self-evident, but we will all at some point encounter a situation where we're a bit dazzled by someone's star power, and worried that they will overshadow us. It's essential to be mindful of this negative human instinct, to keep it in check and exorcise it. The only chance you have to build a truly great venture is to find people who are better than you at what they do and celebrate them every step of the way. You need to program your ego to recognize that their success is your success.

Interestingly, I've learned that self-confidence and success do not always correlate the way we might think. Sometimes people start off being self-confident and attain success. Then age or random circumstances cause us to develop insecurities. We start questioning whether we've still "got what it takes" to lead and succeed or think we need to prove ourselves. At junctures like these, it's critical to step back and study our internal feedback, looking for legitimate issues that we can correct to get back on track and ferreting out the critical chatter that will only hold us back.

And yet, on the other side, a proper dosage of insecurity can be a huge driver for success. Shimon Peres, the great Israeli statesman and Nobel Prize winner, once emphasized this point. I was at a dinner at the World Economic Forum in Davos when he asked, "Do you know what all of us here have in common? We are all insecure." The audience—CEOs of large corporations, heads of state, intellectual luminaries, and a handful of fledgling entrepreneurs like me—was perplexed. But Peres continued and illuminated the truth of his statement: "Some level of insecurity is okay. It is what has brought us all this far. It is what drives us every morning to achieve more, to not rest on our laurels. It is what has pushed you to work harder and longer." As long as it doesn't dull our ability to criticize ourselves, a little insecurity can propel us forward.

LEADING BY EXAMPLE

Leadership is like driving a manual-transmission car. You need to use different gears depending on the occasion. When things are going well and your team spirit level is high, you want to contribute to that positive energy. At the same time, it's also your job to discourage euphoria and help keep everyone grounded and attentive to the challenges ahead.

Howard Schultz of Starbucks once gave me this advice: "Success can hide a lot of your weaknesses and failures." Especially when a business is expanding, you have to be careful not to get overconfident. Your role as a leader is to be on the lookout for things that are not going optimally and for competitive threats. In times of great momentum, your job is to celebrate the triumphant moments while keeping things in perspective and appropriately cautious.

My own way of reaching this balance is often to offer praise *and* ribbing at the same time. If one of my team members delivers an incredible success on a sales account, my instinct is to commend them and also tease them to keep their focus on aiming higher. For example, after two years of efforts, when John Leahy and Todd O'Rourke came back from a Trader Joe's meeting with the news that they had finally secured approval to add four more flavors to our assortment, I said, "Great work. Now we need to get the other eight flavors onto their shelves to get our fair share based on our market performance."

In contrast, when things go wrong for your team or your company, you need to shift gears. Your role is to inspire your team to look beyond the immediate failure and keep perspective on your vision for the future. It's at those times, when someone has stumbled—and particularly when they made a mistake that they regret—that you want to stand by them, sharing the responsibility for the failure and reminding them of the great work they're doing overall. You don't want to waste the opportunity for learning and improvement that failures bring us. But you do want to use a caring tone and cultivate a supportive environment.

Another part of our culture is that no one is too proud to do any task. I believe that everyone in a company should pitch in, including the executives and certainly the CEO. When at a trade show, or at an event, I carry boxes like everyone else. A friend once told me that it's not very "presidential" for me to be picking up boxes and ringing up sales. "You need to carry yourself like the head of the company you run now, and not be doing all of these tasks," he said. I tried that for a bit, but it did not feel right to me, and I went back to my original "nonpresidential" approach. It feels much better to be in the trenches with my team. It might appear to some that by not doing something more CEO-like I'm being inefficient and not delegating tasks to others. For the KIND culture, it works far better to highlight that there's no task too small or insignificant for any of us to do it.

KIND'S MARKETING TEAM: A CASE STUDY IN TRUST

As KIND has grown, marketing and new product development are the areas where I have continued to contribute most. They're the sides of the business that I love the best, and it seems to be where I can add the most value. So it's been harder for me to give up ownership in those areas as we've hired more specialized team members.

Branding is where we occasionally conflict. That's a natural pain point, because our marketing-team members want to introduce fresh new concepts, while I'm the brand protector. As the founder of the company, I understand the brand's heritage and how to keep it consistent. We're so careful, so obsessive about the details at KIND, and we can't lose that part of our identity. It's not smart for me to give up all the power in this area. But I do have to transmit that knowledge so my marketing team can become the brand protectors too. To an extent, this is true with all new team members who join us. If the KIND

DNA gets into their systems and they understand the brand's personality intimately, they will be able to reach independent decisions that are consistent with our brand promise.

Our marketing team has had some spot-on ideas. Our motto started as "Be KIND to your body, your taste buds, & the world." Then it became "Do the KIND Thing for your body, your taste buds, & the world."

Then the team had another idea: change "the" world to "your" world. Initially, I was skeptical: Why change our motto? Why fix something that is not broken? But upon reflection, I realized they were right. The new version is much more consistent with our brand. It's about taking ownership and responsibility of *our* shared world.

One of the problems marketers have when they first join a company is they always think the old way was wrong. There's a lot of change for change's sake in marketing. That can cause a lot of unnecessary work, or it can cause harm to the brand. But this idea made absolute sense.

Another example of marketing insight from my team: Our logo featured two horizontal white lines, above and below the word "KIND." We had grabbed the logo out of the design on our packaging, where those lines appropriately separated the logo from other descriptors. The team observed that if the bottom line wasn't there in certain configurations, it would release KIND. It's not just the psychology of graphic design; it also helped us get the word KIND out there. Not as many people know our name as know our logo. Getting rid of the extra white line helped us make the word "KIND" synonymous with our products in a way it hadn't been before.

Our brand has gone through a subtle evolution over the last ten years to make it consistent. Erica Pattni first helped me rationalize and codify some rules that I had been following in my mind. As we grew and needed others to reach decisions without my input, she helped put those guidelines in writing.

In other areas, the marketing team has come up with ideas that I have overruled because I felt they didn't mesh with our brand history. Recently my marketing team wanted to partner with a hip beverage brand. I am wary about partnering with other brands; I worry we're going to lose our authenticity by pairing with ephemeral brands. So we set guidelines: The other brand has to be consistent with our values, there has to be a huge upside, and the partnership has to advance a goal we can't accomplish by ourselves. For this beverage brand, I wasn't sure that the opportunity met our criteria. We put the deal on hold until we could consider it more fully.

In another instance, my marketing team wanted us to switch our black-based packaging to all white in some situations, including on print ads. I vetoed that idea. But in other areas we achieved smart compromises. Our field Jeeps—which we deploy to sample products across twenty-four markets—felt forebodingly dark and unfriendly in all black. We agreed to use sparkling white Jeeps with a black bar grounding our colorful KIND logo.

I also pushed back on an attempt by our web-design team to use cutesy fruit icons to represent ingredients in our products. This is an absolute for me: We don't use fake pictures of food. We don't even use photographs of ingredients, since most food companies have abused this technique so much that subconsciously consumers are already programmed to distrust them. We only use images of our actual products. Our brand is about authenticity, and we never deviate from those guidelines.

For the same reason, I said no when the team suggested wavy

and circular lines in some of our graphic design. We're a straight-line brand, and we're disciplined about being transparent and straightforward. Curvy lines would suggest something different—movement, motion, fluidity. This may sound overly dramatic, but design provides the consumer with cues about what a brand means. We know who we are, and we need designs that represent us.

This was also the problem with a new tagline that the marketing team proposed: "Trick Your Taste Buds." I found out about it when our patent attorney asked me to sign off on the trademark application.

"I don't like the idea of using 'trick' along with our transparent brand," I emailed back to the attorney and our team, "even if I understand it is a joke about how something so healthy should not be so delicious, we don't want to use that line of thinking—we are all about highlighting that, YES, you CAN do something healthy and delicious, no tricks involved, quite the opposite."

One of our brand directors, Katie Reimer Nahoum, reminded me that this tagline is one we have used specifically in the context of Halloween, where the use of the word "trick" is a clever and appropriate play on words. "We want to educate consumers that KIND is better than candy," she explained patiently. I agreed to keep it as a seasonal tagline in that context.

But I've never agreed to try the kinds of marketing tactics that I feel apply better to other products or services. For example, my team occasionally suggests that we give out headphones or other gadgets as gifts. In some cases that may make sense, but as a general rule, KIND is such a hot commodity that people covet it. The product is king. When creating incentives, gifting, or promotions, I'd much rather give out KIND products. When your product is something people naturally want, there's no reason not to put the spotlight on your own lines.

TRUST AND MOVING FORWARD

In early 2013, Starbucks was changing its food strategy. They had decided on a 360-degree program that would involve selling Starbucks-branded products at other retailers as well. Howard Schultz, Starbucks' CEO, had been very transparent with me about the fact that Starbucks was considering selling in its stores only items in which it had a stake, and that eventually this could mean the discontinuation of KIND products from their stores. While Starbucks represented less than 5 percent of our business at the time, they were a formidable strategic partner. The upside of growing with them, or downside of losing them, was quite significant in my mind. It was an iconic retailer with shared values. KIND had never lost an established account, let alone such a great retailer.

In an effort to change the course of their plans, I asked Howard to let us explore a few more ideas. He agreed to send one of his trusted executives, Jeff Hansberry, for a final try at this. Our team brainstormed creative options that we could present to Starbucks to see if we could preserve the partnership. Some among my team were adamant that we should move on and accept that our strategic vision was not compatible with Starbucks' direction. I understood their point, but before I gave up, I wanted to challenge my team and myself to come up with out-of-the-box ideas—using the AND philosophy—that could address both partners' goals. We invested all our creative energy in the meeting, to prove to Jeff that we would be a loyal and invaluable partner for years to come.

After the meeting, Jeff agreed to call me within a week to let me know of Starbucks's final decision.

CHAPTER 10

OWNERSHIP AND RESOURCEFULNESS

Building a Culture with Staying Power

It was the spring of 2013, and flowers were blooming in New York. I had promised Michelle that we would go away for a romantic vacation just before the birth of our fourth child, but we couldn't find the time, and we ended up spending a single night at a hotel in downtown Manhattan. When I noticed that KIND bars were not among the minibar offerings, I immediately called the manager to pitch to him while my wife waited patiently.

Early next morning, Jeff Hansberry called on my cell phone.

"Do you mind if I take this?" I asked Michelle. "I'm so sorry, it's the call I've been waiting for from Starbucks." She smiled and said it was okay.

"Daniel," Jeff said, "we really appreciate your efforts and creativity. We value you a lot. But we've decided to part ways. We have a very clear path for what we're trying to achieve." He assured me that we would have a smooth transition out of Starbucks stores.

A big weight hit my chest. I took a deep breath and thanked Jeff for the call. I told him that Starbucks had been nothing but a pleasure to work with, that I respected the decision, and that the door would remain open if they changed their mind. "I will continue trying to convince you that rekindling our relationship will benefit Starbucks."

I hung up the phone, looked over at Michelle, and told her Starbucks was out. I felt bad for ending our mini-getaway with somber news. Michelle went home to see the kids and I went to the office.

How was I going to share the news with my team? Until that point, all discussions with Starbucks had been confidential, and only a handful of my team members knew that Starbucks was entertaining a different strategy.

On my way to the office, I called board member Fred Schaufeld. His advice was not to diminish the news or sweep it under the rug, but to use it as a rallying point to challenge the team. John Leahy, our president, was of a similar opinion.

Their advice resonated with my sense that, as our team had grown exponentially over the last few years, my foremost priority was transmitting our values to all of them. If I wanted to ensure that our ownership culture—rooted in an entrepreneurial spirit of resourcefulness and resilience—was ingrained in our team members' minds, here was an opportunity to foster a sense of shared responsibility. When things are going well, you run the danger of starting to think your success is inevitable and your company is invincible, even if nothing could be further from the truth. Here was a humbling reminder that we should not presume anything and we should always maintain our humility and hard-work ethic.

I scheduled a company-wide conference call a week or two later where I covered a number of issues. There was a drumbeat of good news to share, which helped contextualize the Starbucks loss. KIND Healthy Grains Bars had begun hitting stores, and our introduction of the new line to home-shopping channel QVC led to $500,000 in sales of the new bars in their first day.

When it came to talking about Starbucks, I did not disguise how disappointed I was. I took this loss personally, and I used it to highlight several points. I recalled I had worked for many years to get us into Starbucks because of its unique retail positioning. I was upset with myself that I had not succeeded in retaining the account. I explained to the team that it had nothing to do with KIND's performance, but rather with a strategic direction that Starbucks was pursuing. But the context gave me the chance to re-stress, just as I had at the Natural Products Expo a few weeks before, that every relationship must mean everything to us. Now more than ever, that message reverberated: We could not take anything for granted.

I challenged the team to get KIND into as many coffee stores as they could. And they did. First, we identified large, midsize, small, and independent coffee chains and shops aligned with our brand. We started booking participation at all the specialty-coffee trade shows. We deployed some of our veteran team members to call on the coffee trade and build a new channel of distribution. We got into a ton of loyal independents who loved KIND, as well as into well-regarded chains like The Coffee Bean & Tea Leaf and Peet's Coffee & Tea.

We also took our Blueberry Vanilla & Cashew flavor, which of our own volition we had sold exclusively at Starbucks, and made it available to our other accounts in all channels.

At the same time, I resolved to think creatively about how to listen to Starbucks' needs and how to regain their business. I knew every day consumers walked into Starbucks stores looking for a KIND bar—they wrote to us, sent us emails, raving about their morning routine pairing a Starbucks coffee with a KIND bar. I knew that we were adding value to Starbucks. How could we deploy our values—grit, transparency, resourcefulness, creativity—to win them back?

INCULCATING RESOURCEFULNESS

When you're the owner of an underfinanced start-up, every penny spent is a penny you feel coming out of your pocket. Resourcefulness is crucial. Here at KIND, we strive to teach and preserve this ownership mindset when allocating resources. We try to look at every question from a point of view of resourcefulness: How can we get *everything* we need *and* get it at the lowest possible price and on the best possible terms?

I am not a fan of budgets. They're artificial, and they induce people to think in artificial ways, instead of thinking creatively. Of course, in large organizations, there must be a process for deciding how much money each department gets for its initiatives. But I find that it's much more effective to empower team members to think like owners and use budgets as a guideline—one that they aim to beat. We want them to think, "This is my company and I care where the pennies and dollars go. Can I do more with less?" The thought that a team leader will have their budget cut next year if they don't use it up (as is common in corporate America) is counterintuitive to the mindset I want to engender in my team. It is the antithesis of how an owner thinks.

As discussed earlier, a culture of resourcefulness is different from a culture of scarcity. During PeaceWorks' early years, my relentless focus on frugality often misallocated a valuable resource: my team members' time. For instance, I insisted that we chase down every single overdue payment. My theory was that we had to squeeze the last penny out of each situation, because we desperately needed the money, and because some arbitrary deductions by distributors or retailers were unauthorized and unjust. But two hours spent hounding a delinquent account that owed us $80 could have been better spent drumming up new business.

Once the company had enough money that we were no longer fighting to make payroll every month, I began to shift my emphasis from frugality to resourcefulness. Now we focus on being resourceful, coming up with creative solutions to problems. We still try hard not to waste money, which depends on our team members acting like the owners they are. The difference is that now we have the flexibility to invest where we think it will help expand our business.

OWNERSHIP AND COURAGE

Ownership requires courage. There are more upsides to ownership than just being an employee or being just one of many investors, to be sure. But owners shoulder all of the downsides as well. You are answerable to yourself (and to one another, if you are part of a team of owners). If things go wrong, you have to be responsible for all solutions including generating all necessary resources—financial and human—to make things right. Ownership can take a lot from you. It often feels like riding the world's biggest and scariest roller coaster.

But ownership of your brand also gives you a level of control and predictability. We learned how dangerous it was not to control our fate when the makers of the Australian brand we had been importing decided to change their formula. We did not control the manufacturing or the formulation of the Australian line and could do nothing about their decision to add sulfates and sorbitol to their products. We thus committed never again to place our future in the hands of another company.

It wasn't easy to take ownership of product manufacturing—we had never done it before. In the beginning, we did not have the resources to manufacture KIND in the United States, so we started by having KIND manufactured for us in Australia. I tried to convince my Australian manufacturer to set up operations in the United States, but he resisted. Manufacturing in Australia had a lot of disadvantages: The Australian dollar kept getting stronger and we had a number of problems managing the foreign exchange rate; more important, overseeing the manufacturing process abroad was extremely challenging. As soon as we were able to, we began manufacturing some of our product in the United States and eventually moved the whole operation here.

I often think back and sincerely wonder how I had the temerity to pursue this path—it looks scarier in retrospect. Perhaps it's like when you are climbing a mountain: Looking forward and taking baby steps is far less intimidating than staring down the precipice once you are up the cliff. Perhaps it didn't cross my mind because I started with a mission to pursue peace between Israel and its Arab neighbors and I didn't think I had any other option but to pursue that which I believed in. Or perhaps it was from watching my dad. But perhaps to some small degree it was also connected to formative experiences I had as a kid. These included developing the courage to stand up before audiences when I performed magic shows.

I did my first magic shows in front of my parents, then my siblings, then my cousins, then the children of family friends who were less forgiving and would comment on where I was hiding the rabbit. That slow progression to increasingly demanding audiences probably stretched my ability to withstand increasing amounts of pressure.

When I was about twelve years old, my dad took me to compete in an international professional magic convention in Acapulco. I can't say that my performance was particularly distinguished. I remember vividly standing backstage before my act. I had never appeared in front of an audience of three or four hundred strangers before, and I was truly scared. An older magician gave me a tip that I use to this day: "Imagine that every one of these people is a flower: This one is a lily, this one is a rose." That trick works by relaxing you, taking away the fear of presenting in front of a large audience. For me the flower idea works better than the typical technique of imagining people naked. You wouldn't want to imagine most people in a large audience naked.

My experience with performing magic shows also gave me

one of my first platforms to spur my imagination. Because magic is greater than the sum of its individual components, performing magic forces you to think creatively. We tried to replicate this effect with KIND, which for me is, well, magical. We followed the AND philosophy to try to make one plus one equal four—to make the whole bar taste much better than the mere aggregation of its individual ingredients. By challenging those false compromises and coming up with a magical new path, we end up creating more value for society.

TAPPING THE HUMAN SPIRIT

Ownership carries with it a commitment to excellence. When it's your baby, you're going to work harder than anyone. That's why we give stock options to all of our full-time team members—from entry-level team members to seniormost executives. This aligns incentives because every person in our team has a direct economic stake in our long-term success.

While it helps to align incentives, it is not enough. Ownership above all is an attitude. You can have a stake in a company yet lack an ownership mentality. Many public companies issue stock to their employees but their mindset remains as employees rather than co-owners. Inversely, some enterprises are privately held but manage to create a collaborative intrepid soul that approximates the sense of true ownership. Ownership is about tapping the human spirit, about a sense of personal power and the responsibility that comes with it. This approach recognizes we are part of something bigger than ourselves—one big family—and have entered an implicit pact to be loyal to one another and think of our shared enterprise ahead of ourselves.

The problem we have at KIND is that we've had a few team members overdo it. I've had to say, "This is a marathon, not a sprint." Burnout is a real concern.

Keeping up with demand has been challenging for our manufacturing team. Forecasting is extremely difficult for a fast-growth company, and as we grow, the stakes get higher. Underestimating demand can get us in trouble with retailers if we can't keep their shelves stocked. On the other hand, overestimating needs at these levels can bring down companies that invest hundreds of millions in a new factory that then sits idle. As it happened, demand for the new KIND Healthy Grains Bars has exceeded all expectations and our manufacturing team is strained to keep up. As much as I appreciate their work around the clock to build new capacity, I also worry they will break down. I press them to overinvest in talent and support.

There's a tension between everyone doing their part and the responsibility we have to our families to balance work and life. You need to constantly ask yourself what you are balancing. Work has a way of hijacking you. If you let each urgent work crisis drive you, rather than setting priorities, you may lose a sense of equilibrium.

When everyone on your team feels they have the power and responsibility of co-owners, you can expect everyone to pull their own weight in the way that best fits their lifestyle. The work ethic at KIND is just as strong as when we were starting out and would stay in the office until 3 or 4 A.M. But now we consciously encourage our team to incorporate and balance their responsibilities to their families.

As the company grows, and as society evolves, we have to recognize that team members may have duties at home. Our ownership mentality helps managers feel confident that providing flexibility to their team will not decrease productivity. This is easier said than done, but we are working on it.

I don't pretend that everyone has the same stake I do in the company. But I do my utmost to create a culture where a sense of ownership puts everyone on a shared path, where merit and good ideas trump seniority. Of course, there is a chain of command, and I do have the final word on key decisions. But when you create an environment in which everyone is treated with dignity and equality, and people are encouraged to speak up and contribute, the best ideas tend to win.

Treating investors with dignity also pays off. When I decided to create KIND, I could have simply closed PeaceWorks and started afresh, or created a different legal entity. It wasn't immediately obvious that KIND should be part of PeaceWorks and that PeaceWorks investors and team members should benefit from the new KIND venture. The concept, mission, products, and brand were all different. But I felt that the right thing to do was to honor their support and belief in me and give them a stake in the new products. I was doing what I thought was right, not what would maximize my short-term financial interest. Because I launched KIND within the original legal entity that all my earlier investors had joined, they were able to participate in the phenomenal growth of KIND, even after we spun off and separated PeaceWorks from KIND a few years later.

How did this move pay off for me? It set up a track record of principled leadership. It paid off in increased loyalty. When people recognize that you take care of your partners, they appreciate that and want to work with you. What we're building at KIND is a long-term approach to stakeholder relations. It's the same idea as insisting that all my team members have a stake in the company. I do it because KIND benefits when every team member acts and thinks like an owner.

LOYALTY ABOVE ALL

A prerequisite for creating a culture of ownership, with no politics and no backroom gossip, is loyalty. I feel strongly about this value. Someone who makes a mistake with good intentions is always going to rank higher in my book than someone who makes fewer mistakes but isn't loyal to our team. As the company grows, I strive to ensure that the spirit of constructive communication will prevail.

The rule of thumb here is, say whatever you need to say in front of the people affected. We don't talk behind a person's back. If something needs to be said, then the person affected should have the right to hear constructive criticism that will help that person grow. If it does not have the potential to help someone, it probably does not need to be said in the first place.

This is one of the hardest things for managers and human beings to do. Nice people are normally uncomfortable having to critique others. But shrinking from the task of providing candid feedback ends up hurting the team more. I ask my managers to learn this delicate skill in order to provide their respective team members with the chance to change course when necessary and always improve.

Loyalty and ethical conduct make me want to reciprocate and be loyal in return. More than a year before Starbucks decided to part ways with us, they had shared the outline of their strategic direction. Around the same time, we were seriously evaluating taking KIND public. We were growing at a rate more typical of the tech sector, close to doubling revenues every year. Health and wellness was the fastest-growing segment within the trillion-plus-dollar food-and-beverage space. Many banks wooed us to do a public offering.

I worried theoretically about the ramifications for KIND stock if Starbucks removed our products from their stores soon after KIND went public. While I was deliberating, I emailed Howard Schultz and requested a time to talk. I was alone with my twin boys Andy and Jonah when Howard called, but did not want to burden him by telling him I was babysitting. While the boys played quietly in the background, I rushed to walk him through all the reasons why we were adding value to the Starbucks relationship and why they should stick with us. Besides my anxiety about the business matter, I was nervous that Andy and Jonah, who were just eighteen months at the time, would start going wild, so I was talking nonstop and at a mile a minute (and if it is hard to understand me with my accent normally, I can only imagine what I sounded like). Howard finally interrupted me.

"Daniel, stop," he said. "Listen to me. We're not going to do anything to harm your plans. We're going to continue carrying your products for now. You understand our strategic direction. At some point in the future, we may stop carrying your products, but it will not happen now, and we will not interfere with your decision to go public." The elegance with which Howard spoke to me was remarkable. Someone else could have tried to use this leverage to extract concessions from us. Howard was way above that.

I admired the way that Howard took the high road in this

situation, and I bore it in mind fifteen months later, when, in the fall of 2013, Starbucks replaced our bars with fruit and nut bars made by a brand they owned. We debated whether KIND should fight back. After all, it was quite intimidating for one of the best retailers in the world to be entering our space. We explored dozens of options to counteract them. But we decided to be grateful for the opportunity they had given us to do business with them in the first place and maintain a cordial and respectful relationship.

The media was interested in the story and reached out to find out what had happened. I felt a duty to be loyal to Starbucks while at the same time I had an obligation to manage this loss. I got this balance right with most of the media coverage. In an article about Starbucks removing outside food brands in favor of brands that it owned, *The Wall Street Journal* quoted me as thanking Starbucks: "[KIND] appreciates the opportunity Starbucks gave it and respects the company's strategy." In a CNBC interview, I conveyed how highly we thought of Starbucks. But in one magazine article, one of my answers came off as insufficiently appreciative of the enormous value that Starbucks brought to us.

I felt bad that I let Howard down. I had promised myself that I would never forget the considerate way in which he had handled his relationship with us. I sent Howard a handwritten letter apologizing for this incident and expressing my hope that we could maintain our personal relationship. I also reaffirmed my conviction that KIND would be a great strategic partner to Starbucks, and reiterated that our doors would always remain open.

SUSTAINING EXPANSION: TO SELL OR NOT TO SELL

After thoroughly researching the issue and talking to several bankers, equity analysts, and fellow entrepreneurs, I opted against pursuing an IPO for KIND for several reasons. First, we were operating well without the need for cash from the public market. Second, I didn't want to start getting distracted planning quarter by quarter, obsessing about the stock price (and having my team obsess about stock volatility), managing to Wall Street's expectations, or going on road shows to brief equity research analysts and funds. Third, I felt it would be impossible to control our stock price because the health and wellness field in which we compete is currently so hot. Our shares would invariably skyrocket beyond any sensible or sustainable number.

If you have a short-term horizon, exorbitant trading multiples may sound appealing to take advantage of that euphoria. For me, the thought that someone might use his or her pension to buy our stock at $100 and then potentially, after any hiccup, lose their money when the stock hit $50, was discomfiting. I also learned that public companies tend to be magnets for plaintiffs' lawyers who would sue right before the IPO and hold the companies hostage to earn a payoff.

Of course, had we gone public, we might have been able to turn our stock into a currency for acquisitions. In our case, perhaps because of lack of vision on my part, I did not and still have not identified any company that I want to acquire. I would rather we do things ourselves.

When you go public, you get more media attention, because

everything you do or say matters to the markets. That was an attractive feature of going public—it would give us a bully pulpit to share KIND's way of business. But again, where we stand today, we felt we could convey our story without having to deal with all the headaches of going public.

The last benefit that did weigh heavily on me was that going public would have provided our team with a liquidity mechanism. Even if I did not want to sell my stake, they might want to buy a home or a car, and holding an illiquid stake in a private company did not help them meet those goals or make those purchases. I was afraid, though, that if the market got out of control, we would issue stock options to new team members that could later turn out to be underwater and worthless. That could be demotivating to them. I didn't want the value of my team's stock to be at the mercy of the public market.

Instead we have found other ways to create liquidity for our team. We took on a small amount of debt to pay a dividend to all. (My definition of a small, manageable, and safe debt level is less than two times your earnings.) We created a loan program to help team members exercise their stock options. We do our best to pay out generous bonuses. Eventually, we even created a tender offer program where, under certain conditions, the company bought back team members' stock at attractive appreciations over their original grant price.

Friends have asked me why I don't sell while the selling is good, in case the company later falters or implodes. This is part of a fundamental conversation about who we are as a company and what I want my role to be as the founder. From my vantage point at the center of this company, KIND is a sustainable business and can bloom for decades longer. I think we have a resilient platform for enormous growth and change, and I don't see it stopping. I think this is just the beginning. We've built KIND by avoiding fads and thinking about the long term. Most important, we are having so much fun reinventing rules and growing while making this world a little kinder, and I don't want to compromise that mission.

I shared earlier that, years ago, when I was thinking of selling the company in favor of focusing full-time on my work for peace in the Middle East, board member Jim Hornthal told me, "Daniel, you can have far more impact on society guiding KIND than with pure philanthropy alone."

"But, Jim," I replied, "how can I properly focus on the philanthropic work I want to do if I'm also running KIND?"

"You keep talking about the AND philosophy. Why don't you recognize that you can continue guiding KIND *and* advance your work with OneVoice?" said Jim. "In fact, KIND will help you open doors that being the head of a foundation will not. It gives you credibility and a platform for enormous change."

Over the years, I've come to appreciate Jim's advice. I still feel torn at times that I don't have enough time to pursue some of the additional public good ideas I have. At the same time, I have a seat at the table at events I wouldn't have been able to access if not for KIND's success. I understand now that if exercised wisely, that seat can also help me do some good. Most important, as we continue to fine-tune our social impact model with the KIND Movement, the potential for building bridges is exponentially increased.

As I have said, my goal is not just to make KIND products the most trusted products in health and wellness. It's also about turning KIND from a company into a movement and a state of mind. Ideas like the KIND exchange, #kindawesome cards, and KIND Causes allow me to impact more people in dire need, and to help reinvent the way people see companies.

ENDURING PARTNERSHIPS WITH LONG-TERM GOALS

Even though I decided not to go public or to sell the company, in late 2013 I did need to come up with a way to create liquidity for my private equity investors, VMG. KIND would not have achieved all it has without VMG's mentorship and partnership. We had originally agreed with them on a timeline of five years until they would exit and get a return for their fund's investors. In the summer of 2013, I started exploring how to finance this.

In the end, we took on a lot of debt to buy out VMG. It was extraordinarily expensive and to some degree painful to have that debt on our books. But because we had grown so much and they were tenacious negotiators, they received an exceptional return on their investment. I didn't want to carry this much debt, so I also started carefully vetting prospective equity investors equipped with tools to help take KIND to the next level and ended up partnering with two solid investors that I sensed are long-term-oriented.

Most investors are transaction-oriented and most entrepreneurs are relationship-oriented. Investors flit like bees from deal to deal and just want to maximize their returns on each, without caring whether they revisit those flowers again. Entrepreneurs are the flowers turning the sun's energy into honey day in and day out. They are often at a disadvantage, because investors are experts in deal-making. Entrepreneurs make widgets; investors' widgets are the deals themselves. For me, it was important to choose investor bees that stuck to their flower beds.

STRONG & KIND

As we were working out the details of taking on a new equity investor, we were also working on an exciting new product line: savory bars. As of the close of 2013, all successful nutritional and granola bars had one thing in common: They were sweet. For years, I had thought that there should be a huge opportunity in the market for a savory bar. Millions of people buy savory snacks like potato chips, corn chips, and pretzels with no nutritional density, just empty calories. Why couldn't KIND bring a savory bar to life?

And yet we knew that several respectable companies with distinguished product-development records had tried and failed on this front. Did it mean consumers just didn't care for such product and we'd be doomed to fail if we tried? Initially we drew the conclusion that consumers associated nutritional bars with sweet flavors, and that they would be turned off by savory versions.

Then we realized that our use of nutritionally rich almonds as a prime ingredient gave us an advantage others might not have enjoyed before. Consumers are used to eating savory trail mixes and mixed nuts with savory flavors, so we reasoned that a savory KIND bar might be more easily embraced by the consumer.

This puzzle kept us entertained for years. We worked really hard on the recipes. Our team worked hundreds of hours perfecting and balancing the flavors until we felt confident KIND would deliver on this opportunity. Eventually we cracked the code. We designed a bar that we believe appeals to everyone but in particular would be attractive to men—in flavors like jalapeño and Thai sweet chili. The bars tasted so good (and felt so wholesome) that samples went flying out of the office, and we found ourselves craving them; we knew we were on to something.

We were also excited about the fact that these savory bars would not be a substitute for the original KIND bars. They would be complementary. Sometimes we crave something sweet—like a KIND Fruit & Nut bar; sometimes we crave something savory—like these new bars; and sometimes in between—like a KIND Nuts & Spices bar.

Still, the experience was unfamiliar for consumers, so the branding and positioning of the line would need to be executed flawlessly if we were to have a fighting chance of making this a successful launch.

Initially we were thinking of the brand name KIND Bold, but it sounded too generic. A lot of brands use "Bold" as a descriptor. Among the hundreds of brand names we considered, we mulled over "Strong" because in addition to the bold flavors, the bar contained ten grams of protein. But "Strong" felt too aggressive and militaristic. We were trying to appeal to millennial males, but didn't want to alienate female consumers. We were stuck. Weeks went by and we couldn't unlock the ideal brand name.

Then one night in late June 2013, I found myself having dinner with a group that included Jennifer and Peter Buffett, who shared that some of their charitable work centered on redefining what it meant to "be a man" in America. "Instead of the stereotype that you need to be hard and tough, we are encouraging a conversation to show that being nice is not incompatible with being masculine," Jennifer said. "It's strong to be kind." It was a lightning bolt for me.

Her comment brought back to me an idea I had in the early nineties to start an apparel company called PeaceWear. I wanted to build a marketing campaign around the slogan "It's Cool to be Kind." I imagined the tough guys of that era—Sylvester Stallone, Al Pacino, and Robert De Niro—participating in hip videos that would show them looking really rough, as if they were about to pounce on someone, only to surprise the viewer as they performed a soft, kind act. They would then gruffly look over at the camera and say, "It's cool to be kind."

Not to worry, I didn't determine to revive that campaign idea. But that stream of consciousness helped me finally unlock the value proposition for the new line of KIND bars. We needed to celebrate the juxtapositions. We needed to invoke the AND philosophy. We literally incorporated an ampersand—the universal symbol of AND—to craft our new brand: Strong & KIND, showing that you can be both things at once.

Kindness and strength are not normally thought of as going hand in hand. But as the Buffetts pointed out, in fact it often takes strength to be kind when it most matters—when someone is being bullied, or when it may be embarrassing to stand up for those who are down. Strong & KIND evokes the courage to act with humanity when others may not.

The name also evokes the strength derived from kind ingredients, including ten grams of all-natural protein (strength) from unprocessed almonds, seeds, and legumes (kind ingredients), not from processed soy or whey or from any artificial compounds. In addition, the name suggests the experience of strong, bold flavors in a nutritional bar that is also kind to your taste buds.

It seems deceptively simple now but it took us months to figure this out. When dealing with line extensions, traditional branding relies on hierarchical relations: a parent brand and a sub-brand underneath it. Nabisco's Ritz crackers is an example: that legendary triangle adorns and validates its sub-brands. New lines under a parent brand tend to rely on two formats: New line by Parent brand; or Parent brand's New line. In our case, we had considered "KIND's Strong Bars" or "Strong, by KIND." Instead, we literally decided to think with AND, and created a non-hierarchical relationship among equals—Strong & KIND—which allowed us to spotlight the interesting juxtaposition of values, and to celebrate the AND philosophy.

Strong & KIND bars launched in March 2014 and received an enthusiastic reception. To promote the new line, we have begun identifying "ordinary citizens" as well as celebrities and sports figures who we feel embody the brand's twin ideals: showing strength of character *and* a kind soul.

THE COMEBACK

As we worked on Strong & KIND, Starbucks was still on my mind. I had been brainstorming for months about ways to attain Starbucks' objectives and ours. Independent of the business opportunity, I had a desire to reestablish my personal relationship with Howard Schultz, who, more than a great CEO, I see as an exemplary leader. I called him to catch up personally, and after a personal update, even though I wasn't actually planning on pitching anything to him that day, the conversation turned to whether we could find a way to rekindle our business relationship. I shared some ideas that Howard found intriguing. He agreed to explore them. The next eight months were a roller coaster of good-faith efforts by both teams to try to make things work. It was not an easy journey. Starbucks had a number of strategic constraints that precluded some of our ideas. We were also concerned about the risks involved in working with a major retailer that, after all, was also a competitor at the time. It was not a process for the faint of heart.

The entire effort tested every one of our core values: Could we *think with AND* and make sure we would satisfy all of Starbucks's needs while also *being true to our brand*? We created exciting new flavors that were designed with Starbucks in mind: a Salted Caramel Dark Chocolate Nut bar, and an Almond Coconut Cashew Chai that I consider masterpieces from our new product development team. Could we align our *purposes* to make the partnership even more meaningful? Starbucks aficionados often treat strangers behind them in line with a free Frappuccino. We co-created a promotion that celebrated our shared values: free KIND bars to commend and inspire KIND acts by Starbucks consumers.

Certainly we needed to demonstrate *grit* and perseverance, as on many occasions the effort looked like it was going to unravel, considering the complexity of the process and the many obstacles both companies needed to overcome to rekindle our partnership. In that environment, *keeping things simple* and being straightforward and *transparent* helped us develop the relationship of *trust* that helped both teams get through difficult moments.

I developed a deep relationship of *empathy* with their team, and even when they reached decisions that were adverse to ours, I did my best to put myself in their shoes and understand their decisions. *Trust* was also integral when we designed a communications strategy that would be consistent with all of Starbucks' diverse strategic objectives.

In the fall of 2014, Starbucks brought back KIND products into its stores.

Building a business or a social enterprise is not easy. Building a business *and* a social enterprise is even less so. The more ambitious the goal, the more likely it will encounter false starts along the journey. The Starbucks experience is one example of what it takes to get there. Starbucks, like every other customer, can always decide to change its strategic priorities. We can never take them—or any of our other customers—for granted. It is thus all the more essential that we approach every relationship with the sense that it means the world to us. And when things do falter, it is essential that we not lose our tenacity. Rather, that is the time to invoke our *originality* and sheer gumption—to *own* the challenge and think boundlessly—to get them back. How we behave in those instances, how we confront obstacles, how we handle ourselves in every single interaction, with every single human being we come in contact with, defines who we are and who we will become.

OUT INTO THE WORLD

By the time this book went to print, we had sold over a billion KIND bars. The time had come for us to start expanding internationally. In the fall of 2014, we started defining a strategy for our international growth: which countries we would penetrate first, whether we would go it alone, hire a distributor, or enter into joint ventures.

International expansion intimidates me a bit. At other growth points along the way, I have benefited from my prior failures to draw the right lessons on what not to do. But we were entering new frontiers with no earlier experiences or failures to draw lessons from. As I find myself facing new challenges, I embrace the excitement of finding new team members who can teach us how to fulfill our values and mission in their respective areas of expertise, and inviting them to be co-owners and partners who help us take KIND to the next level. I hope the tenets that KIND adheres to will engrain in all of us certain standards that lift us up in our personal lives and behavior—values that will make all the difference in helping us get more enjoyment out of life and achieving more every day.

What is the next level? As I've said before, my goal is to make KIND synonymous not only with a great product, a healthful brand, and a reliable company that our consumers trust and love, but also a state of mind that informs our community. We want KIND to become a movement that millions of our community members feel ownership of. We want KIND to touch their lives in authentic ways that inspire them to join us on our journey of making this world a little bit kinder and more delicious, every day and every moment. And when someone says, "Do the . . .", we hope people will complete the sentence in their mind, "KIND Thing!" and the thought will evoke our vision and imbue these words with meaning. Will you sign on?

CHAPTER 11

MADE TO MATTER

Creating Value from Creativity and Values

Competition is increasingly fierce in the current retail and consumer goods arena. As markets become more efficient, rival manufacturers arduously try to outmaneuver one another for consumers' loyalty. Tensions between manufacturers and retailers are also on the rise, as stores launch their own brands and manufacturers start selling online directly to consumers. Surviving requires impeccable aptitude and Kissinger-like diplomacy. But thriving—rather than merely surviving—calls for more than that. It calls for thinking with AND and questioning the very essence of a business dynamic or relationship.

A phenomenal example of this is the Made to Matter alliance that Target, the iconic retailer with close to 2,000 stores in North America, has forged with socially responsible brand leaders in the health and wellness space. KIND was not an original member of the Made to Matter initiative (we got involved in mid-2014), but as I learned about it, I was struck by the parallels between the tenets I have shared in this book and the values that have enabled Made to Matter to work and thrive, unleashing enormous value for Target, participating companies, consumers, and their communities.

Target has a rich history of partnering with up-and-coming entrepreneurs to build exclusive design-driven brands. Mike Hockenberry, vice president for brand development at Target, has seen the value of this approach, which led him to collaborate with a like-minded thought partner from Method, an important Target vendor, to create what would become known as Made to Matter (MtM).

Eric Ryan, cofounder of Method, maker of biodegradable nontoxic household cleaning and personal care supplies, was in a pub having drinks with Lisa Roath, his senior buyer at Target. He commented on how many of the founders in the natural products community knew each other, were "similarly wired," and frequently exchanged ideas. "Many of our companies have created similar cultures with a deeper purpose beyond profit," he explained. "We are all motivated by using business as an agent of change to champion environmental or human health."

"Sounds like the Nat Pac," she joked, with a fun play on the Rat Pack.

But the joke sparked an idea: Lisa and Eric imagined hosting a Nat Pac retreat to build a collective picture of where the natural products category is headed. "If Target could partner with us," Eric reasoned, "we could further accelerate the growth of natural products penetration, which would benefit all of our businesses."

When Lisa and Eric shared the idea with Mike Hockenberry,

Mike also saw the potential. "While guests [this is how Target refers to their shoppers] love these brands and [these health and wellness companies] were all growing in double digits, it was still a real challenge to achieve the scale needed to really move the industry the way large consumer packaged goods firms could," he explained. "But if we combined the equities and passionate consumer followings of these brands with the financial resources of Target, the sky would be the limit."

So, in December 2013, Mike and Lisa invited the founders and CEOs of thirteen companies to meet at Cavallo Point Lodge for a retreat (the group of 2014 brands later grew to sixteen, and KIND was not part of this initial gathering, so all of these impressions stem from interviews with those who were). The participants did not know what would come out of the gathering, which took place at the foot of the Golden Gate Bridge by San Francisco Bay on an expansive green space with restored historic buildings. It was cold and windy outside. Inside, the atmosphere was much harder to describe.

Competitors eyed one another carefully. John Replogle, CEO of Seventh Generation, the largest producer of environmentally safe household products, and a direct competitor of Method, was among the guests. "As I approached the meeting," John reflected, "my mind started to race and a creeping paranoia entered my head as I pondered the fact that Eric was the mastermind behind this effort. Zero-sum mindset thoughts floated around."

But the power and potential of this gathering reigned supreme. "[Any negative] thoughts were immediately erased as I entered the room," said John Replogle. "There was palpable energy and camaraderie as we gathered, hugged, greeted, and reconnected." It didn't hurt that John had ample experience forging collaborative alliances in his past job at Burt's Bees, where competitors had defined natural product standards together.

Eric approached John with an extended hand and said, "Welcome to Nat Pac."

John embraced the outstretched hand and gave Eric a warm pat on the back.

"It was time to get to work together, as collaborators in conjunction with Target, to build a richer future for the consumer," John recounts.

"The spirit was incredibly collaborative, transparent, and open," said Eric. "We recognized that a rising tide raises all boats and that the collective opportunity was not to swap market share from each other, but accelerate growth, innovation, and making better choices accessible to the consumer."

It all sounds so logical in hindsight, but we need to appreciate that all of this involved *questioning ingrained assumptions,* particularly those fortified by the daily grind of competition. The biggest assumption to be shattered was that to succeed, a rival needs to suffer. Thinking with AND, those gathered were able to brainstorm how to create more value for all stakeholders, to make the pie bigger rather than to just divide the pie. Several ideas emerged at the retreat but the strongest was to create some form of marketing event that could drive growth across the diverse categories and leverage Target as a national platform.

LEADERSHIP MEANS TRUST
AND SHATTERING CONVENTIONS

The next challenge was to sell the leadership at Target on the plan. This, too, was tackled in an unorthodox manner. Ordinarily, this would be an internal pitch by a Target executive to Jeff Jones, executive vice president and chief marketing officer at Target. But Eric and John offered to join Mike Hockenberry on the presentation and "show Jeff the passion [they had] for the program." Mike knew it was unprecedented, but he understood that he'd get one shot at presenting the program and related funding request, and would get a yes or no answer.

"Trust us," Eric persisted. "There's a solid business case here, but it doesn't capture the all-in devotion of the leaders of these iconic natural brands."

Mike made the unconventional decision to let go and allow his partners not only to be involved, but to lead. In the meeting, Eric focused on the passion of the vendors and their willingness to invest in exclusive innovation, while Mike discussed the overall impact for Target and its guests. He presented a strong business case based on how these brands were outperforming the market, and emphasized the importance of collaboration for innovation. "We have assembled the most successful innovators and entrepreneurs in the industry, and they've designed an unparalleled alliance focused on the greater good." They proposed a marketing program in the spirit of "design for all," where social entrepreneurs were treated as the "designers" and creators.

After only thirteen minutes, Jeff said, "I love it. This is what a modern take on a design partnership looks like. Target is all in."

This program also aligned with Target's need to further differentiate its essentials offerings, which have become an increasingly large and important component of the business, from those of its competitors. While Target had a formula dialed in for delivering on both the "expect more" and "pay less" side of the Target brand promise in apparel and home, essentials were imbalanced and missing some of the special sauce that makes the Target shopping experience so unique. Made to Matter would enable them to spotlight Target's emerging focus on wellness as a key point of difference.

Made to Matter was conceived on four key principles, "the four legs of the table," as Hockenberry calls them: Health and Wellness—products that help guests along the journey toward living healthful, happier lives; Exclusive Innovation—groundbreaking new products that guests can find only at Target; Social Responsibility—all participating companies share the mission to strive to make our world better; and Collaboration—individual agendas are left at the door to focus on a shared vision: healthier guests and healthier communities.

While Mike Hockenberry championed the program and its implementation within the merchandising team at Target, Carolyn Sakstrup was helping get MtM off the ground on the marketing front. One problem: 2014 was already upon them. How were they going to fit MtM into their 2014 marketing plans, which were designed and cemented months in advance? She sat down to meet with some of the participants and was struck by the uniqueness of the opportunity. "These competitors were sitting in a room together practically arm in arm. They barely had to open their mouths for me to sense that this was the coolest thing I would have the chance to be a part of in my time at Target." It wasn't typical for Target to invest its own marketing dollars to support campaigns that were specific to vendor brands. Normally it is the reverse: As is the case with many large retailers, national brands invest their dollars to be featured in Target campaigns. "This was going to have to be a place where we would make an exception," Carolyn thought. "The investment on their side, far more valuable, frankly, than pure marketing funds, was breakthrough collaboration and innovation that would deliver truly differentiated access to some of the best new products in the natural space, only at Target."

AN ENVIRONMENT FOR THINKING BOUNDLESSLY

One of the most exceptional aspects of MtM is how this deep partnership enables the manufacturer and retailer to cooperate on innovation. A key reason the program really works is that Target provides a lower-risk platform through which entrepreneurs can introduce new products. "Target's ability to create scale and make options accessible to millions of guests, combined with the MtM brands' ability to innovate, is a magical combination," says Hockenberry.

For example, early in 2014, Ido Leffler, founder of Yes To, and a MtM partner, asked Hockenberry, "Mike, within your business what's a category that is in dire need of disruption?"

Out of the lines he was responsible for at the time, Mike replied, "Paper tableware and cutlery. The designs could be so much more exciting, fun, and trend forward!" Leffler had been exploring an effort to help feed hungry children. By November 2014, Target and Leffler launched Cheeky, a design-driven line of paper tableware where they pledge that every purchase also provides a meal for someone who is hungry. Hockenberry describes this as a "cycle of innovation." "Our trust and partnership removes risks and obstacles and makes us faster, and we fill the pipeline with brands like Cheeky, which are prime candidates for MtM in the future."

Creative juices also flow out of the competitive dynamic of the program. According to Eric Ryan, "The idea was that the spirit of competition would push everyone harder, benefiting all participating vendors and Target. After all, Coke wouldn't be where it is today without Pepsi." The first year, all participants were invited to pitch their exclusive innovation in a *Shark Tank*–style setting. Ryan had recommended this dramatic backdrop because he "wanted to give it the sense of an audition, where the best product concept received the highest support."

Innovation truly is at the center of MtM, and innovation increasingly inspires society. Eric Ryan feels creative thinking is the fundamental passion of millennials in particular. "These days, it's more aspirational to be an inventor or start a business," he shares. "Millennials' life-hacking mentality means that they embrace emergent ideas that improve upon the status quo. They are a generation of cultural mix masters who have been modifying music, images, and even their own identities all their lives." My sense is that millennials will also be best positioned to question the prevailing assumption that business and social objectives have to be pursued separately.

OVERCOMING CHALLENGES
THROUGH GRIT AND PURPOSE

As the MtM alliance shifted to execution mode, an understanding of what a big undertaking it would be became undeniably clear. Traditionally, when Target creates design differentiation programs, marketing and internal product development work with a designer to create a range of products. Executing this program across sixteen vendors and multiple categories had never been done before and would require a new level of collaboration between marketing, merchandising, and the vendor partners.

As with anything this big, there were many challenges and obstacles to getting it off the ground.

The merchandising team needed to make a very significant investment of shelf space and premier promotional locations in store and on Target.com, and the program was competing with other major priorities such as critically important Back to School and Back to College seasonal programs. Moreover, this had to be coordinated across multiple business leaders within Target, each with his or her own unique priorities. In many cases, looking in isolation at the short-term economic value of the MtM assets being requested from these individuals, the correct decision would have been to allocate resources to other business priorities.

Given the size of the investment, there needed to be marketing value in the program not only to drive Target's natural and organic products business for a few months, but for the Target brand as a whole. "We were asking for an internal investment equivalent to one of our 'designer' programs," recalls Hockenberry. "In addition to driving sales and traffic, these programs advance Target's brand image and historically are conducted within the apparel and home businesses, not the essentials businesses such as food, health care, or household cleaning. This would be one of Target's big bets for the fall of 2014."

To make the business case, the MtM team devised a "tip of the spear" program and argument for supporting Target's strategic growth platform of health and wellness, carefully balancing the short-term economic benefits with long-term strategic value. They argued that the unprecedented collaboration would result in media buzz. They explained that Target's reputation as a health and wellness destination would be enhanced. And they emphasized that game-changing innovations would help drive new guests to Target. In short, that the whole would be greater than the sum of its parts.

The boldness of the request, and the stark contrast between the immediate resources being solicited for a risky proposition at the expense of "sure bets" with a precedent, made some question "if the juice was worth the squeeze." One of the merchandising teams reviewed their Back to School program and proposed to reallocate some of their in-store promotional locations away from MtM and over to more traditional Back to School food brands and products. At some point, the entire program almost unraveled as healthy skepticism drove some critical Target team members to question the viability of the exercise. What made this crisis particularly hard to resolve was the scope of the MtM program and the number of people involved.

And those executives at Target who had staked their reputations on getting MtM off the ground also had to bear the risk that smaller suppliers, who were not as sophisticated logistically as the multinational conglomerates, might fail to deliver. Target was dedicating national marketing support for these products so it was vital that the products would hit the shelves on time. Sixteen small vendors with limited supply-chain capabilities were now all launching innovations simultaneously, some into new categories.

As one of the executive sponsors, Mike Hockenberry was under a lot of pressure. He was worried that these setbacks were the first dominoes that could lead to the whole thing falling down. Feeling very discouraged one day, he called some of the vendor partners to check in. "They reminded me what we were really doing here," he recalls. "I remember talking to Rich [Richelieu Dennis, founder of SheaMoisture], who was telling me about how he was trying to help fight Ebola in Africa. Rich was dealing with enormous challenges to create an economic infrastructure for a village in Sierra Leone so they could purchase finished goods and create more value in Africa than if they just bought the natural resources. When I asked about some of the challenges Rich was facing, he replied calmly, 'Sure, it's a little overwhelming, but there is no choice, and we can make a difference, and if we don't, who will?' Suddenly my challenges seemed so insignificant." I understood perfectly how Mike felt. Issues like these—whether dealing with Ebola or poverty or internecine conflict—very quickly put our challenges into perspective.

The sincerity of purpose of the participants gave Mike the grit and the gumption to stay focused on the Made to Matter mission. "Neil [Grimmer, cofounder and CEO of Plum Organics] had just calculated they were going to be able to donate an additional 100,000 smoothie pouches to feed undernourished children in the United States. John from Seventh Generation was devising a plan to win with natural diapers and leave a little less waste for our grandkids in a category driven by hundreds of millions of dollars in marketing." Mike said, "I was able to take advantage of the passion of the founders to help keep me motivated and my spirits up when things were tough."

If you ever meet Mike Hockenberry, you will not mistake him for a peace-and-love pacifist. He is a serious businessman with a cultlike devotion to the Target consumer. That is why I found his self-confessed transformation after being exposed to the power of social entrepreneurship so interesting. He once told me, "Made to Matter has changed my whole outlook on business. If you would have asked me three to four years ago, I would have said it all boils down to economics and I'm working for the money, to survive. Made to Matter opened my eyes to something so different, so authentic, so much more. I now see I have the ability and the responsibility to do my little part to change the world, too, and I always knew Target did, but I see now so clearly how. All the typical daily challenges at a large corporation, which used to be quite discouraging, now are so insignificant to me. What gets me out of bed is what I can do that will really matter."

COLLABORATION ROOTED IN
TRANSPARENCY, EMPATHY, AND TRUST

Made to Matter would have been impossible without a bedrock of trust. On a cold night in January of 2014, shortly after the Cavallo Point retreat, the principals gathered to share their innovations with the group, which included several of their foremost competitors.

The evening began with some introductions. John Replogle went first: "I'm John, and I'm the CEO for Seventh Generation. I make soap." Eric Ryan followed: "I'm Eric, cofounder of Method. I make soap that's better than his soap," he said teasingly as he pointed to John. Mike Hockenberry went next: "I'm Mike from Target. I'm the executive sponsor for Nat Pac. I use his soap." He pointed to Rich Dennis from SheaMoisture. When it was Rich's turn, he said "I'm Rich, with Sundial Brands. We make SheaMoisture. I don't need to brag about my soap because it's Mike's favorite." Competition was the eight-hundred-pound gorilla in the room. The group began to break down barriers by hitting them head-on through humor.

At one moment, Neil Grimmer from Plum Organics volunteered to hold a board showing the innovation that was being presented by Paul Lindley, CEO and founder of Ella's Kitchen, a direct competitor. As Paul described it, "I was a little apprehensive as I felt the Ella's innovation was pretty groundbreaking, and I thought I trusted Neil, but didn't know." Paul asked Neil to give a scout's pledge, and they both committed playfully but tensely to "do [their] own thing" and develop their own great innovations.

Paul approached Mike afterward and asked what controls were in place to prevent others from misappropriating ideas. Mike looked him in the eyes and just shared frankly, "None. It's all about mutual trust." He did reassure Paul that he knew Neil personally and knew him to be a man of integrity. "It was a defining evening in my relationship with Neil and in deepening my belief that collaboration and competition can and should coexist for the greater good," Paul shared.

The most surprising thing is that it was only the beginning. From then on, Neil and Paul have become great friends, even enjoying some vacation time together with their families. Prior to that evening, Neil recalls having bumped into Paul at trade shows and "always felt like [we were] two animals sizing one another up. During those brief run-ins, I think we were both slightly suspicious and somewhat guarded, but always had a healthy amount of intrigue and respect for each other." But everyone's frame of mind shifted when Hockenberry encouraged them to think differently: "This is going to be unlike any meeting you have had before. We are going to focus on the future of the Target guest who's seeking out better options. We are looking for your thought leadership and all of us, whether friends, competitors, or both, must choose collaboration for us to accomplish these lofty goals." Neil concluded that "as simple as that sounds, it's a radical idea in the American business landscape. Many will tell you it's crazy. I found it refreshing. Little did I know at the time, but it was an idea that also resonated heavily with Paul, and it was the beginning of a deep friendship."

"I grew up in Africa," Paul told Neil once, "and there is a fantastic African proverb that says, 'If you want to go fast, go alone. If you want to go far, go together.'"

Trust and transparency were essential not just between competitors, but also between the manufacturers and their host retailer, Target. Typically, vendors are presented with clear and detailed parameters and guidelines of a program or investment that Target wants them to make. Vendors get to propose what they have, and the buyer then decides whether to proceed or to decline the proposal. Hockenberry changed the rules because he realized that trust was paramount for a successful business relationship, and that transparency and candor were the basis for that trust. "This will be unlike any interaction you've had with Target and likely any retailer before," he said. "Target doesn't have the answers. This is *our* program, not Target's, not any one vendor partner's, but ours collectively. Target's goal is to support your mission." This vulnerability made Mike uncomfortable: What if the group crossed boundaries or went after sacred cows? What if the ideas didn't create a commercially viable program? But he knew he needed to establish that vulnerability and step back to give his partners the room to lead. "The opportunity is not for you to take share from one another but to grow the pie by making America happier and healthier." The tension in the room began to dissipate as everyone realized the common thread that brought them together, and how collaboration—rooted in trust, transparency, and empathy—could accelerate everyone's mission.

OWNERSHIP AND RESOURCEFULNESS

The principals in Made to Matter feel total ownership over the alliance. This did not happen by chance. It was a goal of those who conceived the program, and it may be among the most important factors in Made to Matter's success.

KIND was not a part of this program in its inaugural year, but we were invited to join in 2014, and Target asked that I personally be in on the MtM discussions. As I shared earlier in the book, I now seldom participate in any sales calls. The relationships with our retail partners are managed by Chuck Engle, our formidable senior vice president of sales, and by John Leahy, our president and my mentor and partner in crime. I had never been to Minneapolis, let alone understood Target. Erin Riley, a director of sales on our team, managed Target beautifully. But here was Mike Hockenberry insisting that I had to show up if we wanted a shot at being a part of this program.

"It is critical that we have the founders/CEOs of the vendor partners engaged in the program because they drive the mission-oriented culture for their brands," Mike later acknowledged. In addition, at least at KIND, innovation is something I am deeply involved in, and for Target it was very important that the founders or CEOs be committed to innovating with them in exchange for all the investments that Target would make in their brands and new products.

"When selecting brands for the program," Mike also said, "we're thinking about the brand and its mission, whether the products help people live happier and healthier lives, *and* the fit and willingness of the founder to engage as we need them to."

Once I showed up, I understood how smart this whole strategy was. First, I developed personal relationships with the Target principals and saw their authentic passion for KIND. John Leahy, Chuck, and Erin had all shared how devoted our new partners at Target were, but I only fully appreciated it once I saw it with my own eyes. It was also fun to experience Target's culture and see the energy and innovation oozing out of the corridors and elevators in their headquarters.

No less important, Mike gently pressed for me to join a gathering with the other principals, and during that gathering, the Target team ensured the process involved the vendor partners in key decisions and presentations. Sometimes you have to let go of the reins and let your team members or partners drive in order to get the most out of them. In MtM's case, a committee of five of the vendor partners serves on an advisory board. They get input from other vendors, which they feed back to Target to help shape the program.

Even proposals are now pitched in partnership. The drama of the *Shark Tank*–like presentations had its strengths, but for 2015, pitching was done collaboratively to emphasize the shared ownership of MtM. Instead of having the vendors come in and pitch their programs to the buyers, the buyers and vendors worked together to co-own the program and then made the pitch to the MtM committee.

Vendor partners are now also helping to identify and bring on board other new brands. Justin Gold of Justin's is one example of a fantastic social entrepreneur who is connected to the program through Phil Anson, the founder of EVOL frozen foods.

STAYING GROUNDED AND
KEEPING THE BRAND PROMISE

The launch of Made to Matter coincided with an unexpectedly difficult period for Target. Criminals had broken into Target's databases and accessed shopper credit-card information. Criticism was widespread and hard feelings reigned at the time. Target's stock price was in a decline, as was consumer confidence. As Carolyn Sakstrup put it, "What was, 'Wow! That must be so great to work there! I LOVE Target!' was now 'Wow. That must be hard these days.'" It was a difficult environment for Target team members.

But in that environment, MtM resonated more than ever, not just for Target guests, but for the entire Target team. MtM helped focus attention on Target's core brand values. The fascinating and unusual collaboration generated interest from the media. The launch of the program helped Target shift the conversation toward what makes it special while earning a heavy dose of goodwill from consumers and media alike. The press was overwhelmingly positive, as was consumer sentiment. "Made to Matter is what made me excited to show up at work every day," said Sakstrup.

"No one's ego likes to hear [that you've let someone down]," Carolyn wrote on her blog. She concluded with great introspection and honesty:

> Trading ego for humility, though, [is] one of the
> more beautiful sentiments a relationship can know.

It is the bedrock of commitment, growth and progress. To those consumers who do love us, who do feel let down, but who are still pulling for us, I would tell you, as much as any large corporate entity is capable of doing so, Target loves you back.

Consider this latest collection a big hug.

And what a hug it was.

KIND Innovation Timeline

1994
PeaceWorks founded as a "not-only-for-profit" business

PEACEWORKS

2002
OneVoice founded

ONEVOICE

2004
KIND is conceived and launches KIND Fruit & Nut line of bars.

KIND FRUIT & NUT

2008
KIND PLUS is introduced as a line of all-natural whole nut & fruit bars with a natural boost

KIND PLUS

2009
First iteration of KINDED trackable cards launched

KIND You've been KINDED

2010
First iteration of Do the KIND Thing is launched where causes try to inspire the most kindness for $40K in grants

Do the KIND Thing

2011
KIND Healthy Grains Clusters is launched, marking KIND's first introduction into a new category

KIND HEALTHY GRAINS

2012
KIND Nuts & Spices is launched as line of bars made from whole nuts & spices with only 5g sugar (or less)—and nothing artificial

KIND NUTS & SPICES

2013
KIND Healthy Grains Bars are launched as first "chewy with a crunch" offering in the granola bar category
KIND Causes program is launched

KIND HEALTHY GRAINS

KIND causes

2014
STRONG & KIND is launched as first-ever savory offering in the healthy snack bar category

STRONG & KIND

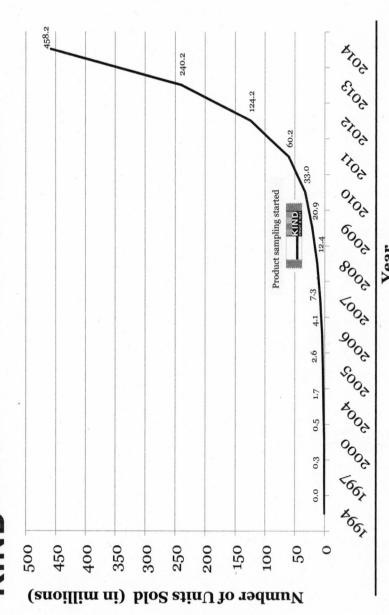

KIND Growth in Units Sold

Number of Units Sold (in millions)

500
450
400
350
300
250
200
150
100
50
0

458.2

240.2

124.2

60.2

Product sampling started

33.0

20.9

12.4

7.3

4.1

2.6

1.7

0.5

0.3

0.0

Year

1994 1997 2000 2004 2005 2006 2007 2008 2009 2010 2011 2012 2013 2014

Growth in Distribution

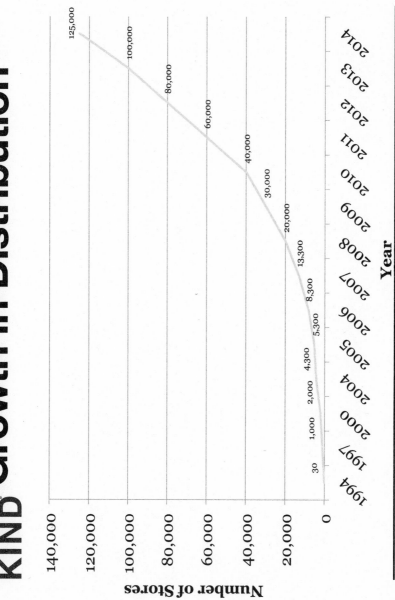

KIND Growth in Team

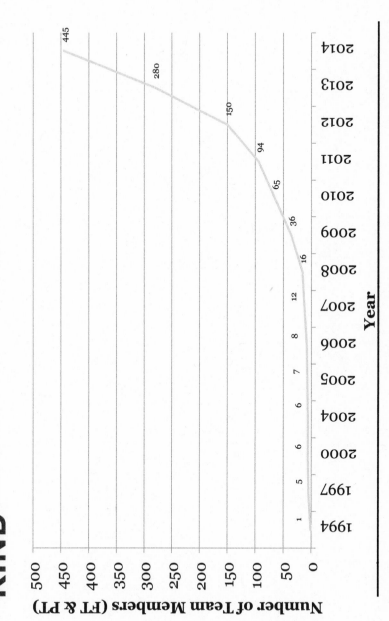

Number of Team Members (FT & PT)

Year

ACKNOWLEDGMENTS

Writing and editing *Do the KIND Thing* took a lot longer than I imagined. I am immensely thankful to my wife, Michelle, for being so infinitely patient and supportive, as always. I am so blessed for Michelle's love, for how she makes me laugh, and for how she keeps me grounded.

Natalie, Andy, Jonah, and Romy, I hope that a few years from now when you are reading books, the values in *Do the KIND Thing* will help you find passion and purpose in life. I hope you'll find the lessons in this book worth the many hours that I had to miss playing with you. I love being with you guys. Remember, my kids, the most important thing is for you *to be united*!

To my mom, Sonia Lubetzky, who keeps us together; to my dad, who lives inside us and whose life revolved around his children; and to my siblings Ileana, Tammy, and Sioma: I am the luckiest to have your unfailing love and support, and we are so blessed to have such a beautiful family.

Those who know me know that brevity is not my strong suit. And with that, I was fortunate to have a partner in Chana Schoenberger, who spent hundreds of hours with me compiling, writing, and organizing the many stories I wanted to share in these pages. Not only would this book have been impossible to write without her, but Chana also became a psychoanalyst, a teacher, and a friend along the way. Thank you for your partnership, Chana.

Thanks to Jennifer Joel for being such an extraordinary agent, thinker, and friend. Jennifer's intellect, judgment, and knowledge about publishing and writing awed me. Her great advice and the extra time she invested guiding me and helping edit the book really added immeasurable value.

Thanks also to my editor, Marnie Cochran, for her excellent editorial skills, and for her guidance, patience, and brilliant advice. I really appreciate the commitment and passion she showed toward our project. Thanks also to the entire Ballantine and Random House team. Beyond being so impressed with your dedication and professionalism, I really enjoyed working with all of you: Libby McGuire, Richard Callison, Ryan Doherty, Jennifer Tung, Quinne Rogers, Toby Ernst, Denise Cronin, Cindy Murray, Susan Corcoran, Lisa Barnes, and Melissa Milsten, whose equally brilliant sister, Sara, coincidentally worked with me at PeaceWorks in the mid-nineties. And thanks to Jennifer Rodriguez for leading the copyediting process, to Briony Everroad for copyediting with such attentiveness, and to Tom Pitoniak and Eva Young for proofreading the manuscript.

My chief of staff, Julianna Storch, my assistant, Rebecca

Halpern, and my director of communications when this project started and vice president of strategic development when it ended, Elle Lanning, were exceptionally supportive during the entire process. Together with our general counsel, Justin Mervis, they kept me out of trouble with all their wise advice. Thanks also to Joe Cohen, KIND's senior vice president of communications, for his input.

Particular thanks also to my dear friend, Joshua Ramo, who I look up to and admire, for taking time from his busy life, prolific writing, and strategic work to provide comments on my manuscript.

I am grateful to my cousin Serge Bluds, for helping me confirm certain facts about my dad's experiences during the Holocaust by drawing from his film archives.

A friend who kindly reviewed the first draft of my manuscript said it read like an Oscar acceptance speech because of all the people it named, and the acknowledgments and honors it provided at every turn of the page. Out of deference to the reader, and against my initial instinct, I edited out scores of instances where I had found a way to insert the names of team members, strategic partners, mentors, and friends in retail and elsewhere who contributed to PeaceWorks, KIND, OneVoice, and Maiyet, or to me. Rather than listing every colleague and team member here, I want to acknowledge and thank everyone who has at one point or another helped make a difference on this journey.

To my initial investors, my first team members and interns, and the first retailers, suppliers, distributors, brokers, and strategic advisers who believed in me and gave me a chance, I am most grateful to you. Without your pioneering support, neither

PeaceWorks nor KIND would have risen and succeeded. Also thanks to all donors, volunteers, activists, trustees, and advisers of the OneVoice Movement, for making a vision come true.

To all the advisers, board members, friends, investors, colleagues, natural foods community members, retail partners, and mentors who I've been blessed to work with and learn from, thank you.

The week I was writing these acknowledgments, my wife and I attended a dinner that David Bernstein, our intellectual property counsel, had invited us to. The waiter smiled at me and said, "Hi, Daniel." It was Dzavid Mollabeqiri, or Djavo as I used to call him, the superintendent at 245 East Eighty-fourth, who twenty-one years ago had helped me carry boxes into that infamous windowless basement where it all started, and who always smiled and helped me out when I needed. Djavo was such a supportive and friendly figure, and yet I hadn't thought about Djavo or seen him in years.

Like Djavo, thousands of others have entered my life and contributed to making my journey richer, with a pat on the back when things were not working out, or with a hearty laugh when we were having fun, or with both a pat on the back and a hearty laugh when we were having fun *and* things were not working! I want to thank all those people, including the ones I have not seen in two decades, as well as the security guard that opened the door and the friendly stranger that shared a smile this morning, for the unrecognized warmth they bring to our world every day—and for any role they had in helping KIND rise.

KIND is becoming a very special brand, company, and state of mind because of our loyal consumers. To all our consumers,

I am infinitely grateful for your trust in us. We will do our best to never disappoint you.

The exclusive chapter "Made to Matter: Creating Value from Creativity and Values" in this special edition of *Do the KIND Thing* was written in collaboration with, and with rich contributions from, Mike Hockenberry, Eric Ryan, John Replogle, Carolyn Sakstrup, Neil Grimmer, and Paul Lindley. Their affiliations are described in that chapter. They provided all the critical content without which this chapter would have been impossible to write, and I am grateful for their partnership.

Above all, thanks to my amazing team members at KIND. From the entire management team to the team members who joined this morning, I am so proud and so grateful and so blessed to be able to learn from you every day. May the tenets in *Do the KIND Thing* help all of us continue to extend our values toward our shared undertaking.

Sincerely,
Daniel Lubetzky

INDEX

ABOUT THE AUTHOR

DANIEL LUBETZKY is a pioneering social entrepreneur known for integrating social objectives with sustainable market-driven forces to forge new business models that build bridges between people. He is the CEO and founder of KIND Healthy Snacks and the KIND Movement. He is also founder of PeaceWorks and OneVoice, and cofounder of the apparel company Maiyet. Lubetzky has received numerous awards and recognitions for his humanitarian efforts and his business practices; among them he's been named one of America's Most Promising Social Entrepreneurs in *BusinessWeek*, one of 25 Responsibility Pioneers by *Time*, one of the Creativity 50 by *Advertising Age*, and one of the 100 Most Intriguing Entrepreneurs at the Goldman Sachs Builders and Innovators Summit. He has received Entrepreneur of the Year awards from both *Entrepreneur* magazine and Ernst & Young. He lives in New York with his wife and four children.

www.kindsnacks.com

Facebook.com/KINDSnacks

ABOUT THE TYPE

This book was set in Bembo, a typeface based on an old-style Roman face that was used for Cardinal) Pietro Bembo's tract *De Aetna* in 1495. Bembo was cut by Francesco Griffo (1450–1518) in the early sixteenth century for Italian Renaissance printer and publisher Aldus Manutius (1449–1515). The Lanston Monotype Company of Philadelphia brought the well-proportioned letterforms of Bembo to the United States in the 1930s.